AHARON APPELFELD

AHARON APPELFELD

From Individual Lament

to Tribal Eternity

Yigal Schwartz

Translated by Jeffrey M. Green

Foreword by Arnold J. Band

Brandeis University Press
PUBLISHED BY UNIVERSITY PRESS OF NEW ENGLAND
HANOVER AND LONDON

1 – 4187

Published with the support of the Jacob and Libby Goodman Institute for the Study of
Zionism and Israel

Published by University Press of New England, Hanover, NH 03755

© 2001 by Brandeis University Press

Printed in the United States of America

5 4 3 2 1

Library of Congress Cataloging-in-Publication Data

Shovarts, Yig (R) al.
  [oKinat ha-yaohid ove-netsaoh ha-sheveot. English]
  Aharon Appelfeld : from individual lament to tribal eternity / Yigal
Schwartz ; translated by Jeffrey M. Green.
    p. cm. — (Tauber Institute for the Study of European Jewry studies)
Includes bibliographical references and index.
  ISBN 1–58465–139–3 (cl. : alk. paper).—ISBN 1–58465–140–7 (pa. :
alk. paper).
  1. Appelfeld, Aron—Criticism and interpretation. 2. Holocaust, Jewish
(1939–1945), in literature. I. Title. II. Series.
  PJ5054.A755 Z8913 2001
  892.4'36—dc21   00-012584

Published in Hebrew in 1996 as "Individual Lament and Tribal Eternity: Aharon Appelfeld:
A Picture of His World" by Magnes Press and Keter Publishers, Jerusalem.

THE TAUBER INSTITUTE FOR THE STUDY OF EUROPEAN JEWRY SERIES

The Tauber Institute for the Study of European Jewry, established by a gift to Brandeis University from Dr. Laszlo N. Tauber, is dedicated to the memory of the victims of Nazi persecutions between 1933 and 1945. The Institute seeks to study the history and culture of European Jewry in the modern period. The Institute has a special interest in studying the causes, nature, and consequences of the European Jewish catastrophe within the contexts of modern European diplomatic, intellectual, political, and social history.

The Jacob and Libby Goodman Institute for the Study of Zionism and Israel was founded through a gift to Brandeis University by Mrs. Libby Goodman and is organized under the auspices of the Tauber Institute. The Goodman Institute seeks to promote an understanding of the historical and ideological development of the Zionist movement, and the history, society, and culture of the State of Israel.

RICHARD BREITMAN, 1992
The Architect of Genocide: Himmler and the Final Solution

GEORGE L. MOSSE, 1993
Confronting the Nation: Jewish and Western Nationalism

DANIEL CARPI, 1994
Between Mussolini and Hitler: The Jews and the Italian Authorities in France and Tunisia

WALTER LAQUEUR and RICHARD BREITMAN, 1994
Breaking the Silence: The German Who Exposed the Final Solution

ISMAR SCHORSCH, 1994
From Text to Context: The Turn to History in Modern Judaism

JACOB KATZ, 1995
With My Own Eyes: The Autobiography of an Historian

GIDEON SHIMONI, 1995
The Zionist Ideology

MOSHE PRYWES and HAIM CHERTOK, 1996
Prisoner of Hope

JÁNOS NYIRI, 1997
Battlefields and Playgrounds

ALAN MINTZ, editor, 1997
The Boom in Contemporary Israeli Fiction

SAMUEL BAK, paintings
LAWRENCE L. LANGER, essay and commentary, 1997
Landscapes of Jewish Experience

JEFFREY SHANDLER and BETH S. WENGER, editors, 1997
Encounters with the "Holy Land": Place, Past and Future in American Jewish Culture

SIMON RAWIDOWICZ, 1998
State of Israel, Diaspora, and Jewish Continuity: Essays on the "Ever-Dying People"

JACOB KATZ, 1998
A House Divided: Orthodoxy and Schism in Nineteenth-Century Central European Jewry

ELISHEVA CARLEBACH, JOHN M. EFRON, and DAVID N. MYERS, editors, 1998
Jewish History and Jewish Memory: Essays in Honor of Yosef Hayim Yerushalmi

SHMUEL ALMOG, JEHUDA REINHARZ, and ANITA SHAPIRA, editors, 1998
Zionism and Religion

BEN HALPERN and JEHUDA REINHARZ, 2000
Zionism and the Creation of a New Society

WALTER LAQUEUR, 2001
Generation Exodus: The Fate of Young Jewish Refugees from Nazi Germany

YIGAL SCHWARTZ, 2001
Aharon Appelfeld: From Individual Lament to Tribal Eternity

RENÉE POZNANSKI, 2001
Jews in France during World War II

Contents

Foreword, by Arnold J. Band   xi

Preface to the Hebrew Edition   xvii

Preface to the English Edition   xxi

Explanation of References   xxv

I.   **"For There I First Breathed in the Blossoming": Literature and Memory**   1

II.   **A Beautiful but Unknown Resting Place: Literature and Place**   29

III.   **In God's Image, or Dust and Ashes: Literature and Religious Anguish**   95

Notes   143

Bibliography   163

    Aharon Appelfeld: Poetry, Fiction, Essays, and Lectures   163

    References and Other Sources   169

Index   183

Photographs follow page 102.

IN MEMORY OF

NAOMI,

MY BELOVED SISTER,

WHO WAS TAKEN FROM US BEFORE HER TIME.

Foreword

Outside the Hebrew reading community, critical recognition of Aharon Appelfeld as one of the most significant writers of fiction dealing with the Holocaust was granted belatedly, in 1980, after the publication in English of his novella, *Badenheim 1939*. The subdued yet haunting tones of the book, its web of symbolic details, and its deliberate avoidance of scenes of atrocity attested to the rare craftsmanship of the author. It was clear that a new, precious voice had been added to the already crowded shelves of Holocaust literature that had found increasingly receptive audiences after the trial of Adolf Eichmann in the early 1960s. Since then, many of Appelfeld's novels and short stories have appeared in English and other languages, invariably to enthusiastic critical acclaim.

The Hebrew reader, of course, was familiar with Appelfeld's fiction since the publication of his first collection of stories, *Ashan* (Smoke), in 1962, but since Holocaust fiction could not find a receptive audience in Israel during its early decades, his readers were few. The demands of the Zionist ethos, its adulation of positive, masculine action and rejection of Diasporan passivity, essentially condemned Holocaust fiction to denigration. While it is true that Appelfeld was included in Gershon Shaked's influential volume of essays, *Gal Hadash Basipporet Haivrit* (The New Wave in Hebrew Fiction, 1971), his books had nowhere near the sales of other writers, such as Yehuda Amichai, Amos Oz, A. B. Yehoshua, Amalia Kahanah-Carmon, and Yehoshua Kenaz. With the maturation of Israeli society, however, the horizons of reception expanded, and fiction about the Holocaust, the lives of women, and the Oriental communities are accepted as normative, particularly since the early 1980s. Today, a half-century after the horrors of World War II, it is abundantly clear that no serious consideration of the fiction generated by that catastrophe either in Israel or in America or Europe can exclude the work of Aharon Appelfeld.

Still, the association of Aharon Appelfeld only with the literature of the Holocaust restricts our vision of his artistic scope. Reading Appelfeld only as a Holocaust writer drastically diminishes the range of his concerns and

blurs the nuances of his texts. This was true even in his first widely read
translated novella, *Badenheim 1939*. The reader expecting a stark confrontation with the atrocities of the death camps did not find it in that
book. Its absence was actually the enigmatic source of terror. Paradoxically, most of Appelfeld's stories do not deal with the war years, and, if
they do, the perspective is deliberately oblique, carefully avoiding the
landscape of agony.

This paradox should alert us to the fact that there is much more to Appelfeld—or, for that matter, to many other gifted so-called Holocaust
writers—than testifying to the Holocaust, however important that might
be. Among the strident tones of the atrocity, the creative voice of the individual author is often muted or lost; it then becomes the task of the critic
to identify and recover this voice, to help it assert its identity and humanity. This goal shapes the rubrics of Yigal Schwartz's study of Appelfeld's
fiction, *Aharon Appelfeld: From Individual Lament to Tribal Eternity*.
Rather than tracing the trajectory of Appelfeld's writing over the decades,
Schwartz explores three major areas: the recovery of childhood memories; the perennial search for a secure haven; the problems of Jewish identity. These rubrics allow Schwartz to delineate a more complex portrait
of the author as he appears in his fictions.

Schwartz's portrayal of Appelfeld corresponds uncannily to Appelfeld's own recent (1999) autobiography, *Sippur Hayim* (The Story of a
Life), which was actually published three years after the appearance in
Hebrew of Schwartz's book. In it the years of World War II are placed in
their context between the childhood pastoral (1932–41) and the time of
rehabilitation and creativity (1944–99). Throughout this book, the adult
Appelfeld, now a man in his sixties, attempts to recapture and understand the events of his life beginning with his first childhood memories
and continuing through his emergence as a significant writer. Within this
"story of a life," the Holocaust and its agonies are crucial, but they are
not the totality of his experience. The early chapters attempt to re-create
the fragmentary memories of childhood, many of them erased by the
events between 1941 and 1944; similarly, much attention is devoted to
the painful adjustment first to life in the refugee camps and the prestate
Yishuv and, later, to Israel through the 1950s, where Appelfeld slowly
forged his talents as a Hebrew writer.

While the narrator of "The Story of a Life" realizes that his reactions
to events are shaped by his keen sensitivities, he analyzes his personal development by situating himself in specific, trying narrative contexts. He,

like Schwartz, is trying to understand through his fiction the formation of the adult writer who now lives in Jerusalem and writes these stories. While the suffering of the Holocaust years are crucial and formative, they are by no means the only experiences that affect the human being we call Aharon Appelfeld. Both Schwartz's study and Appelfeld's autobiography are, indeed, attempts to recoup the child that was erased by the searing experiences of World War II and to understand the often painful rehabilitation of the child after the war, thus leading to the mature writer who created not only an impressive body of fiction but a whole life with family, children, friends, and work. Schwartz demonstrates that the act of rehumanization involves both the reconstruction of childhood and the subtle, oblique yearnings of the unconscious.

In his autobiography, Appelfeld is aware of the difference between the pastoral life of his pious maternal grandparents in whose home he enjoyed his summer vacations, and his secular parents who enjoyed the cosmopolitan, secular life of Czernowitz, where Appelfeld spent most of his childhood from 1932 to 1941. Though the city was under Rumanian control for most of this period, the cultural ambience was that of the Habsburg Empire: the architecture, the trade, the cultural tastes, and the language were that of Vienna. This was a city of high culture; it nourished in Appelfeld's days such other brilliant writers as Paul Celan, Dan Pagis, and Rosa Auslander. Appelfeld spoke German to his parents and barely comprehended the Yiddish of his maternal grandparents whom he visited in their rural home. The comfortable economic conditions of his parents and their doting on him, their only son, insulated him from the increasing hostility of the gentile population in the late 1930s.

The sudden shattering of this secure world in July 1941, when German and Rumanian troops murdered his mother and closed both him and his father in the Czernowitz ghetto, are never clearly portrayed in either his fiction or his autobiographical essays. The same is true for subsequent horrors: the deportation eastward sometime in the late fall or early winter of 1941 to Transnistria, the long marches through the snow in that hostile territory beyond the Dniester River, the prison camp in the Ukraine, the separation from his father, his own escape from the camp, the work in the house of a Ukrainian prostitute in the winter of 1942–43, and subsequent wanderings and work chores in Ukrainian forests and farms until the area was liberated by the Soviet army in 1944 and he was attached in some support capacity to the advancing troops. The trauma of these years in the life of a sensitive early adolescent must have been profound since they generate an eerie silence; Appelfeld rarely writes about that three-year period, and it seems to constitute a barrier through which he attempts to penetrate, a Herculean effort described by Schwartz in the first part of his book. In his second part Schwartz expands this investigation by demonstrating how places and spaces—forests, fields, dawns, rooms, and cellars—are used by the narrative voice to shape and anchor a sense of self. What the narrator observes and describes become metonyms for an emerging, re-created self.

Appelfeld's wanderings from the Ukraine through Rumania and the Balkans to Italy sometime after late 1944 together with a group of similarly orphaned and traumatized adolescents achieves greater articulation in his fictions than does his childhood, partly because he was already a bit older and experienced, partly because he was in less danger of being killed. Many of his early stories, in fact, deal precisely with the years in Italy, 1945–46: though he is surrounded by equally brutalized survivors, the sun is warmer, food is available, and the sea is blue. In Italy he began to learn Hebrew, a language he knew nothing of since he had but a minimal Jewish education in Czernowitz. Hebrew, the language of his creative life, was the embodiment of the painful struggle toward rehabilitation, always in the framework of Jewish relief organizations usually staffed by Hebrew-speaking teachers sent from Palestine to prepare this lost youth for their new life in the Zionist community.

Like thousands of other orphans of his age, he was taken by ship to Palestine, where he had no family and was expected to be rapidly acculturated to the life of the Yishuv. In his autobiography his recollections of his struggle to adjust are among the most painful in the book: the tensions between the expectations of the institutions where he spent the first two years in the Hebrew society and his desperate attempts to make sense of his life since 1941 were never settled. Similarly, the two years he spent at odd jobs before his induction in the Israeli army in 1950, the years of the Israeli War of Independence, are divorced from the momentous struggle going on in the nascent state. Even in retrospect, at the distance of fifty years, Appelfeld does not seem to relate to these tumultuous events that have so deeply etched themselves on the Israeli imagination. One gathers that most of his social contacts were with other survivors, equally alienated from Israeli life.

Army service was another period of humiliations and anomie since he was of slight build and had spent his formative years in ghettos, forced marches, concentration camps, and the forests. He began to find some sort of compatible society at the Hebrew University, where he studied between 1952 and 1956 and was attracted to those professors who presented the culture of Central and Eastern Europe. The names he mentions repeatedly are Martin Buber, S. H. Bergman, Gershom Scholem, and Dov Sadan. And yet Appelfeld's chosen path of study was odd: he chose to major in Yiddish literature, a field of little standing or practical purpose in those days in Israel, certainly of minimal use for one who began to consider a career as a writer in the Hebrew-speaking Israeli society. Appelfeld had already begun to publish Hebrew poetry in 1952 during his military service. In his autobiographical essays he attributes this strange choice to his desire to reconnect with his European Jewish background, a gesture of internal opposition to the Israeli society from which he felt alienated.

Here, too, Schwartz's observations are particularly productive. In the third part of his study, he deals with Appelfeld's complicated relationship with traditional Jewish religious life. Appelfeld's discovery of this life was not a return to lost norms of belief or behavior, for when one examines his earliest years one finds no real Jewish background in the Czernowitz of his childhood. Appelfeld's Jewishness seems to be a combination of a proud cultural stance (Judaism seen through the eyes of a Buber or a Scholem) and a marker of national identity. It motivates, for instance, his scorn for the frequent apostasy of Jews who appear in his stories set in the prewar society of Bukovina or Austria. It does not imply an imperative to return to Jewish religious observance.

The publication in 1962 of *Ashan*, Appelfeld's first volume of stories, was a milestone in his life, the end of the initial struggle to conquer a place in the world of Hebrew fiction, in itself an affirmation of life and identity and the beginning of a lifelong project of re-creating himself through his fictions. His personal life in Jerusalem over the past fifty years, his work as a teacher, his family, and his involvement in the everyday tensions of Israeli life do not appear in his fictions, which are mostly situated either in the milieu of the Holocaust or in the Central Europe of Franz Kafka, Joseph Roth, and Bruno Schultz.

The absence of any representation of Israel, where he has lived since 1946 and so successfully reestablished himself as a creative human being, has puzzled some of Appelfeld's readers and is, I believe, the latent leitmotif of Yigal Schwartz's remarkable study. For Schwartz's three-pronged analysis of this complicated body of fiction attempts to penetrate to the core of Appelfeld's creative persona as it developed over the past five decades, first through a search for a childhood, then through the embodiment of self in space, then through the growth of a complex relationship to his Jewish identity. What we gain through this method is a liberation of Appelfeld from the status of "Holocaust writer" and thus his rehabilitation as a full person, scarred by the Holocaust, to be sure, but who insists that there is human life beyond Transnistria or even beyond the daily exigencies of Jerusalem.

University of California–Los Angeles   ARNOLD J. BAND

Preface to the Hebrew Edition

Aharon (Erwin) Appelfeld was born on February 16, 1932, in a small village called Zhadova or Jadova near the city of Czernowitz in Bukovina.
He was about eight years old when the Germans invaded his native village. First they killed Jews who were innocently walking about in the
streets, including Appelfeld's mother. Later they drove most of the remaining Jews out of the region, including young Aharon and his father,
who were exiled to Transnistria, that part of the Ukraine which Hitler
handed to Rumania in return for taking part in the war against the Soviet
Union. During this journey into exile, Aharon was also separated from
his father. For more than three years he wandered through the fertile and
brutal countryside of the Ukraine, mainly on his own.

In 1946 Appelfeld arrived in mandatory Palestine with the Youth
Aliya. During the first half of the 1950s he began publishing poetry, and
in the second half of that decade he began publishing stories. His first
book was *Ashan* (Smoke), a collection of stories published in 1962.

Appelfeld is regarded as a leading Hebrew author. His work has won all
the important literary prizes in Israel and gained international recognition.
Dozens of critical articles, brief and comprehensive essays, and academic
studies have been devoted to his writing, including two books: *Bayit al
Blima* (House on the Edge of the Abyss, 1989) by Lily Ratok, and *Aharon
Appelfeld: The Holocaust and Beyond* (1994) by Gila Ramras-Rauch.

The present book, written intermittently over the past ten years, attempts to characterize the worldview that emerges from the whole of
Appelfeld's work. I chose three issues that seemed essential to the poetical
and conceptual world of this major author, examining them from uncon-
ventional angles of vision to attain new insights.

The first part is devoted to the way Appelfeld deals with his early
childhood, from which, as he says, he has only blurred fragments of
memory. I trace the process of artistic reconstruction of memory of that
critical period as it was consolidated in successive stages, beginning with
his first literary activity, in the early 1950s, to his novella, *The Age of
Wonders* (1978), which marks the peak of that process.

The second part is devoted to the extensive literary domain that Appelfeld has created over the decades. I trace the boundaries of that domain, describe its various regions and typical landscapes, and examine the reciprocal relations among them. Similarly, I have tried to clarify through whose eyes this fictional world has been created and whether this world is grasped as an object that can be "conquered" by artistic means.

The third part is devoted to Appelfeld's religious attitude. Central in this section is the discussion of the complex tension evident in most of his stories between adhesion to the Jewish tribe and its faith and an affinity with a primitive, non-Jewish experience. In this context I have examined the author's two principal efforts (in *Hakutonet Vehapasim,* 1983, trans. 1983 as *Tzili: The Story of a Life,* and *Katerina,* 1988, trans. 1992) to combine these seemingly contradictory elements. I tried to bring out their artistic logic, including their biographical and psychological roots and also the conceptual consequences that derive from them.

The combination of these three topics has enabled me to develop an original approach to another issue, one a serious discussion of Appelfeld cannot afford to ignore. I refer, of course, to the presence and status of the Holocaust in Appelfeld's work and its meanings in various contexts: artistic, socio-ideological, and the like. The three angles of vision through which I examine the whole of Appelfeld's work form a prism within which the Holocaust emerges as it is conceived in the author's eyes: in a multifaceted and fundamentally paradoxical manner. For example, examination of the Holocaust in the psychological and the socio-ideological contexts shows us, among other things, that Appelfeld conceives of it as a time in which his typical protagonist—an assimilated, Central European Jew between the two World Wars—has completely lost the ties of his identity, already weak and blurred, yet at the same time is granted a flash of metaphysical contact with the deepest roots of his belief.

The Holocaust has a similar status in the context of the purpose of Appelfeld's writing. In one sense, Appelfeld's great artistic endeavor is a mighty struggle to preserve a specific individual ego that was crushed in the Holocaust. In another, Appelfeld repeatedly seeks to reconstruct his point of view as a child at that time—the point of view from which the boundary between the individual and his surroundings is erased and the world is experienced through a precategorical faculty. This effort to reconstruct is depicted as an "Orphic plunge," a voyage to the heart of artistic experience (here the heir of creedal experience), which has two aspects: one is the desire for annihilation and for self-abnegation, which arouses fear and dread, and the second is the feeling of wonderment at discovery and revelation.

The three central subjects presented in this book are discussed in longitudinal sections that cut across large portions of Appelfeld's work. The works to which these longitudinal sections refer in each part of the book were chosen on the basis of two principal considerations: first, the central issue of the respective part; and second, the selection of works discussed in the other parts. I have tried, and I believe with success, to refer to most of Appelfeld's writing: his early works in poetry and prose from the 1950s, later works that have not been collected in books (fiction and drama), sections from works not yet published in their entirety, nonfiction both collected and uncollected (including some not yet been published), and of course collections of stories and novellas. While this examination of Appelfeld's significant literary corpus is thorough and systematic, some discussions challenge the customary norms of academic literary discourse. This challenge derives both from the character of the subject—life and work against the background of a huge emotional and cognitive trauma—and also from my own personal propensities and weaknesses.

Of course this book would not have been published had it not been preceded by the great works of Appelfeld. Reading and studying them have opened hidden domains for me. I was also fortunate in that I have had the privilege of knowing the man who wrote these works. The beginning of our acquaintance was a meeting that Appelfeld initiated—after I sent him a seminar paper that I wrote for my B.A. in 1979—and it continued in dozens of conversations held in various places in and outside of Israel. Some of these were professional literary conversations—between 1986 and 1996 I served as Appelfeld's literary editor—but most were ordinary conversations, though a few also touched on the essence of art. In writing this book, I have used some of what I heard during those fascinating conversations.

This book, in its final form, would not have been produced without the support and assistance of many people. I am grateful to my seminar students at the Hebrew University and at Harvard University, with whom I explored some of the central ideas discussed in the book, and to Professor Nili Gold, Professor Yoel Hofmann, Professor Avraham Holtz, Dr. Avner Holtzman, Dr. Tzvi Tzameret, and Professor Shlomit Rimon-Kenan, who read an early version of the book. Their useful and instructive comments were very helpful while I was working on the final version; Haya and Yaakov Ben-Ari, Idit and Gonen Goren, Dudu Hazanovitch, Michal Felt-zig, Professor Ruth Karton-Blum, Dr. Malka Shaked, and Professor Ger-shon Shaked encouraged me and stood by me at difficult junctures. De-vora Stavi of the Genazi Archives in Tel Aviv provided me with photocopies of Appelfeld's manuscripts. I also thank Danny Benovici of Magnes Press and Yakov Tsoref from Keter, whose experience and wis-dom as publishers permitted the publication of this book relatively soon after the completion of the manuscript; Hila Blum, who helped with the research; Gabriella Avigur-Rotem, who made sensitive stylistic com-ments; and Claire Pagis, who worked to prepare the bibliography and in-dices—as usual, with diligence and with responsibility.

Special thanks to Ben and Yoav, and, of course, and most of all to Sigi.

Jerusalem, 1996   YIGAL SCHWARTZ

Preface to the English Edition

Israeli and American readers have long been puzzled by the virtual absence of contemporary Jewish society in the works of Aharon Appelfeld. Although he has lived in Israel for more than fifty years, and has spent extended periods of time in Europe and the United States, he returns time and again in his writing to the Europe of his childhood and appears to show little interest, his readers complain, in the Jewish experience of the present or even recent past. Behind their puzzlement lies the important question of the relevance of his writing to contemporary readers.

I shall attempt in this study to show that Appelfeld's books do indeed touch on the experience of modern man in the beginning of the third millennium—Israeli, European, and American alike. Surely Appelfeld repeatedly re-creates the world of assimilated Central European Jews between the two World Wars in an attempt to reconstruct the home he never had. But more important, the lives of assimilated Central European Jews exemplify what Appelfeld perceives as the tragic condition of the secular, liberal, and enlightened individual. The Jewish tribe is important to the writer not only for its own sake, but also as the ultimate representative of a cultural idea.

Many of Appelfeld's Jewish characters, particularly those that represent the generation of his parents, have converted, as it were, to the "religion of the enlightenment." According to Appelfeld, they have rid themselves of ancient ties to tribe, tradition, and the creator of the universe, and embraced science, universalistic ideologies, and modern art. But science and ideologies meant to improve the world, and even great modern literature—European and Hebrew literature alike, whose luminaries include Heinrich von Kleist, Franz Kafka, Hermann Broch, Robert Musil, Uri Nissan Gnessin, Yosef Hayim Brenner, and S. Y. Agnon—are inadequate substitutes for the lapsed tribal-religious faith. Modern literature surely plays a significant role. Centered on the individual and guarding his autonomy, literature defends the most important principle of the European Enlightenment, which Fascism tried time and again (and succeeded) to eradicate. By contrast, science and modern ideologies as well as history and theology value the collective over the individual and simplicity over tangible detail. But literature cannot relieve the crisis of faith. Modern Western man thus has no clear direction and, having lost his connection to the fundamental and the primitive, now wanders aimlessly, unaware of whence he came.

Appelfeld is therefore critical of the modern secular experience, which is characteristic both of the Central European Jews who figure in his writing and of his contemporary readers throughout the Western world. Paradoxically—and herein lies the root of the complex nature of the fictional world he has created—he is also critical of fundamentalist yearnings. The attraction of the primitive and the envy of those who espouse a naive religious faith arouse anxiety and deep apprehension in the writer. These fears are hardly surprising when we remember that Appelfeld's formative years saw the darkest elements of fundamentalism and primitivism laid bare. In this context, Appelfeld's extraordinary attitude toward the Holocaust, as well as his poetics, is revealed. The Holocaust has a dual function in all his writing: Not surprisingly, it symbolizes uprootedness, loss, and intense violence and bestiality. At the same time, it is represented as a great earthquake, whose shock waves reunite Appelfeld's modern, assimilated, and alienated protagonists with their heritage and tribe in a religious sphere.

And yet, as is evidenced in all his stories in one version or another, this singular bond endures only for the duration of the Holocaust. After the Holocaust the secular Jew, the modern European, reverts to his previous state: a seemingly full and vibrant existence, at times even suspiciously crazed, that is in truth hollow, devoid of vitality and meaning. The period of the Holocaust, when the child Aharon wandered alone in the wild and fertile expanses of the Ukraine, is perceived both as a total calamity and a mighty metaphysical experience. This dual attitude is expressed in a riveting way in Appelfeld's use of language. On the one hand, he exploits the mimetic-referential potential of Hebrew to create *ex nihilo* worlds of virtual reality. On the other hand, he blurs and undermines the descriptive boundaries of these worlds by juxtaposing the mental modes of characters who experience the world from perspectives that may be termed precategorical. I refer here especially to the perceptions of children, young people, and emotionally and intellectually limited adults. Through the prism of these naive, primitive characters, the world appears as a chaotic and primordial space lacking in clear distinctions between man and beast, sights and sounds, inanimate objects, and living things. The space is threatening and hostile even as it is sublime, magnificent, and pulsating. This strange blend and others like it, concocted in the writer's artistic laboratory, give Appelfeld's fictional world its hybrid nature: a cross between the modern realistic story and the folk tale, between Christian exemplary legends and hasidic stories. The result is a narrative form that may be classified as a realistic folk tale or as a modern rendition of a medieval allegory. These creations are anchored in literary traditions imbued with great moral and didactic substance that comes to life in Appelfeld's brilliant narrative art form.

I am thankful for the generous support of the Fund for Basic Research, the Federman Fund in Honor of Paula and David Ben-Gurion, and the Charles Wolfson Fund of the Hebrew University of Jerusalem, which made this English edition possible. I wish to acknowledge with many thanks the directors of these funds as well as Ahuva Cohen, research director of the Institute for Jewish Studies, and Yehudit Avraham of the Faculty of Humanities at the Hebrew University.

I would like to thank Arthur Samuelson for reading the manuscript and introducing me to the University Press of New England. I am grateful for the interest shown in my book by Jehuda Reinharz, general editor of the Tauber Institute series at Brandeis University, and its warm reception by Phyllis Deutsch, editor at the University Press of New England. I am thankful for the assistance of Miriam Hoffman and especially grateful to Sylvia Fuks Fried, executive director of the Tauber Institute for the Study of European Jewry, for her painstaking attention to the project, her keen critical sense, and her empathy and sensitivity. I thank my translator, Jeffrey Green, whose many translations of Appelfeld's works made it possible for him to appreciate my study; Edna Amir Coffin for her timely translation of this preface; and Ann Hofstra Grogg, for her thoughtful and careful editing of the English manuscript. I thank Maayan Harel for assisting with the preparation of the bibliography and comparison of the English version with the original Hebrew.

I am indebted to Arnold Band for honoring me with an enlightening foreword. Professor Band's wisdom, unusual psychological sensitivity, and his deep acquaintance with Appelfeld's work enabled him to capture my meaning also where I failed to express it adequately.

Neve Shalom, August 2000   YIGAL SCHWARTZ

Explanation of References

The first time a work by Aharon Appelfeld is mentioned, the Hebrew title is transcribed and translated. Thereafter, unless the work has been translated into English, only the Hebrew title is given; quotations from Hebrew texts have been translated specifically for this book. The page numbers cited refer to the Hebrew editions of the works in question. However, when reference is made to an Appelfeld work that has been translated, the English title of the book is given with the Hebrew and used subsequently, and translated passages are taken from the published English version. Similarly, the page numbers refer to the translation. For complete citations, see the Bibliography.

I

"For There I First Breathed in the Blossoming":

Literature and Memory

How do you call it that I receive letters from home,
And home is no more?
How do you call it that I receive letters from home,
And no one is living?

How do you call it that people write me from home,
And no letter is written?
And no letter is sent?
How is it called?

—AVOT YESHURUN

Prelude

By the beginning of 2000, Aharon Appelfeld had published twenty-three
books, including collections of stories and novellas and volumes of essays. In addition he had written dozens of stories, novellas, poems, essays, and plays that were published in periodicals in Israel and abroad
but have not yet been reprinted in collections. There are also novellas he
is now completing, sections of which have been published.

This extensive *oeuvre,* in all its variety, is marked by an unmistakable
intellectual attitude and literary style. From these abundant works, which
fit together like links in a chain, a personal world emerges, almost autobiographical and at the same time with a broad perspective. Appelfeld's
view, with regard to the Jewish world, is more comprehensive than that
of any recent Hebrew author since S. Y. Agnon and Haim Hazaz.

One feature of Appelfeld's literary world that distinguishes it from
much contemporary Israeli literature can be called the "Lot's Wife's Syndrome." His work exhibits nearly obsessive clinging to the traumatic
past, to the experience of the individual Jew and the Jewish community
of Central Europe before the Holocaust, and in particular to the experience of the individual and Jewish community of Bukovina, where he
spent his early childhood. While some of the stories take place after the
Holocaust, in the diaspora or in Israel, these, too, are closely bound to
the Jewish world that was cruelly destroyed.[1]

3

Appelfeld's works draw almost entirely on the landscape of his early childhood. This literary fact would appear to justify the assumption that his early childhood memories have had a decisive influence in shaping his literary world. Other writers provide models. Among them are some who were not exiled (Marcel Proust, Thomas Woolf, David Shahar, Yaakov Shabtai) and some who were separated from their communities, either voluntarily or by force (James Joyce, S. Y. Agnon, Asher Barash, Yonat Sened, and Alexander Sened). All these writers relied on personal memories to build their fictional worlds, whose reality depends on a marvelous ability to draw on fragments of life from the past: splinters of sights, echoes of sounds, hints of fragrance. From partial memories, these writers create living, vibrant pictures.

Memorial Creations in the Absence of Memory

In contrast to the decisive role of memory among these writers who devote their work to time past and their youth, Appelfeld claims to remember nothing or almost nothing about the region to which he "returns" or, more precisely, from which he creates in his works. The phenomenon of effaced memory that leaves a *tabula rasa,* the supreme importance of which has been noted by only two critics of Appelfeld's work,[2] emerged in the content and tone of an interview by Shmuel Schneider, one of the most revealing interviews ever given by Appelfeld. Schneider tried again and again to elicit details about Appelfeld's early childhood. Appelfeld tried to cooperate, but perhaps because of that effort, the interview is full of sentences such as: "I don't remember details," or "My memories . . . are few," or—in reference to the entire period—"There is little certainty and great obscurity."[3] On other occasions, Appelfeld has said that in his stories he repeatedly tries to build a "replica" of the world in which he lived during his first years—an extensive reconstruction, rich in minute detail, that is not based on actual memories.[4]

Appelfeld's work, or at least a large and significant portion of it, is thus a paradox. It "re-creates" an effaced period, or, to use the author's own distinctive phrase: "My work is memorial, but it lacks memory."[5]

Appelfeld's forgetting of his past is a complex phenomenon: his explicit testimony and many of his stories show that erasure of memory took shape gradually, stage by stage, over many years. In part it was a natural process, and in part it was governed by mechanisms of repression and obliteration—which is an important point for us here.

Let me emphasize that Appelfeld's memories of his childhood in Bukovina were few from the start.[6] At the age of eight he was driven from home with his father and banished to Transnistria. He would not see his mother again; she had been murdered in the street near his house. At Mogilev Podolski, one of the stopovers on the march into exile, Appeleld was separated from his father, whom he would not see for sixteen years. From then until the first days of liberation in 1944, the child wandered constantly, entirely alone, in the wide and fierce expanses of the Ukraine.[7]

During this time, Appelfeld says, his experiences wandering in the Ukraine and the few details he remembered from his past in Bukovina became clouded. Details from the present were buried by the overwhelming intensity of the present.[8] Details from the past were buried because they were connected to his Jewish identity, which he had to hide, to disguise, and to repress so that he could continue to survive in the hostile antisemitic environment.[9] Some of the stories in the volumes *Bekomat Hakarka* (On the Ground Floor, 1968) and *Adnei Hanahar* (The Riverbanks, 1968) show the erasure of memory at work.[10]

In 1944 Appelfeld, who was then about twelve years old, was attached to the Soviet army, which was advancing through Bukovina and from there on to Rumania and Bulgaria. In Rumania, Appelfeld stayed for some time in an orphanage in Czernowitz run by Dr. Ginigor (see the photographs following page 102). In Bulgaria, he escaped from the Soviet army and wandered along the roads with some other children to Yugoslavia and then to Italy. In Italy, not far from Naples, they met a monk who took them to a monastery. There, too, the erasing mechanism came into play. The monks, who tried to convert the children, sensed the burning presence of the past in their world. They found an easy solution to the problem, from their point of view. Thus we find that in all Appelfeld's stories about the monastery the children keep raising disturbing questions such as: Who are we? Who were our parents? The monks deny the parents' existence and offer the children answers such as: We are all children of God. Every birth derives from sin.[11]

The tide of erasures that began during the war swelled after its conclusion. According to Appelfeld, the suffering imposed upon him only because he was Jewish created an "obscure protest" within him. As a victim, he adopted the wickedness of the oppressor: "I looked upon everything that was Jewish or seemed Jewish as weak, ugly, and harmful." These thoughts created "a kind of private penal colony, . . . and on its gate a single sign hung: to forget and uproot" ("Al Hargasha Ahat Manha Venimshekhet" [On One Leading and Prolonged Feeling] in *Masot Beguf Rishon* [Essays in the First Person, 1979], p. 38).

On top of this "violent forgetfulness" (p. 38), which continued for years, came another "violent forgetfulness" that began when the boy who had survived the Holocaust encountered the Israel of the late 1940s and early 1950s. Israel was, according to Appelfeld, an ideological country, bursting with the romanticism of the pioneers, spouting clamorous slogans that declared an end to "the old era," "the era of exile," upon the ashes of which a "new epoch" would arise, "an epoch of redemption." Appelfeld, now a new immigrant, felt he had to erase the remnants of his memories and construct a new identity for himself according to the new doctrines. People told him he was expected to change everything: his name, his personality, and even his physiognomy. He had "to resemble a kibbutznik, a moshavnik, a Tel-Avivian in khaki trousers,"[12] or, as he put it more sarcastically, "to become overnight a tall, blond lad with blue eyes, and, the main thing, sturdy."[13]

However, the Zionist metamorphosis that was imposed on Appelfeld in Israel in the late 1940s, like the other metamorphoses that were imposed upon him (but with a difference) in the wild Ukrainian countryside and in the Italian monastery, was not completed. The Israeli melting pot aroused a reaction in him expressed in the partial rejection of the "artificial" Zionist identity, on the one hand, and in faint and hesitant efforts to recover the shreds of his old identity, on the other hand.

This reaction against the Zionist melting pot is reflected in various ways at different stages of of Appelfeld's work. It is caustically dramatized in several early stories that were never reprinted in books.[14] In the first four collections of his stories—*Ashan* (Smoke, 1962); *Bagai Haporeh* (In the Fertile Valley, 1963); *Kefor al Haaretz* (Frost on the Earth, 1965), and *Bekomat Hakarka*—there is hardly any mention of the Zionist melting pot. However, it returns to center stage in the story "Hayom" (The Day), which is included in his fifth collection of stories, *Adnei Hanahar,* and in his early novel *Haor Vehakutonet* (The Skin and the Cloak, 1971), and it is depicted with forthright severity in the novel *Mikhvat Haor* (The Scorch of Light, 1983).

The protagonists of *Mikhvat Haor* are boys who survived the Holocaust and have recently arrived in Israel "by chance." These boys keep finding themselves torn between two imperatives: the imperative to erase the remnants of their earlier identity, imposed by those responsible for them on the Zionist training farm, and the other imperative, fainter and more elusive, to retain, no matter what, traces of their miserable, contemptible old selves, which are at the same time precious.[15]

The emotional and cognitive world that emerges from *Mikhvat Haor,* as from all Appelfeld's stories (including those that take place before the Holocaust) is traversed by two opposing vectors: the involuntary necessity and the desire to erase every bit of memory, and the effort to preserve those few scraps of memory. These two vectors wax and wane, in a kind of pendulum movement. Sometimes the need or desire to forget prevails, and sometimes the need or desire to remember. One way or another, the battle between these "imperialistic" forces takes place on a very small stretch of remembered landscape.[16]

As one becomes aware of the path of cognition and memory that was imposed on Appelfeld, one's surprise is heightened. Where did he quarry the building blocks from which he created this lifelike territory? What is the source of the houses, the streets, the landscape, the characters, the ceremonies, the sounds, and the odors?

The secret of the literary origin of the lost territory of Appelfeld's childhood is in the connection between two components, a tense equilibrium that changes from work to work. One component is the fundamental attitude of the author toward his personal, family, and tribal past. This sharply ambivalent attitude began to take shape in Appelfeld's earliest childhood and was refined during his formative years in the Holocaust. Its most outstanding expression is the eternal struggle between the necessity and/or the desire to forget and the necessity and/or desire to remember and to remind people. The second component is an extensive body of knowledge—historical, sociological, literary, and linguistic—that the author acquired as an adult. These two components—his attitude toward his early formative experience and his knowledge—are indissolubly linked. The knowledge was acquired and shaped by the formative experience, and the latter was refined and embodied in literary form, patterned by the cultural knowledge accumulated with patience and perseverance.

When discussing Appelfeld, it is thus impossible to speak of a process of remembrance in the same sense as the process of remembrance in Proust, Agnon, or Shabtai. It is a process of remembrance in quotation marks, an "artificial" process. Authentic experiences and impressions are relaced by pseudo-authentic experiences and impressions, which were cast and molded in the artist's soul by means of knowledge he acquired later, knowledge that was absorbed and adapted in the pattern of the author's formative experience.[17]

Against this background, it is not at all surprising that Appelfeld, who has always been viewed as a lyrical writer, one from whose works there emerges an almost personal world, poetical, and very stylized,[18] presented the accumulation of knowledge as an essential condition in the formation of a writer: "To be a writer means to gather information for years. . . . Without that it is impossible to write."[19]

The Achilles Heel and the Archimedean Point

One of the criteria by which to measure artistic greatness is the artists' ability to convert an essential shortcoming into a decided advantage, their ability to locate the characteristic that is their Achilles heel and to make it into their Archimedean point, the point upon which it is possible to erect an entire world. Appelfeld certainly passes this test. At an early stage he discovered his Achilles heel—the lack of a true world of living memory—and he made it, or rather the emotional and intellectual struggle with its existence, into one of the central concerns of his work.

Exploring Appelfeld's *oeuvre* from this point of departure, we can identify four main creative tendencies that together constitute what can be called Appelfeld's "journey to the obscure origins"; these to some degree, overlap.[20] The first three creative tendencies took shape during the 1950s and 1960s, and they are characterized by short literary forms: poems, essays, and short stories. The fourth creative tendency—in which Appelfeld's journey reached its pinnacle and to which the central portion of this study will be devoted—began to emerge in the mid-1960s and matured mainly during the 1970s. This creative tendency is clearly marked by the transition from short stories to novellas.

The first stage of Appelfeld's journey to the obscure origins was the most direct phase of personal confession. Between 1952 and 1959 he published dozens of poems, most of which have been ignored by scholars.[21] Many poems focus on his efforts to reconstruct details of the world of his early childhood in Bukovina: the figures who were close to him (mainly the mother), the primal sights (mainly country landscapes), and odors and sounds. As we see repeatedly, these poems overflow with yearning for that entire realm of existence consisting of "bundles of shadows," "remnants of dreams" ("Yatmut" [Orphanhood, 1955]) and nothing more. Nevertheless, or perhaps for that very reason, this primal world, the world of early childhood that floats in the mists of consciousness, does not leave the speaker alone; it takes over his existence.

Here, for example, are stanzas from "Yatmut" and from "Shovakh Hayaldut" (The Dovecote of Childhood, 1955):

ORPHANHOOD

The arms of the walls grasped strongly.
The silence pressed with the muteness of its claws.
The shadows drew remnants of dreams,
The thoughts modeled a statue—
Mother!
Perhaps this evening—which is saddest of all the evenings,
When he so much yearns for warmth;

Perhaps this evening—which is so shadowless—
You will come, the way you came to me in the dream,
The way I saw you yesterday.

THE DOVECOTE OF CHILDHOOD

The red-tiled dovecote of childhood
Awaits me every evening.
The summer has ripened the redness of its fruit
Apples and apples;
A bell rings the hour of autumn
Ding-dong;
The gloaming horizon turned very red
In alien lands—
And the doves of longing in the heart yearn greatly
To return to the dovecote of their dream
On such an autumn day,
Sad,
Yearning
For warmth.

Appelfeld's early efforts to reconstruct details from the world of his childhood were unsuccessful, for two interrelated reasons. First, because he had not yet acquired aesthetic distance or, in the words of the narrator

of the story that reflects his *ars poetica,* "Bagova Hakar" (In the Cold
Height, *Bagai Haporeh*), he was lacking "certain virtues of coldness, that
permit . . . some vision" (p. 136). Second, those efforts at reconstruction
were in fact bound up with a double act of fabrication—the creation of a
fictive poetical world *ex nihilo,* or nearly *ex nihilo*—which Appelfeld
once regarded as the creation of a false magic spell or cutting a window
into "the world of visions."[22] This double act is repeatedly described in
his poems as an extremely serious moral infraction, necessitating severe
punishment. Thus, for example, we find it in two of his programmatic
poems, "Shirim" (Poems, 1958) and "Mishpat" (Trial, 1955):

POEMS

Poems that I make up
By and for myself
Also those that have appeared in a book.
Why are people not flogged today
For rebellious thoughts
Why aren't sorcerers burned
Today in city squares.

TRIAL

Who appointed you as imaginer
Who appointed you in spells
By whose authority do you write
The epistles of your heart.
And where will you come before
The rods of your heart in the evening—
When all the courtyards
Are prepared for justice.

Many of Appelfeld's early poems demonstrate a complex attitude toward the obscure origins: a powerful yearning for reattachment to the
matrix of childhood, only a little of which was not erased from his memory, along with a sharp feeling of the breaking of a taboo that is accompanied by guilt and expectations of severe punishment.[23]

The second creative tendency in Appelfeld's journey to the obscure origins is marked by the distancing of testimony. In place of the personal,
confessional poems that dealt with traumatic experiences almost directly,

we now have short stories written in the second half of the 1950s. Their most conspicuous feature is the submerging of the traumatic elements from the time of childhood, both before and during the Holocaust, within the lives of banal characters on the margins of life in Israel. The outcome of this literary process, which characterizes most of the stories in Appelfeld's first collection, *Ashan,* is a subdued and restrained artistic form.[24]

The distancing of Appelfeld's testimony—that is to say, the objectivization of his formative experience—is reflected on most of the levels of the stories in *Ashan:* in the social typology of the characters (taxi drivers, petty merchants, smugglers); in the point of view (an omniscient, transparent narrator); and in the figurative procedures (emotional digressions, such as giving objects metonymic value and landscapes metaphorical value). However—and this is the central axis of our discussion—the human experience portrayed in these stories is the same as that portrayed in the early poems: a complex attitude toward the obscure past that is marked here (and henceforth in all the author's work) by tension between the necessity and/or the desire to forget and the necessity and/or desire to remember. The characters cannot forget, because the meaning of forgetfulness is the erasure of a critical period in their biography, but they also cannot remember, because memory evokes intense and difficult feelings (sin, guilt) and/or because it is sealed off or erased.

The transition between poetry and the stories of *Ashan* was a necessary step for the young author, apparently preceded by a sober artistic self-evaluation. An indication of this transition can be found in the story, "Shlosha" (Three, *Ashan*), which Appelfeld chose to place at the beginning of his first collection of stories, and not by chance. This story constitutes a link between the poems and the stories of *Ashan,* primarily in the attitude of the narrator, who serves as intermediary between the obscure past and the reader's world.

"Shlosha" is the only story in *Ashan* in which the events take place on the threshold of the obscure past. The plot focuses on three men: an old man, a middle-aged man, and a youth, who have just now escaped from some unknown place and are on their way to an unknown destination. The threesome, and also the narrator (who is apparently one of the three, reporting on the events from a distance in time and place), try to cope with the obscure past in different ways. They attempt to conceal and forget the events of the past and to begin living as though from the start, from the point of departure of the narrative present, from the moment they managed to escape and onward. This effort ends in dismal failure. Within a short time the three realize that every act in the present is stamped with the seal of the past that they cannot or will not remember. At the end of the story the threesome cannot bear one another. "They should have disappeared, each in his own way" (p. 13), because for each the presence of the others is a constant reminder of that obscure past. The moment they separate and stop living as a group seals their fate as individuals as well. The separation marks entry into yet another dead end. This road is blocked because those who travel it try to do the impossible: to flee from their past—that is to say, from themselves.

The narrator in "Shlosha" tries to grapple with the obscure past in a different way: he tries to remember, to reconstruct, to explain, and thus to build a story that will also encompass the events of the past. However, despite the difference in time and place, he repeatedly fails in his endeavor. He does not manage to find the "point of contact" (p. 13) from which he can perhaps try to reconstruct the past. The obscure past remains a "riddle" (p. 13) that swirls above him, as on the first day of his flight, like "a moving body, accelerating, whose whirling cannot be stopped" (p. 7).

Trapped in emotional and artistic distress, the narrator of "Shlosha" reflects the distress in which Appelfeld was trapped when he wrote that story. He, too, it appears, found it difficult to discover the "point of contact" in relation to the events of the obscure past—his early childhood in Bukovina and/or the time of his wanderings during the Holocaust. Against this background it is no surprise that he chose to distance his testimony, if only for a limited period.

The third creative tendency in Appelfeld's journey to the obscure origins is characterized by an effort to extend the socio-cultural range of his stories. Here his education begins to show, the education he obtained in an institutional and noninstitutional manner during the years when, as a teenager, he was in an agricultural boarding school and in military service. He also attended an accelerated pedagogical training course in a teachers' seminary of the religious workers' movement, and at the Hebrew University he took courses in Hebrew and Yiddish literature, the Bible, Kabbalah, and Hasidism. Among his teachers were Gershom Scholem, Yehezkel Kaufmann, Shimon Halkin, and, especially important for him, Dov Sadan, who spread before Appelfeld, as he says, "a broad Jewish map."[25]

In *Ashan*, Appelfeld placed the figure of a single person or a small group of people in the foreground. These characters were unable to cope both with memory and with forgetfulness of events from their narrative past. These events were always connected, as one may surmise from the shadows they cast upon the present, to behavior that was contemptible according to universal ethical standards: overcoming obstacles as part of the effort to survive, "so that you can't say how anymore" ("Shlosha," *Ashan,* p. 8), the real or imagined abandonment of relatives or other companions (in "Aviv Kar" [Cold Spring], "Ashan" [Smoke], "Shutfut" [Partnership], "Al Yad Hahof" [By the Shore], "Sippur Ahava" [Love Story], and others), preference for material benefit over an obligation from long ago ("Bertha" and "Bekomat Hakarka" [On the Ground Floor]). Indeed, in some stories—for example the excellent "Nisayon Retzini" (A Serious Effort) and "Pitzuim" (Compensation)—these actions are connected to an ambivalent attitude to the past in the traditional Jewish context as well. Nevertheless, any connection with the "Jewish tribe" is depicted here, if at all, in the background. In contrast, Appelfeld places the Jewish tribe in center stage in some of the stories in *Bagai Haporeh* and in many stories in *Kefor al Haaretz,* which constitute the third tendency. In these stories, the individual, with his or her universal moral distress, is portrayed in the background.

These developments do not permit us to conclude, as did Gershon Shaked, that Appelfeld decided to take upon himself the task of "becoming a community chronicler."[26] The socio-typological expansion that characterizes the stories belonging to this tendency took place only within the framework of the author's formative experience. The Jewish archetypes in stories in *Kefor al Haaretz*—the intercessor (in "Mota shel Hashtadlanut" [The Death of Intercession] and "Tzel Harim" [The Shadow of Mountains]), the community chronicler (in "Gonev Marot" [The Thief of Visions]), the Jew who tries to regain a concession that had been taken from him (in "Batahana" [In the Station]), and the last in a dynasty of village estate owners (in "Bimlo Hastav" [In the Fullness of Autumn])—are all portrayed in the same fashion: they are swept away by the flow of time because Jewish life arouses in them acute attraction and revulsion. These contradictory feelings do not permit them to renew their connection with the obscure "point of contact," nor do they permit them to detach themselves from it once and for all.

The archetypical situations in stories in *Kefor al Haaretz*—expulsion and emigration (in "Hagerush" [The Expulsion] and "Hakhanot Lamasa" [Preparations for a Journey]), a pilgrimage to a hasidic *rebbe* (in "Haderekh ben Drovna Ledrovitz" [The Road from Drovna to Drovicz])—are also portrayed with the same inner logic: always journeying, on the way, between one place and another. It is not surprising that the predominant metaphor in these stories is the wanderings of the Israelites in the desert, portrayed here as eternal wanderers. Failure to decide between the necessity and/or the desire to remember and the necessity and/or the desire to forget determines the nature of this journey. It is a constant trek through barren, monotonous expanses in a timeless time. Indeed, it is merely apparent motion.

One of these stories, "Sibir" (Siberia, *Bagai Haporeh*), recounts the history of a band of political prisoners, Jews and non-Jews, who transport coal from Siberia to the front in the war against the Germans. This story is characterized by a narrative framework with no natural connection to Jewish archetypes or to the author's formative experiences. Nevertheless, in Appelfeld's hand the journey of these political prisoners on the trans-Siberian railway—a journey that seems to have a clear direction and goal—becomes an eternal journey, explicitly compared to the mythical journey of the Israelites in the desert (p. 93). The endless character of this journey is connected repeatedly to the struggle between two contradictory forces: poignant flashes of precious memories of the past, which are symbolized by fire, and an enormous desire to sink into utter oblivion, symbolized by sleep and the soft snow.

I Throw Myself into My Life Again

The fourth tendency of Appelfeld's journey to the obscure origins is the most complex. It is a fascinating mixture of features of the early tendencies: the personal-confessional mode, the distancing of testimony, and the problematic connection with the tribal tradition. The novellas that belong to this corpus—*Keishon Haayin* (Like the Pupil of the Eye, 1973), *Tor Hapelaot* (The Age of Wonders, 1978; trans. 1981), and *Mikhvat Haor*—all relate to the *Bildungsroman* tradition and to the autobiographical mode of fiction. That is to say, they are presented as memories of life by one of the protagonists writing in the first person.[27]

Appelfeld's many coming-of-age stories and choice of the autobiographical mode of fiction during the 1970s were not coincidental. They derived from a principled decision once again to grapple with the subject of the obscure past. However, that decision, which gave rise to the three novellas mentioned above and, with certain reservations, to the collection of lyrical essays, *Masot Beguf Rishon,* was not made in a vacuum. It was preceded by important searches for direction evident in some of the stories in Appelfeld's second collection, *Bagai Haporeh,* and also in some of those in the third collection, *Kefor al Haaretz.*

Appelfeld included three coming-of-age stories in *Bagai Haporeh*: "Masa" (Journey), "Kittie," and "Masaotav shel Andriko" (Andriko's Journeys). Though set in various historical times and places, these stories share certain common features: all describe adolescents whose past is obscure, either entirely or almost entirely, and whose consciousness and psyches are limited. The process of adolescence itself is presented with harsh and contradictory feelings of exaltation and guilt that are interconnected, in various ways, to two "secrets": the "secret" of Jewish origin and the "secret" of sexuality.

Another common feature of these stories is their manner of conclusion. In the final scene it emerges that the process of adolescence has been incomplete. The initiation ceremony departs from conscious struggle to enter a symbolic or visionary arena. Just such an initiation ceremony, frightening and making one shudder, is experienced by Kittie in the story that bears her name. Toward the end of the story, German soldiers burst into the convent and drag her from her hiding place in the cellar "to behind the fence." The story ends with two short passages that the distant narrator defines sarcastically as the "final ceremony":

> Kittie had grown taller in the cellar, and when she was taken out into the light in her white nightie, she seemed taller than her height. A train trailed behind her.
>
> She was led along the narrow paths to behind the fence. How wonderful that event seemed to her, as though skimming through space. Now they were not people. Angels grasped her arms. And when the shot was heard she stood for another moment in wonder at the revelation. ("Kittie," *Bagai Haporeh,* p. 58)

"Kittie" and the other initiation stories that belong to this corpus herald Appelfeld's return to the subject of the obscure origins. At the same time, it should be noted that these stories contain striking distancing mechanisms. All these adolescents are, as mentioned earlier, limited in their psyches and consciousness: Kittie is not male, like the author, but female; and "Masa" and "Masaotav shel Andriko" take place outside the region of the obscure origins, which is represented here (and in other stories, as we shall see below) by the Holocaust. "Masa" takes place at the end of the nineteenth century, and "Masaotav shel Andriko" takes place right after the Holocaust. To these distancing mechanisms must be added, of course, the symbolic-visionary concluding scenes.

The effort to contend once again with the obscure origins undergoes a dramatic transformation in several stories published in *Kefor al Haaretz,* one of which, "Baeven" (In Stone), conveys the whole collection's *ars poetica.* The first-person narrator of this story testifies to the nature of that change, or at least part of it. This narrator, who is an adult, describes what happened to him in a monastery where he was taken in as a child. He begins the story with the following lines:

> I throw myself into my life again. Let that not be thought of as a sin. Like a wanderer I shall trail alongside the stream; how mighty are the days in their flow. No dam will be erected here. Nevertheless the arm reaches out like an oar, trying to anchor itself for a moment; the head turns back, wanting to call the places by name. The sights are formless, as though made of a single element. You know that in this trial something of yours has been lost, and perhaps it has faded already. Nevertheless you are drawn to it as though into the depths. ("Baeven," *Kefor al Haaretz,* p. 72)

To this point, nothing is new: the effaced memory, the compelling force of nature, feelings of loss and sinfulness accompanied by what is grasped as "the theft of visions," yet the head turns back again and again. All of these are motifs that typify the author's first effort to "throw" himself into his "life again" in the poems that dealt with failed re-creations of the lost world of childhood. The innovation of "Baeven," at least on the overt level, comes in the following two passages.

Here is the first:

> My primordial life was lost somewhere in the small village. I was never there, but still I know every tree in it, the babble of the water, the sky that flows above it. Sometimes it seems to me that no one can describe it like me, for there I first breathed in the blossoming, laughed at the touch of the wind on my lips. ("Baeven," *Kefor al Haaretz,* p. 72)

This passage presents a true fact: a childhood that has been extinguished. Moreover, the speaker declares that not only has he no early memories from the place of his childhood, he also has no later memories, for he has never returned. Yet, despite these facts, he claims emphatically that he has an intimate acquaintance with fundamental visions of the place. Moreover, sometimes it seems to him that he can describe them better than anyone else, solely on the basis of several primal, sensory experiences.

The narrator moves on and, in an apparently offhand way, makes an astounding declaration: "I had a mother, a father, a sister. I have already fixed them in my heart. I made them my companions, to whom I can make myself known daily. No one can take them from me; they are mine" ("Baeven," *Kefor al Haaretz*, p. 72).

The adult narrator of "Baeven" thus experiences a cognitive process, at the end of which he legitimizes the act of creating an imaginary family that he places in his heart as though it is his own. As a child in the monastery, the narrator underwent a similar process. The child joins a group of stonecutters who are working in the courtyard of a monastery, erecting walls, and he carves figures into the stone, which he calls "my father" and "my mother." At the end of the story, these stone figures are recognized, and the monk orders that they be sanctified. Sanctification thus comes from without, and from an alien authority, whereas later legitimacy, which the adult narrator gives to the creations of his spirit, comes from within, after a difficult struggle lasting many years.

The difference between the creation of the crude carvings of the family that the boy made in the monastery and his later reference to this act, now as a more mature and experienced artist, is analogous to the difference between Appelfeld's two efforts to return to his primal life. With the first effort Appelfeld creates, as the speaker in the poem "Yatmut" states, a crude statue of his mother that was hewn from musing and fragments of dreams. In the second effort, about ten years later, Appelfeld returns to the same subject, but this time as a more mature artist, skilled in the secrets of aesthetic distance and rich in culture.[28]

The astonishing declaration of the adult narrator in "Baeven," giving life to his imaginary family, is marvelously consistent with Appelfeld's revolutionary step as heralded in "Bimlo Hastav." This is Appelfeld's first story in which a real family is portrayed—father and mother, son and daughter, and even a grandfather. Rather than isolated figures, an actual couple, a pair of people who function as a couple, or a small group of people whom deceptive fate has joined together, here we have a full nuclear family, anchored in the living tissue of relations, a family that is, by its nature, unique and at the same time endowed with universal validity. It is difficult to exaggerate the importance of this innovation in Appelfeld's work, both against the background of the emotional and artistic difficulties that hindered him until he allowed himself to begin this act of creation, and also because the family permitted Appelfeld—for the first time—to link up with the heritage of the tribe in a manner that can be called nearly organic.

On the importance of the family in this context, Appelfeld has said the following:

> First of all the family. By means of it we lived in cities and villages, in destitute stores and splendid commercial establishments. For the family is Jewish history in miniature; in it are found remnants of believers, believers from habit, those who are distant without thinking about it, those who are intentionally estranged, apostates for their own pleasure, and apostates out of spite. Everything that was widespread during the past hundred years was represented in it. Anarchists and communists, Zionist and Bundists, and the more extensive the family was, the greater was the division. ("Edut" [Testimony], *Masot Beguf Rishon,* p. 9)

This idea of the family, vital both in theory and in fact, is realized in the Rappaport family in "Bimlo Hastav." The father, through whose eyes we see the narrated world, represents the rural Jewish aristocracy under the merciful Habsburg dynasty ("Bimlo Hastav," *Kefor al Haaretz,* p. 67). He is an "astute" man who tends to see his personal fate "through the broad prism of history or social science" (p. 71). The paternal grandfather lives in a small village, Prinovka, "where everything still follows the old order, every day they rise for prayers, and on the holidays they travel to Sadgora" (p. 70). The mother still has "feelings of devotion that she took with her from her parents' home, and which developed in the shadow of her educated husband, in opposition to all of his ways" (p. 68). The son, who is close to his mother's heart, is entirely different. His father foresees a future for him as "a new Jew," "as one who fills coffee houses and stock exchanges and manages a small factory" (p. 66). However, the daughter, who is close to her father's heart, is about to marry the Polish teacher of the village, and she will almost certainly abandon Judaism.

In Appelfeld's conception, the Rappaport family is "Jewish history in miniature," both in view of social typology and also in view of the psycho-cultural process the family has undergone, upon the last stage of which this story focuses. Here, family members lose the "thread that pass through the characters, joins them, makes them attentive to one another" (p. 71). All members of assimilating Jewish families in Central Europe between the two World Wars underwent a similar process, which Appelfeld was to depict in the course of his career,[29] a process that cannot be halted. The father of the family, Mr. Rappaport, who tries unrelentingly to find the point that connects the members of his family, knows very well that there is no such point, and the family is doomed to destruction. "The matter in itself has already been determined—he concluded to himself—just why did this termination take place so slowly?" (p. 70).

The conclusion that emerges from this trailblazing story is clear: the Jew as described here has only a semblance of existence. This is, to cite the educated father once again, "the final metamorphosis," "a scrap of dream," "a colorful bubble" (p. 71), and no more.

Here we must stop and ask about the source of this harsh view. Does it derive from objective research, or is it from Appelfeld's formative experience, forged during the Holocaust and projected upon the experience and fate of an entire group? The answer is—and this is another innovation heralded by this story—that both are correct. In "Bimlo Hastav" Appelfeld deals for the first time with the assimilated Jewry of Central Europe. That community, into which he was born but whose characteristics, in all their types and varieties, he came to know through extended and persistent study, was tailor-made to fit his formative experience. From historical studies and personal testimony, the assimilated Jewish community of Bukovina between the two World Wars appears to have been a society in a precarious condition. As it passed from Habsburg to Rumanian rule in 1918, it cut itself off from its tribal-national-religious roots and continued to look toward Viennese-German culture, which at that time was already more of an illusion than a true culture.[30] The existential status of that community, as described in historical studies and personal testimony, is consistent with the existential status of Appelfeld's lost childhood world as it emerges in his stories. These are two rich and variegated worlds that float in the air and can be called, following the intellectual father in "Bimlo Hastav," "colorful bubbles."

The essential turning point expressed in this short story would almost certainly not have been possible without an additional, seemingly technical innovation—a bifurcated point of view. Mr. Rappaport contemplates the world, like all the central characters in stories in *Kefor al Haaretz*, from within, as a protagonist taking part in a lifelike world, and also from without, as an observer and commentator examining his family, which represents, as noted, the entire Jewish tribe. In the latter case he is like an anthropologist or, rather, a pathologist observing a patient's death in view of preparing a postmortem report. This is the candid gaze, aesthetic (and chilling), so typical of the narrative method of the youthful observers in *Keishon Haayin* and in the first part of *The Age of Wonders*.[31]

Colorful Bubble

In *The Age of Wonders,* Appelfeld's literary art reaches one of its highest
and most impressive peaks, achieved through a refined and precise focus
and the integration of the tendencies that characterized the author's journey to the obscure regions from the mid-1950s on. The novella consists
of two separate and distinct parts: the first, entitled "The Age of Wonders" like the entire novella, describes the history of an assimilated Jewish family in Austria on the threshold of the Holocaust, seen through the
eyes of an adolescent boy named Bruno. This part opens with an account
of the mother and son's trip in an elegant train that is taking them "home
from the quiet, little-known retreat" (p. 3). They are returning to a small
Austrian town named Knospen. This part ends a few days before Bruno
is due to become Bar-Mitzvah, with an account of another journey that
the mother and son make. This time a cattle train takes them from their
hometown to somewhere unknown and entirely different. The father's
absence from the two journeys that frame the plot of this part is no coincidence. A well-known Austrian Jewish author, he keeps abandoning his
family, first in symbolic fashion and then, with the outbreak of the war,
in actuality, as he flees to Vienna and takes refuge with an Austrian Christian socialite.

The second part of the novella takes place, as its title says, "Many
Years Later When Everything Was Over" (p. 175). It opens with Bruno's
journey. He has reached the age of his father in the first part of the book
and now is traveling from his home in Jerusalem back to "the town of his
birth" (p. 177) in Austria. This trip takes place after Bruno has experienced a mental breakdown and a failed marriage.

This part also ends with a train trip and it is told, it must be emphasized, from the perspective of an ostensibly omniscient narrator. Bruno
stands on a platform, "empty of thought or feeling. His eyes focused va-
cantly on the blinking railway signal, waiting for the brass plate to fall
and the whistle of the engine to pierce the air" (p. 270). Between the two
parts of the novella—as in two other books by Appelfeld (*Shanim Veshaot* [Year and Hours, 1978] and *Hakutonet Vehapasim* [The Cloak and
the Stripes, 1983]) that consist of separate parts, one set against the background of events preceding the Holocaust, and the other against the
background of events following it—stands a pure white page.

The Age of Wonders can be taken, it seems—at least by an incautious reader who knows Appelfeld's biography superficially—as a literary autobiography.[32] This form is a literary or artistic composition that is not fictional but presents the life of the author, or sections of it, and is committed to the authenticity of the facts thus recounted. However, classifying *The Age of Wonders* among a distinguished group of literary autobiographies written by Holocaust survivors[33] is a mistake that results from the following:

First, there is a similarity between the early life of the main protagonist of the novella, Bruno A., and Appelfeld's early life: childhood in a region of the former Austro-Hungarian Empire, the interruption of that childhood by the Holocaust, and immigration to Israel. Second, fictional characters in *The Age of Wonders* can be mistaken as representing people who also have an extraliterary existence. In this context, mention of the father's relations with famous contemporary Jewish Austro-Hungarian authors, such as Franz Kafka, Stefan Zweig, Jacob Wassermann, and Arthur Schnitzler, is very important. The father is described as a major Austrian writer, and he might be mistaken for a prototype of the authors who belonged to the "Viennese circle" (p. 150). He is even said to have had an unsuccessful meeting with Martin Buber (p. 62).

A third reason for possibly mistaking this book as autobiographical is the manner in which the physical and human landscapes are described. *The Age of Wonders,* especially the first part, is replete with subtle descriptions of places, institutions, and character types, chiaroscuro, physical gestures, odors, and sounds. These subtle descriptions create a realistic fictional world, detailed and convincing, that seems to draw upon actual memories. A fourth reason why one might mistake *The Age of Wonders* for a literary autobiography is that the first part is presented as an autobiographical work by the central character, young Bruno. The use of an autobiographical narrator repeatedly tempts the incautious reader to ignore the intangible partition that divides fictional autobiography from actual autobiography. Finally, apparently explicit testimony of the author himself is misleading. In an interview with Shmuel Schneider in 1982, Appelfeld declared that *"The Age of Wonders* is an effort to recreate my childhood."[34]

However, the effort to read *The Age of Wonders* or any other book by Appelfeld as a literary autobiography has no real basis, for the following reasons: First, Appelfeld gives the protagonists of his book and the places of his setting fictional names.[35] These fictional names signal that the reader must not ascribe to the book any extraliterary, autobiographical

intention. Second, the resemblance between the details of Bruno's early
life and those of Appelfeld's early life is slight. I refer to the most basic details: birth dates, the father's profession, the mother's occupations, and
the history of the parents before the outbreak of the war. The similarity
between the details of the adult years of the author and his fictional character is likewise slight.

Third, the effort to view *The Age of Wonders* as a literary autobiography is undermined from the start by Appelfeld's frequent and specific
statements on the poverty and weakness of his memories from his childhood home. In this context it is noteworthy that Appelfeld returned, or
rather was taken back, to the region of his childhood at the end of the
Second World War where, for a few months, he was in an orphanage in
Czernowitz managed by Dr. Ginigor. He did not return again until 1998,
nor did he wish to go back! (Here he is similar to the central protagonist
in "Baeven" and unlike Bruno in *The Age of Wonders*.)

Another indication that *The Age of Wonders* is not an artistic or literary autobiography emerges when we examine Appelfeld's statement on
this matter in its full context:

> All my years I have tried to make a reconstruction of my childhood. To
> re-create it piece by piece. To fill voids. *The Age of Wonders* is an effort to
> re-create my childhood. Since there is little certitude and much obscurity, it
> is a replica. It is an archaeological excavation within myself. It is in fact a
> creative process.[36]

The choice of words must be noted. Appelfeld does not speak of flashes
of recollection but of a "reconstruction," a "re-creation." Rather than
fragments of visions, scraps of voices, and delicate odors, there are
"voids." Instead of a feeling of solid certainty or at least a sudden illumination, there is "little certitude and much obscurity." In another interview, Appelfeld discussed the nature of this reconstruction: "It was important to me from a personal and cultural point of view to re-create my
home, the place where I was born. I lost everything at an age when one
still has no awareness. It was important to me to recover those years, the
surroundings, to fill the voids, the vacuums."[37]

If we cannot classify *The Age of Wonders* as a literary autobiography,
we must ask what genre we can assign it to. A related question pertains to
the nature of the creative process that Appelfeld took on when he sat
down to write this novella. As he has said that this process is a re-creation

of autobiographical details, we must try to clarify the source from which he mined the abundant details in his book and, more important, the artistic principle that guided him.

In answer to the first question, *The Age of Wonders* can and must be defined as an "imaginary autobiography."[38] This term refers to a work that has two subjects: one is fictional (that is to say, it derives its authority from its inner logic and artistic texture) and explicit, and the other is imaginary (that is to say, it is built on details whose source is the imagination and/or education of the author) and implicit. Regarding the subject of such a work, two different statements may be made, each of which is correct. In the present instance, we may say that *The Age of Wonders* consists primarily of episodes in the life of a fictional figure named Bruno and in the lives of the characters around him. Secondarily it consists of episodes in the life of a fictional persona named "Aharon Appelfeld" and in the lives of the characters that "surrounded" that persona.

I have placed the author's name in quotation marks because the implicit subject of *The Age of Wonders* is essentially imaginary. The fictional and explicit subject of the novella cannot guide us to episodes in the life of Aharon Appelfeld himself, or to those who surrounded him, as happens in a "fictional autobiography"—because Appelfeld, who stands behind all the abundant details and "facts" mentioned in the book, remembers hardly anything of his early past. In other words, the manifest subject of *The Age of Wonders* is not a model of the actual life of the author. It is a model of the life that he could perhaps have had under historical and socio-cultural conditions like those it depicts.

The answer to the second question regarding the nature of the creative process that Appelfeld took up in *The Age of Wonders,* has already been intimated in my short discussion of "Bimlo Hastav" (which is, as noted, the first story in which Appelfeld created a world that represents the region of his obscure origins), and it is consistent with our view of the novella's genre. Bruno's biography and the biographies of the characters around him—like most of the details in the novella that create a lifelike context—are carefully selected from the broad reservoir of knowledge that Appelfeld acquired about the history of the Jewish people during the past century, especially the assimilated Jewish community of Bukovina between the two World Wars. The principle of artistic selection is the degree to which the details suit the author's basically ambivalent attitude toward the past, expressed in tension between memory and forgetfulness.

The tension between memory and forgetfulness is expressed in *The Age of Wonders* both on the cognitive level (as in the story "Shlosha" and others written during the second creative tendency) and on the sociocultural level (as in the archetypical stories of the third creative tendency, in *Bagai Haporeh* and *Kefor al Haaretz*). That tension, which is anchored here in a personal and family context, is examined again and again through a moral prism: the memory and forgetfulness of the personal past and/or the memory and forgetfulness of the collective past (traditionalism as against assimilation) are repeatedly measured against concepts of loyalty and betrayal.

The validity of the principle of artistic selection that I have presented here becomes clear when we inspect some conspicuous details of Bruno's "biography" in its light. For example, Bruno's father is portrayed as a well-known Austrian author because he must represent, as a chosen exemplar, the "uprooted" existence of the assimilated Jewish community of Bukovina. It was a Jewish community that was about to lose all affinity with its tribal roots, on the one hand, and refused to acknowledge that the culture to which it sought to be attached, German culture, was about to eject Jews from it, on the other. Bruno's father is also represented as an author because of the accusation of parasitism. It would be difficult to lay this accusation against a man whose line of work was "productive," such as a man who installed motors in flour mills (as Appelfeld's father's did). Moreover, Bruno's father abandons his family at the first sign of trouble, most certainly an act of treachery against the family circle (the "small circle") that fits in perfectly with the position of a confirmed assimilationist, a position that was taken as a betrayal of the Jewish tribe (the "larger circle").[39] This double betrayal is reflected, in a complex and subtle manner, in Bruno's ambivalent attitude toward his father, on the one hand, and toward the heritage of the Jewish tribe, on the other. Bruno's divorce from his wife, a Holocaust survivor, and his return from Israel to "the town of his birth" (page 177), at exactly the age his father was when he last saw him, represent the effort to grapple once again with the obscure and traumatic past. However, this time Bruno seeks to understand his father's viewpoint, which is so problematic, for he also abandoned both his family and his tribe.

The Age of Wonders is not, therefore, a literary autobiography—a work that reveals episodes of the author's life and is committed to the truth of the facts portrayed in it. Rather it is an imaginary autobiography—a work that reveals details of the life of a fictional character and fashions an imaginary life, a life that might have been that of the author. Hence we infer that the detailed depiction of people and landscapes in *The Age of Wonders* is in fact, a "colorful bubble" ("Bimlo Hastav," *Kefor al Haaretz,* p. 71), lifelike but with no more than a weak connection to an extraliterary reality. This novella, which serves here as a prime example of all Appelfeld's later belletristic writing, is a closed circle of illusion, created by the mental projection of the situation of the self upon the condition of the tribe, and of the reciprocal projection of the condition of the tribe—as it is visualized in the author's mind's eye, according to his formative experience—upon the condition of the self.[40]

The Presence of Absence

The validity of the principle of selection presented here becomes clear when we try to understand three other artistic decisions made by Appelfeld. Each touches upon the representation of time in the novella: Why did the author choose an imaginary alter ego who encounters the horrors of the Holocaust precisely at the age of thirteen and not, for example, at the age of eight—the age at which he himself had to confront those horrors? For what reason did the author take the trouble of emphasizing that Bruno's Bar-Mitzvah ceremony would take place during the Holocaust? What are we to make of the fact that the entire period of the Holocaust—including the date Bruno's Bar-Mitzvah was supposed to take place—is represented as a blank page?

Indeed, this disruption of time has three central causes, all consistent with one another. First, Appelfeld chose a protagonist of the age of thirteen because he already had, to use Dov Sadan's expression, a true power of memory. Second, *The Age of Wonders* deals with the problem of Jewish identity, a problem most effectively portrayed in relation to the age when a Jewish child joins the tribe and formally connects with Jewish tradition. Third—and this is the minefield at the center of the novella—by incorporating the initiation ceremony within the horrors of the Holocaust and representing it as a blank page, Appelfeld has placed the most significant events in the book, those that are supposed to have given Bruno's character its final shape, beyond the boundaries of the text before us.

The white page between the two parts of *The Age of Wonders* brings me back to my starting point—the issue of "erased memory" that leaves a "blank slate." Again, as in "Shlosha," the story that opens Appelfeld's first volume of stories, the question arises as to whether it is possible to build a life story on a memory from which the decisive period has been completely or almost completely effaced. This question is made acute in *The Age of Wonders* (and in all of Appelfeld's other coming-of-age stories) because the novella is related to a literary genre whose *raison d'être* is, as Franco Moretti has pointed out, the harmonious resolution of identity conflicts.[41]

The careful reader of *The Age of Wonders* will approach this question with caution. For at least in one respect it cannot be denied: the "alien magic" and the "forbidden spells" of the poems, which Appelfeld again presented in his first stories as sinful acts, as a "theft of visions," were turned, with an enormous effort of consolidation and distillation that took many years, into "wonder." That is to say: a variegated, pseudo-realistic world at this time, in *The Age of Wonders,* reached its peak of perfection. The nature of this wonder can be learned from the author himself:

> Thus the train speeds. It speeds inward and on its way it gathers up faces and years. The more it travels inward, the *wonder* never fades: everything is known, known to the depths of the years. The writer, who by the nature of his work deals with introspection, is surprised that on this course not only does he discover himself, but also the scattered souls of his tribe, which have been humiliated and rejected and lost in oblivion. ("Al Harga-sha Ahat Manha Venimshekhet," *Masot Beguf Rishon*, p. 40)

However, in another respect, which must also be taken under consideration when we try to answer the decisive question before us, it is difficult to ignore the heavy feeling with which we are left after finishing *The Age of Wonders*. The place of the delicate and sensitive boy in the first part of the novella, who describes the world about him with rich vitality, fluent and precise, is taken in the second part by a man who may have some sensitivity to the landscape but who is emotionally crippled, weary, coarse, bitter in his soul, and violent. Yes, and even slightly inarticulate— a quality that the author takes care to emphasize by attaching an omniscient narrator to him to give voice to his feelings.

What is the source of this radical transformation in Bruno's personality? Is it a result of the trials he had to withstand during the Holocaust? Perhaps the trials from that period did not change him fundamentally but only revealed and brought out what had existed in him potentially as a child. It is very difficult, indeed impossible, to determine the source because of the blank page that separates the two parts of the book, a blank page whose pure whiteness glistens with dread.

The Age of Wonders is either an imaginary autobiographical novella or a truncated imaginary autobiographical novella, and its form reflects the story of a life that has gone awry. It is a life story that is traversed by a psycho-existential fault line that cannot be bridged. A similar psycho-existential fault line traverses other stories by Appelfeld. It is the life story of all the assimilated Jews of modern Central Europe during the past century.[42]

In conclusion, let us pose one more question, one necessitated by the entire discussion. Again and again, Aharon Appelfeld, as we have shown here, creates and perfects colorful, lifelike bubbles and then describes, with precise observation, the way they burst. Why?

With great caution, it may be suggested that this process is the necessary artistic result of the persistence of two apparently contradictory tendencies. One is to connect with the obscure origins, expressed in imagining all these colorful bubbles that reflect, by their nature, both private and collective experience. The second is to detach from the obscure origins—an effort to terminate the condition of mourning, which is both private and collective—expressed in the deliberate bursting of these colorful bubbles. However, neither of these two tendencies—the simultaneous presence of which characterizes, as Sigmund Freud stated, all traumatic loss[43]—can be fulfilled, and for the very same reason: the tortured and humiliated origins will forever remain obscure.

This eternal paradox determines the purpose of Appelfeld's art, which—as the following parts of this book seek to show—is to make present the existential feeling of absence from which there is no escape (here Appelfeld follows Franz Kafka, who was for him, in his words, "not only a teacher but a redeemer" ("Edut," *Masot Beguf Rishon*, p. 15). This existential feeling of absence was not created, as many critics have maintained, as a result of the "black hole" left by the Holocaust in Appelfeld's biography. It is an existential feeling that was produced at a prior stage in the author's life, in his early childhood, and the "black hole" left by the Holocaust always serves "only" as a frame of reference and as a very powerful metaphor.

The author's desire or need to illustrate this existential feeling of absence determines the character of his poetical world. This world is partially realistic and partially imaginary, a trustworthy and convincing world and at the same time dreamlike. The extended family that Appelfeld creates for himself—that, as he says, represents "everything that was common during the past century" ("Edut," *Masot Beguf Rishon,* p. 9) in the Jewish tribe—is a marvelous demonstration not so much of what he had and lost (his actual family and the memory of his family) as of what he never had (the feeling of a rooted, familial-tribal existence). This sense of non-existence is at the root of Appelfeld's being as a creative artist.

II

A Beautiful but Unknown

Resting Place:

Literature and Place

It is not easy to name the places, to overcome the mixture of darkness and light that sometimes blurs boundaries but deprives ordinary objects of their familiar stability. At first I believed that by sorting I would fulfill the duty of clarifying, but the matter is not as easy as I had imagined.
　　—"GONEV MAROT" (*Kefor al Haaretz*)

Prelude

Aharon Appelfeld began his literary career as a writer of fiction by portraying the states of consciousness of isolated and alienated Holocaust survivors set against an Israeli environment limited to small and remote places in Jerusalem and Tel Aviv in the early 1950s.[1] Later in his career, Appelfeld expanded the scope of his fiction in both subject and (the two are interconnected) place. Overall, the geographical dimensions of Appelfeld's corpus are imperial. The borders of this imaginary realm encompass an enormous, though not contiguous, territory: from Siberia and the Ukraine in the East to Germany in the West, from the Carpathian Mountains in the North to Italy in the South, as well as various regions of the Land of Israel.[2] The expansionist tendency in the work of a writer of fiction, as in the fiction of any group or generation of writers, its extent, and the types of territory included in the imaginary realm, as well as the manner of literary portrayal—all require careful scrutiny if we are to understand an author's poetical and cognitive world.[3]

First this examination will focus on the writer's intentions. Did Appelfeld unconsciously expand the boundaries of his fictional realm in a seemingly coincidental fashion? Or did he have a master plan in advance, a kind of general map, which he filled in systematically, over decades, stage after stage?

Appelfeld does not appear to have charted a master plan before beginning to write stories. However, such a plan did take shape in his work at a rather early stage. We can observe it by examining the "history" of his fictional realm. Its boundaries were already firmly established in his first three collections of stories, all published in the first half of the 1960s—

Ashan, Bagai Haporeh, and *Kefor al Haaretz.* In the succeeding thirty years Appelfeld filled in blank regions in this realm whose boundaries had been set. While he portrayed regions he had written about earlier from a new point of view, he did not venture beyond "his" territory.

The structure of this realm, its inner logic and basic laws, were also determined at a rather early stage. By the mid-1960s a clear division was established between primary and secondary areas. The principal and marginal traffic arteries were demarcated, the central groups of citizens were defined on the basis of various affiliations, and the laws of existence and survival were established.

That Appelfeld's fictional realm was built on an early master plan can be learned from the author himself. In an interview with Shulamit Gingold-Gilboa in 1983, Appelfeld referred to himself as an "architect" and explained: "For years a person is like an architect building a city and planning bridges, lighting, roads, tall buildings, low buildings—thus the personality has already built the construction that suits it. The working-out of details comes afterward."[4]

What kind of architect is Aharon Appelfeld? With what school of architecture may he be identified? I prefer to answer, or, rather, to begin to answer this question, negatively. Appelfeld is not a strictly realistic writer. Anyone who looks for a "slice of life" in his stories will be sorely disappointed. The realm that Appelfeld has created does not depend on the evocation of a specific social and historical context.[5] On the contrary, the various regions of his realm are consistently portrayed as entirely detached from their historical and social context. They are semi-autonomous worlds, isolated and sealed off.

Nor is Appelfeld an ideological writer. It is impossible to derive a clear lesson from the nature of the spatial structure of his stories, in contrast to the spatial structures of stories with explicit morals. Certainly one cannot infer a clear political, philosophical, religious, or other doctrine from them, as can be done, for example, from *romans à thèse.*

Though Appelfeld does have a strong interest in ideas, they are always refracted through a complex personal prism and in ambiguous fashion. His stories employ finely tuned structural and stylistic devices that defy any attempt at deriving unequivocal lessons. This feature of his art belies the efforts of certain scholars and critics in Israel and the United States to present Appelfeld as a "Zionist author," an "anti-Zionist author," or even a "self-hating Jewish author."[6]

What, then, is the relevant "architectural school" for our discussion?

Perhaps it may be called "lyrical-contemplative." The "master plan" of those who belong to this school, of which Appelfeld is an outstanding representative, is based on a combination of two main components: an emotional position on the one hand, and an intellectual (though not ideological) position on the other hand. The master plan of Appelfeld's fictional realm is based on a complex combination of the author's ambivalence regarding his personal past, as the child of an assimilated family in Central Europe who was "caught" in the Holocaust, and his view of the situation of the Jewish tribe in the modern age, portrayed as a period of uprootedness and loss of direction.[7]

Finally, in section 3 of this chapter I will try to ascertain the vantage point from which Appelfeld portrays his fictional realm. Stated differently, I shall try to clarify through whose eyes we view the fictional spaces. Are they the eyes of a detached narrator, who describes the world he has created from a distance of moderating tranquility? Or are they the eyes of an involved narrator, who describes the world he has created without any barrier, like someone who once again experiences in literature a traumatic experience from which he cannot free himself? Perhaps, as I shall try to show, we view the world before us through both sets of eyes—or, to be precise, through the eyes of a detached narrator who consistently "surrenders" to an involved narrator and to his way of seeing the world.

In this connection, I shall also try to evaluate the consequence of this literary technique, which is central to our discussion. Can it be said that the entirety of Appelfeld's works shows that he views the fictional realm he "conquered" as his own? Or perhaps we have here (as I believe is the case) an author who "conquered" a realm that he knows full well is not susceptible to "conquest." The territory belongs, both psychologically and artistically, to a twilight zone where there is no separation between biographical and historical reality, between dream and nightmare.

The following discussion is based upon a comparative examination of the prominent regions in Appelfeld's fictional realm, while taking the processes of their creation into account. This examination will be proceed mainly, though not solely, on the basis of theoretical distinctions made by Gabriel Tzoran.[8] Tzoran maintains that literary space includes three distinct dimensions: the topographical dimension (space as a static entity, a kind of map that is not dependent on the organization of time and language in the text), the chronotopic dimension (organizational principles that are imposed on space by events and motion—the action of the plot), and the textual dimension (organizational principles imposed on space by the fact that it is portrayed in a linguistic text).

Among these three dimensions there can be, as I see it, two principal models of reciprocal relationships. The levels of organization can reinforce each other and present a unified and clear image of reality. Alternatively, they can exist in tense equilibrium and exhibit a nonunified and blurred image of reality. The fictional realm created by Appelfeld is definitely founded upon the second model.

Section 1:
The Realm and Its Regions

It is very easy to lay out the topography of Appelfeld's realm. It comprises two principal regions, an intermediary region that separates them, and a "zone of banishment" on the margins of the realm.

The two large regions are Central Europe, which I shall call here, to use Appelfeld's expression, the "Land of the Cattails" and the Land of Israel. The distinction between these two regions is based on two main sources—upon our extratextual knowledge and upon a large number of pairs of topographical contrasts to which the text calls our attention. These contrasts derive from the horizontal and vertical dimensions of the world, from patterns that relate to the quality of things (colors, materials, types of objects), and also from the ontological characteristics of the space (pairs such as hostile versus friendly space, traditional versus secular space).

In Appelfeld's fiction, some of these contrasting pairs, which differentiate between the two large regions of the realm, are to be expected, while others are surprising. Among the expected qualitative contrasts is one based on light: the European region is frequently characterized by bitter cold and soft light, whereas Israel is frequently characterized by bright, dazzling light and oppressive heat. The contrast in the climate of the two regions, which cuts through all of Appelfeld's works, serves as a central structural element in some of his stories. The early story-sketch "Yuli" (July), pivots entirely around the tension between two journeys: one the central protagonist makes on foot through the streets of an Israeli city, which lies in the "violent heat" of the peak of the summer; the other the imaginary journey made by the same protagonist to "the place of origin," to his childhood where "the snow piled up on itself, and it already touched the windows." Similarly, *Haor Vehakutonet* revolves almost entirely around the tension between the region of cold and snow, defined as the true Jewish geography (p. 138) and the hot and arid region, portrayed as an alien and alienated place.

Most of the ontological contrasts are less expected. Thus, for example, the European space is characterized as violent and murderous, and it always contains two ethnic groups: gentiles (mainly Ruthenians) and Jews of various kinds.[9] However, the Israeli space, which is violent but not murderous, contains only one ethnic group: Jews of various kinds and nobody else. This contrast is present in the novella *Mikhvat Haor,* which takes place mainly on the Zionist youth farm, and also in *Bartfuss ben Almavet* (in *Hakutonet Vehapasim;* trans. 1988 as *The Immortal Bartfuss*), which takes place throughout the city of Jaffa, which is, of course, a city with a mixed Jewish and Arab population.[10]

The large regions of Appelfeld's realm are thus clearly distinguished from each other. Nevertheless—and this is a central point—they are built on the same topographical pattern. Both realms contain three main geographical reference points by means of which the reader is required to build two alternative, competing, horizontal-hierarchical arrangements of reciprocal relations. The first arrangement is based on relations between the center and the margins as they are in geographical-historical reality—what is known to us from our extratextual knowledge. The second arrangement is based on relations between the center and the margins as they are in the fictional reality—what we apprehend by the manner in which the realistic spatial components in the story are presented anew, in "distorted" form. Naturally the second arrangement—the narrative, fictional one, which is not consistent with geographical-historical reality—reflects the author's emotional and cognitive attitudes.

In all the stories set in the Austro-Hungarian region, tension is created between these two spatial arrangements. First there is the "historical triangle": its center is Vienna, Prague, or Budapest; the marginal area on one side is Bukovina or small towns of Galicia, and the marginal area on the other side is hasidic centers in the Carpathians or small provincial villages in Galicia. Second, there is the "fictional triangle": Bukovina or small, provincial Austrian cities are in the center while either Vienna or Prague are on one side as a marginal area, and, with the same degree of importance, the hasidic centers in the Carpathians or small towns in Galicia are the marginal area on the opposite side.

Parallel spatial-structural tension is created in the longer stories that are set in the Israeli region. The historical triangle has either Jerusalem or Tel Aviv as the center, with small agricultural settlements (Zionist training farms and various kibbutzim) on one side, and small cities (Jaffa, Beersheba or Netanyah) as marginal areas on the other. Then there is the fictional triangle: a small agricultural settlement (a Zionist training farm) or a smaller city (Jaffa) stands in the center, and the marginal areas consist of a large city and, with the same level of importance, another agricultural settlement or small city.

The structural similarity between the two large regions is also reflected in the character of the vertices of the fictional triangles and in the structure of reciprocal relations between them. The primary vertices of these triangles—that is to say, the places where the central events of the plot take place, the arena of the action—always include various blends of the principal existential possibilities of the fictional world. Those options are also presented in the marginal vertices, but here, always, in an extreme and unequivocal form. Thus, for example, the arenas of the action in the Austro-Hungarian stories (villages, small cities, and resorts in Bukovina and Austria) always include various blends of assimilation and a throwing off of the yoke of morality, on the one hand, and traditional and conservative moral tendencies on the other. The diverse and generally contradictory components of this blend appear in their pure form at the other two vertices of the fictional triangles: assimilation and the throwing off of the yoke of morality are presented as strongly typical of the Jewish inhabitants of Vienna, Prague, and Budapest; and, in contrast, retaining tradition and an insistence on moral norms are presented as typical of the Jews of the Carpathians and Galicia. A very similar logic also underlies the mutual relations among the vertices of the triangles in the stories of the Israeli region and those of Italy, the intermediary region.

The Land of the Cattails

> [He] turned his eyes inward to find the place on the map he bore with him and suddenly he knew, with the simple certainty with which things are revealed to you in times of light—that the village lay in the Carpathians, and snow covered the mountains in that season, and the gentiles were sleeping their winter sleep now.
>
> —"BAMEKOMOT HANEMUKHIM"
> (IN THE LOW PLACES, *Kefor al Haaretz*)

The topographical pattern described above did not immediately take shape in Appelfeld's consciousness at the start of his literary career. He formed his first literary structures without an overall plan. As he stated in an interview with Edna Evron in 1994: "In my youth I hadn't yet seen the entire neighborhood. I thought I had built just one house, and I didn't know about the possibility of building another."[11] The first "house" that Appelfeld built in the framework of his neighborhood thinking was, it seems, the house in "Bimlo Hastav." In this important story, which I have already discussed from other viewpoints,[12] Appelfeld schematically sketches the topographical-thematic structure upon which, in the course of his career, the major stories of the Land of the Cattails were to rest.

The originality of "Bimlo Hastav" in the present context is expressed in the following variables. It is the first story to describe Jews living in their "natural habitat"—the Rappaport family, who live at a time close to the First World War on a rural estate that the family has owned for several generations. Furthermore, in this story Appelfeld's fictional triangle is presented for the first time, with most of its central characteristics. The arena of action is a provincial rural estate in Bukovina. This setting is anchored in a topography defined by two main reference points on the margins, which represent various and opposing tendencies within the *Zeitgeist* combined in the estate. This is how the spatial-thematic structure appears from the point of view of the father of the family, Mr. Rappaport:

> Standing aside, slightly hidden, the eye was free to wander, whether to the east toward Bessarabia, or toward the railroad tracks that led to Vienna. This was a quiet focal point, that joined together without sensing that it joined opposite spirits. ("Bimlo Hastav," *Kefor al Haaretz,* p. 67)

The expression "a quiet focal point," which subtly combines contradictory elements within itself, conveys the status of the rural estate that joins together "opposite spirits": the spirit of secular, free, even libertine modernism, the wind that blows from Vienna, the capital of "the Hapsburg Empire, the realm of mercy" (p. 67); and the traditional-conservative spirit, the wind that blows from Bessarabia. This combination conveys the situation of the father, a Jew with secular education who respects the Jewish tradition. He senses the "seduction" in the name "Vienna," but it also "occurs to him to travel to Prinovka to ask his old [father's] advice, and at the same time to rest a little, because in Prinovka everything still follows the old order, every day they rise for prayers, and on the holidays they travel to Sadgora" (p. 70).

The rural estate and the father are essences that combine opposing existential components within them. But these combined essences are on the verge of disintegration, and the well-educated Mr. Rappaport knows this very well: "Indeed he was the last of the dynasty here" (p. 70), and his family was soon to fall apart. Each of the components will move on its own "in constant motion until it dissolves like a colorful bubble" (p. 71). This is a vision of spiritual decline, the early signs of which are evident in the separate inclinations of members of the third generation of the family. The son is tightly bound to Vienna, and his father already sees him in his imagination as a "'new Jew,' . . . one who fills coffee houses and stock exchanges and manages a small factory" (p. 66). The daughter, by contrast, casts her lot with the Polish teacher, who has recently come to open the school year in the Ruthenian village. She is about to marry him and abandon Judaism.

The novella *Keishon Haayin* is built upon exactly the same pattern as "Bimlo Hastav." The arena of action is a family estate in the provinces, portrayed, like the estate in the earlier story, as a quiet focal point that joins together contrary spirits: the spirit of loyalty to the old Jewish tradition, and the spirit of assimilation and rejection of tradition. The same spatial-fictional triangle is presented in these two rural stories, though the relations among the vertices of these triangles are portrayed differently and they are set in different historical periods. In "Bimlo Hastav" the members of the Rappaport family themselves represent the "opposing spirits." By contrast, in *Keishon Haayin,* we have a family that is all of a piece, more or less. The Hoffman family, which lives on an estate, combines within it, in loose equilibrium, traditionalism and assimilation. The opposing spirits that ultimately undermine the family's delicate balance are introduced by relatives who appear, as though by chance, from the "great city," on the one hand, and from remote villages, on the other. Aunt Paulina arrives from Prague, bringing with her the decadent spirit of the life of assimilated Jewish artists in the magical city. Uncle Paul arrives from a Ruthenian village, bringing with him the failure of his effort at assimilation into the simple folk. Religious and poor relatives bring ghosts from the familial-tribal past.

The "invasion" of representatives of the opposing spirits at the Hoffman estate heralds the family's demise. This is both a spiritual and physical end—not only a spiritual ruin, as at the end of "Bimlo Hastav." At the close of the novella, the family moves to Vienna, where they receive deportation orders and are sent to their doom. The difference between the two endings is anchored in the difference in the historical background:

"Bimlo Hastav" is set, as noted, in the period preceding World War I.
Keishon Haayin is set just before World War II.

The first part of *The Age of Wonders,* like *Keishon Haayin,* concentrates on the process of a family's disintegration on the eve of World War
II, and this family, too, is more or less of a piece. Here the process of disintegration is described by means of human encounters of two kinds.
There are meetings with representatives of the "opposing spirits" who
"invade" the home of the A. family in the small Austrian village of Knospen, either directly or indirectly: the famous actress Charlotte, who, in
the family living room, announces the establishment of a "Jewish order"
(p. 36); Yetti, the simple girl who brings to the house "a breath of fresh
air from Father's native village" (p. 97); the critic, Michael Taucher,
whose articles "reveal" the "certain beauty, but . . . parasitic beauty" of
the father's stories (p. 72); Aunt Theresa, who converted to Christianity
and was hospitalized in a Christian sanitorium, from whose letters "it
was clear she was enchanted by the life of the convent, and it was only
the beauty of the landscape to which her senses were opening" (p. 75).
Other encounters with the opposing spirits take place during the family's
journeys in their small city and in various places around it: the grand-
mother, Amalia, who was forgotten in a sanitorium for thirty years, returns and predicts a "harsh judgment awaiting her daughters who had
converted to Christianity in the world to come" (p. 49); and the anonymous female admirer whom the father meets in the train and who ex-
poses his detachment from everything happening around him; the artist
Stark, the son of a Jewish mother and a Christian father, who decided to
have himself circumcised and whom the family visits, after the event, in a
miserable Jewish home; the rabbi of the community, who refuses to hold
a Bar-Mitzvah ceremony for Bruno, declaring: "'A home in which the religious precepts are not observed and the sons are not circumcised does
not deserve to be called a Jewish home'" (p. 167). These and similar encounters reveal the weakness and alienation of the family. Against this
background it is no wonder that the story ends as "our door stood open
and strange people walked in and out as if the house were a public hall"
(p. 153) and the family itself is scattered in every direction: the father
abandons them for Vienna, and the mother and son "were on the cattle
train hurtling south" (p. 174).

Appelfeld's health resort novellas (*Badenheim, Ir Nofesh* [Badenheim,
Resort Town, 1975; trans. 1980 as *Badenheim 1939*]; "Hapisga" [The
Summit, 1982; trans. 1985 as *The Retreat*]; and *Ritzpat Esh* [Fiery Ember,

1988]) are based on the same spatial-thematic structure as "Bimlo Ha-stav," *Keishon Haayin,* and the first part of *The Age of Wonders.* The in-novation here is in the specific character of the setting (a place of recrea-tion, at least ostensibly), the way in which the opposing spirits are presented; and—though only in *Badenheim* and *Ritzpat Esh*—the loca-tion of one of the marginal vertices of the spatial-fictional triangle.

The Retreat takes place in late 1937 in the "Institute for Advanced Studies." This is an isolated spot on a high mountain in the Austrian provinces, and its mission is to bring about "reform of body and soul" (p. 103) for people who suffer from "Jewish abnormality" (p. 126). The therapeutic methods are, among other things, physical activity, healthful country food, regular sleep, the battle against "melancholy," and devel-opment of a "correct" German accent.[13]

In this institute, which has long since shed its great aspirations, dwell a group of middle-aged Jews, most of whom were fired from their jobs be-cause of their Jewishness and whose families have abandoned them. This human collective has a role parallel to that filled by the nuclear family in "Bimlo Hastav," the extended family in *Keishon Haayin,* and the ex-tended family with its chance encounters in *The Age of Wonders.* It repre-sents the opposing spirits so typical of the Jewish community of that time and place: the great Balaban, the founder of the institute, who tries "to turn the sickly members of his race into a healthy breed" (p. 63) and to instill in them "the lessons of nature, the virtues of the horse" (p. 61); Lauffer, in whom "all the Jewish vices were personified" (p. 97) but who refuses to change; and Herbert Zuntz, the enlightened journalist, who tries to resolve the conflict, to find some middle way among the contra-dictory paths.

The opposing spirits represented by the residents of the institute are connected, as in the works already discussed, to the tension between the sinful metropolis and the primal purity of Jewish Ruthenian villages in the Carpathians. Lotte, the former actress in a provincial theater, has two contradictory dreams of place. The first one is to obtain "a grant to go to Vienna. To Berlin. To be free for a year from the chains of the provincial theater, to see the world, breathe the atmosphere of true theater, great theater" (p. 77). The second is to find "a resting place by the side of some simple man in a remote cottage where the bread was fresh and warm, vegetables grew outside the windows, horses grazed in the meadow and the fences were covered with creepers" (p. 66). Needless to say, these two visions appear here as artificial and groundless—just like the "noble

idea" by whose light the institute was established. At the end of the novel
all the members of the group are gathered, despoiled of their property
and looking with dread at Herbert, who returns from the village at the foot
of the mountain, battered and bruised by the blows of Ruthenian thugs.

In *Badenheim* and *Ritzpat Esh* the opposing spirits are represented by
the same structure, with one significant difference: the Carpathian village—the constant marginal vertex of the earlier stories—is exchanged
for other places that have the same spatial-thematic function. In *Badenheim* the place of the Carpathian village is taken by "Jewish Poland," and
in *Ritzpat Esh* by the Land of Israel.

In Badenheim, a health resort for assimilated Jews that gradually becomes a prison camp, a harsh struggle is waged between two camps: the
Austrian camp and the *Ostjuden* camp. The former is composed of totally assimilated Jews who yearn for Vienna and its luxuries. The latter
wish to return to the "origins"—that is to say, to Poland—for as Dr. Pap-
penheim, who in the past "brought the moist breath of the big city with
him" to Badenheim (p. 2), says, " 'We all lived in Poland once, and we're
all going back there' " (p. 52).

In *Ritzpat Esh* a similar struggle is waged in the heart of Rita Braun, a
capricious assimilated Jew who is vacationing with several old friends in
a small and remote Austrian village named Pracht. Like Lotte in *The Retreat,* Rita has two contradictory visions. On the one hand, she yearns for
the big city, with its charms and seductions, and on the other hand, she
dreams about Palestine, "the holy land . . . [where] she would have forgotten her miserable marriage, her muscles would be strengthened, and
she would marry a simple, straightforward farmer" (p. 59).

The struggle between the two existential possibilities, represented at
the vertices and margins of the two spatial triangles, culminates—with
great irony and horror—in the victory of the "purifying possibility." The
vacationers in Badenheim are transported in the train that will carry
them to "Jewish Poland," whereas Rita abandons her friends and her son
in Pracht and begins a mad journey in the course of which she has hallu-
cinations about Palestine and, significantly, loses the last vestige of her
dignity and decency.

Appelfeld made a more conspicuous change in the portrayal of the
Austro-Hungarian fictional triangle of his novels in *Beet Uveona Ahat* (At
One and the Same Time, 1985; trans. 1990 as *The Healer*) and *Timyon*
(Oblivion, 1993; trans. 1998 as *The Conversion*), and, in another version,

in *To the Land of the Cattails* (trans. 1986; published in Hebrew 1990–91, 1992 as "El Eretz Hagomeh") and *Ad Sheyaaleh Amud Hashahar* (Until the Dawn Rises, 1995). In the group of works mentioned earlier, the action of the plot takes place almost entirely in a small, remote location. The other places mentioned in those works are primarily representational. In contrast, in all the works mentioned just above, the main action takes place at two vertices or in one of them and on the way to another, or on the way between the two. The action of the first part of *The Healer*, which is set in the second half of the 1930s, takes place in a tiny village in the Carpathians, and the second part takes place on the way back to Vienna and in Vienna itself. The first part of *The Conversion*, which is set in the second decade of the twentieth century, takes place in a provincial Austrian city named Neufeld, and the second part is set in a village named Rosow in the Carpathians. The central action of *To the Land of the Cattails*, which takes place just before the outbreak of World War II, is set on the road between an Austrian town named Schoenburg and a village named Dratscincz in Bukovina. The central action of *Ad Sheyaaleh Amud Hashahar* takes place during the mid-1930s in a small Austrian town named Heimland and on the way from it to the hasidic village of Vizhnitz, which is located in the heart of the Carpathians.

The change in the spatial-fictional triangle of these stories is not a trivial matter. It indicates a phenomenon that distinguishes the latest stage of Appelfeld's fiction. The central figures here take their fate into their own hands. Some seek purification in the place of their origins (close to the tribal home and/or to nature): the mother, Henrietta, in *The Healer;* Karl in *The Conversion;* and the mother, Toni Strauss, in *To the Land of the Cattails*. Others wish both to purify themselves in a place of origin and also to take revenge against the gentiles: Blanca in *Ad Sheyaaleh Amud Hashahar* sets fire to many churches on her way to Vizhnitz. However, one way or another, in all these stories, the process of purification is an apparent or a tardy return. The characters who had at least seemed to detach themselves from the vain attractions of dazzling, urbane Austrian life do not succeed in rejoining the opposite, rooted way of life.

The town planning of the stories that are set in the Land of the Cattails includes another central architectural principle, one that reflects the existential situation of the two large groups of residents in the region: Jews and gentiles. The fictional space in the stories of the Austro-Hungarian region, or, to be more precise, the actualized space in which the action of

the plot takes place, is always divided into two existential zones: the first
zone is that of Jewish life, described as a small territorial enclave, surrounded on all sides by an enormous borderless expanse; the second zone
is that of gentile existence, and it includes the entire space, except for that
of Jewish life.

These two groups relate very differently toward the regions where they
live. The gentiles take the space for granted, and they adapt to it marvelously. By contrast, the Jews view the space where they live as alien and
hostile. They feel different, deviant. They do not fit in, and in the end they
are expelled from the space without any fuss. Their foreignness, as the
youthful narrator of *Keishon Haayin* states prophetically, "continually
grows on them like a skin. The [Ruthenian] village surrounds them as
with heavy fetters" (p. 80).

The difference between the gentiles' and the Jews' relation toward the
surrounding space stands out especially in the stories of the Land of the
Cattails that have a rural setting ("Bimlo Hastav," *Keishon Haayin*) and
in the village sections of the other stories of the region (*Katerina* [1988;
trans. 1992], *The Conversion, To the Land of the Cattails,* and *Ad Sheyaaleh Amud Hashahar*). The father of the family in "Bimlo Hastav"
clearly expresses the nature of this difference:

> But it seemed that the kind of arrangement that we're used to in the human
> realm began to develop among the plants, too. On the one hand, and
> mainly, large plants whose foliage is always imbued by an expression of
> wildness, and on the other hand—as though to show contrast, pampered
> plants with slender stems. If the wind just blows on them—they'll be up-
> rooted. ("Bimlo Hastav," *Kefor al Haaretz,* p. 69)

The contrast pointed out by Mr. Rappaport is also mentioned in *Keishon
Haayin,* but in a slightly different version:

> The [gentile] servants stood outside like forces of nature. In the winter their
> movements narrow, and they are as slow as bears. They hit slowly, snore
> rhythmically, and when it's cold they shift a heap of coal and kindle fire in
> it. How meager we were compared to them. Butterflies on whose antennas
> thin sadness always trembles. And even if you uproot them from here, they
> always know what the season is. And we're more sensitive every year, and
> always surprised. Suddenly we sensed: a distant melody knocks on the
> shutters of the house, a soundless melody. We didn't know how it was

called, how you drive it away, how you wrap yourself in its whispering woe. We were like winter birds that a forgotten, uncomprehended melody has reached. (*Keishon Haayin,* in *Kemeah Edim* [Like a Hundred Witnesses], 1975, p. 197)

This passage contains all the components of the contrast between the relations of Jews and gentiles to their surroundings.[14] The gentiles' life cycle is adapted to that of the natural world. In the winter, for example, they are as slow moving as bears. In contrast, the life cycle of the Jews does not suit that of nature. They are like winter birds that have forgotten the meaning of the secret call to leave for warmer climes, and they are relegated to cold regions and fated to die.[15] The gentiles, like "forces of nature," are a permanent fixture of the landscape, whereas the Jews are transient, like butterflies that perish the day they are born. The gentiles stand outside; open spaces never frighten them. In contrast, the Jews are shut up at home; and they view open spaces and nature as wild and dangerous. The gentiles work in the fields, cut down trees in the forest, and swim in the river, while the spatial existence of the Jews is expressed in sporadic outings for picnics and mainly in contemplation of the landscape through their own "natural space"—the glassed-in veranda that looks out at the courtyard and the surrounding fields.[16]

What is the character of that Jewish existence, for which nature and the Ruthenian peasants serve as mirrors in all the stories of the Land of the Cattails? Appelfeld himself provided a partial answer to this question in an interview with S. Shifra in 1975: "The landscape is an illustrative element that is placed [in these stories] in opposition to a certain Jewish way of life. The Jew, who was urban by nature, against his will in some measure, viewed the landscape as a demonic element. The fields, the forest, were a source of fear . . . In the eyes of the Jewish intellectual [as in the family in *Keishon Haayin*] nature is seen as life, and everything outside of nature is death."[17]

The combination of these two contrasting pairs in Appelfeld's remarks—nature and life versus the Jew and death—creates a chilling equation that is also present in his fiction. This equation portrays the life of assimilated Austro-Hungarian Jews as fundamentally decadent. The rural families in "Bimlo Hastav" and *Keishon Haayin,* the bands of vacationers in *Badenheim, The Retreat,* and *Ritzpat Esh,* Karl, Martin, and Freddi in *The Conversion,* the mothers and their children in *To the Land of the Cattails* and in *Ad Sheyaaleh Amud Hashahar*—all the Jews of the Land of the Cattails suffer from the same ailment: they are all afflicted with what can be defined as diminution of the will to live. This affliction is expressed, among other things, in prolonged emotional aridity, accompanied by bouts of depression that have no clear cause.[18] Indeed, all of them are characterized by attraction and subtle sensitivity to delicate sensory stimulation: to the smallest nuances of light and shade and hue,[19] voices and sounds,[20] and fine tastes.[21] Another characteristic of these "pampered plants with slender stems" ("Bimlo Hastav," *Kefor al Haaretz,* p. 69) is an awareness that although nature is the source of life and creativity, they nevertheless feel revulsion for everything natural—and attraction for cultivated and artificial things.

These symptoms, which characterize all the assimilated Jews of the Land of the Cattails, seem to derive from two interconnected phenomena: detachment from the natural environment and the tribal tradition, on the one hand, and excessive cultural delicacy, on the other. According to the stereotypes of decadence, these phenomena typify societies that have gone beyond the peak of their historical-biological development and are now undergoing an irreversible decline.[22]

It must be emphasized that Appelfeld's disintegrating families and vacationers glow with subtle and refined beauty, but this beauty is always depicted as the sickly aspect of creatures that have long since lost their vitality. Hence it is no surprise that Appelfeld's decadent protagonists are identified with beautiful and rare, though artificial, forms of life. Thus, for example, the members of the Hoffman family in *Keishon Haayin* are identified with exotic plants that the mother grows with holy reverence in a greenhouse: the "cactuses, which are similar to petrified animals," and the "red flowers from whose corollas drips thick sap" and whose stems "are attentive like snakes, and bushes from distant lands" (p. 252). Similarly, the vacationers in *Badenheim* are identified with the delicate tropical fish in the aquarium that stands in the hotel lobby—artificial creatures that the vacationers take with them ("holding the bottle wrapped in a green sweater[,] he cradled it in his arms like a sleeping baby," p. 131) on their way to the transport that will carry them to their doom.

The exotic plants, the tropical fish, and the Jews who are enthusiastic about them and feel close to them will all—according to the decadent and deterministic logic that prevails here—suffer the same fate. Indeed, the greenhouse is blown up, the tender fish die, and their owners are "evacuated" in transports, their place taken by those more fit for life.

The Land of Searing Light

Who, like him, is able to describe, in detail and in colorful language, the cruel separation and the hopeless transplanting into the Mediterranean region.

—"BAMEKOMOT HANEMUKHIM" *(Kefor al Haaretz)*

The stories of the Land of the Cattails are populated, as we have seen, by Jews who live in the region of their birth, who speak the vernacular, and who are well integrated in the local way of life and culture. The stories set in Israel—the Land of Searing Light—are populated by Holocaust survivors who have arrived in Israel "by chance," immigrants who do not speak the local language and are not integrated in the local way of life and culture. The demographic difference between the two regions is also expressed by the surrounding population. In the Land of the Cattails stories, this population is gentile, while in the Israeli stories, it is Jewish.

The conspicuous demographic differences between the two large regions could invite different topographical patterns. Thus we might expect that the map of the Israel stories would be ruled by a systemic logic different from that of the Land of the Cattails stories. This is not the case, however. Though the two maps are not identical, the same systemic logic is inherent in both.

A Full Reckoning Cannot Be Demanded

The first houses in the Israeli region were built, just like those of the Austro-Hungarian region, without any town planning. Though young, Appelfeld was aware of this architectural flaw. His first stories and sketches, those which he decided not to include in any book,[23] deal with the efforts of semi-autobiographical figures to draw a map for themselves, a defined topographical pattern that they could use as an emotional anchor. These efforts are portrayed in a fixed spatial and plot pattern: a person who has recently arrived in Israel wanders through the streets of a city unknown to him—Jerusalem or Tel Aviv—and his mind grows weary as he tries in vain to cling to another geographical point of

departure: the regions of his childhood—Bukovina or the Carpathians—
or the area of his wanderings during the Holocaust. Thus, for example, in
"Rega" (Moment, 1961) we are linked to the consciousness of a man
who repeatedly says to himself that he remembers nothing, that he "is
getting lost," and that he "must clarify [for himself] a point of departure
[from which] he can rebuild." The story ends with a chance encounter,
by means of which it appears to that man, for only a brief moment, that
he has finally found the point of departure.

> The man shaded his eyes, but through his eyelids he sensed how the two
> men, whom he had seen earlier from a distance, were approaching. Their
> steps were clearly audible. Now their voices became clearer, especially that
> of the thin one.
>
> "They divided us into two," said the thin man. "They transported us to
> Toltsch, and from Toltsch they took us to Toltzin, and from Toltzin they
> took us to Gubrin. And when there were only a few of us left, they trans-
> ported us to Zarfin, but in Zarfin there was no room, and they took us to
> Farstein. In Farstein only five of us were left, but since there was no room,
> they returned us to Zarfin, and from Zarfin to Gubrin, and from Gubrin to
> Toltzin, and from Toltzin back to Toltsch."
>
> He walked and listed, listed again, until you couldn't know whether he
> was listing for the stones as they rolled down onto the field. He listed and
> counted to himself or shouted into your ears. He counted again and
> listed—as though stoning some evil animal. ("Rega")

In another story from this group, "Hirhurei Kayitz Hatufim" (Passing
Summer Thoughts, 1961) we are linked to the consciousness of a man
who is wandering in the outskirts of an unidentified city, apparently Tel
Aviv. He keeps trying to imagine a "full picture" of the region of his
childhood near the Prut River. The man is aware that he cannot refrain
from this effort, and also that he is bound to fail.

> And so, without noticing, you head south. You've also left the area of
> the housing projects. Yellow expanses are spread before you. Sand, a sea of
> sand. Will you get lost soon in that monotonous yellowness? . . .
>
> Ha, if you gave your imagination a little freedom, the details would rise
> up here and trample. Like herds of sheep on their return from pasture. The
> whole allotment. You're careful not to do that. For can anyone demand the
> whole picture from you? . . .
>
> A soft evening begins to slip over from the firmament. As though it were
> trying to make an appropriate frame for your thoughts. In the twilight it's

easy to sail away. Nothing can stop you. You feel the danger and try to re-
trace your steps. A full reckoning cannot be demanded. But you also can't
prevent yearnings or pain or awareness. Yes, awareness.

You walk and walk but never arrive. Where does the path lead? ("Hirhurei Kayitz Hatufim")

Cellars and Ground Floors, Streets and Squares

The Israeli stories that Appelfeld decided to include in *Ashan,* as well as
the later Israeli stories that were collected in *Adnei Hanahar,* have a different character. This difference is expressed in the cognitive situation of
the characters and also in their spatial pattern.[24] Center stage is occupied
here by characters whose consciousness is totally or partially blocked.
These characters are portrayed as people who have made every effort "to
bury their memories—both from the Holocaust period and from their
childhood—deep in the seabed of the soul. This is a place where no
stranger's eye, nor even their own eye, can reach them" ("Al Hargasha
Ahat Manha Venimshekhet," *Masot Beguf Rishon,* p. 36). The cognitive
situation of the characters in these stories—so different from the cognitive situation of the characters in Appelfeld's first stories and sketches—is
well reflected in the architectural pattern: two spaces clearly separated
from each other. The first space is the main and more significant arena of
the action, always depicted as a small space, dense and enclosed. The second space, the secondary arena of the action, is always depicted as an
open area, lacking defined boundaries and concealing many dangers.

The first space is typically a cellar or ground floor, with many of the
connotations attached to cellars and ground floors in Western culture.[25]
This is the place of unconscious and unprocessed materials, materials
with mightily destructive potential. But it is also the place of the most
vital material, which is saved for times of trouble. Memories from the
past are always stored in Appelfeld's Israeli cellars and ground floors.
These can be memories of the distant past, of childhood in the Land of
the Cattails, or recent memories, from the Holocaust. These threatening
and precious memories are always embodied in secondary characters,
who never venture out of their cellars (at least not of their own free will);
the passing of time and historical events have no influence on them. Bertha is the secondary character in the story that bears her name, and all of
Max's memories are embodied in her figure. He is the main character,

and she always sits "inside, in the small room, [where] life was preserved in its fading frozen state, . . . as though for her there were no cycle of years, . . . no change took place in her" ("Bertha," *Ashan,* p. 61). The "old man" in the story, whose title is translated as "On the Ground Floor" ("Bekomat Hakarka") has a very similar role. The memories of his sister's two sons are bound up in his figure. The "old man" always sits in the ground floor, which is similar to a "dark cave" ("Bekomat Hakarka," *Ashan,* p. 192), "and only he, it seems, is untouched by time" (p. 195).

The cellars and the cellar figures often represent the collective memory of the tribe. Thus the "old man" in "Bekomat Hakarka" remembers all of the Jewish holidays from his "deep and isolated" place (pp. 193–95). Similarly Regina, whom Zeitchik "kept down below in the cellar," looks at him, her patron, with "a look that remained with her from her ancestors" ("Regina," *Adnei Hanahar,* pp. 28–30). Into Shimon Zinger's "rented cellar" "rise [!] scattered remnants of Solocin" ("Akhsanya" [Hostel], *Adnei Hanahar,* p. 36). In the same way, Bronca in "Hasoher Bartfuss" ("Bartfuss the Merchant," *Adnei Hanahar*) has "a simple relationship with her parents, as though she had not been separated from them" (p. 46). Of Kandel's Bronda we are told:

> [Kandel] used to find shelter with Bronda the blind woman. She would secretly let him into her room, in the cellar, and he would quietly burrow into her blindness. It was a narrow room, lit with diluted darkness. A table ran across its length, with a wooden bench, as though stolen from an abandoned synagogue. The wide bed was low. She seldom left her room. The neighbors installed a faucet for her, and she used to wash in a big wooden tub. ("Bronda," *Adnei Hanahar,* p. 12)

Kandel's burrowing into the depths of the unconscious (the cellar and blindness) is an action typical of the Holocaust survivors in Appelfeld's Israeli stories.[26]

This action combines soothing and threatening elements: preservative forces (here, memory of the tribe and the synagogue) and dark, destructive forces (here, the allusion to theft). Other actions typical of those characters who serve a similar function are curling up under a blanket pulled over the head[27] and an obsessive sorting of objects that had belonged to relatives who perished in the Holocaust, objects that had been stuffed into closed and sealed containers (boxes or "rucksacks"), locked and stored in attics or in other remote, dark corners of the house.[28]

The secondary space of the Israeli stories—which surrounds the primary space, the cellar—is typically the street or square on the edge of a large city. Usually this place swarms with people and bustles with vehicles. The street, the movement of cars, the rushing of people, and everything else that threatens to upset the frozen routine that the Holocaust survivors protect in their cellar space, arouse responses of intense dread expressed in various ways. Many of these survivors are described as they walk on the sidewalk, "groping alongside the walls" ("Etzel Harofeh" [At the Doctor's, 1960]),[29] or when they try to cross a busy street or intersection. Often this apparently simple action is depicted in the early stories as a complex and fateful act.[30] Or they are depicted when they think about the "crushing movement" ("Rega")[31] or about the threatening width of the street or the square: "[Everything] is so open" ("Leyad Hamorad" [Near the Downslope, 1960]). The author indicates the great difficulty these characters have in walking in open, public spaces by repeatedly comparing the air to a liquid. Many Holocaust survivors in the Israeli stories move in the streets as though they are moving through "diluted liquids" ("Hakikar" [The Square], *Adnei Hanahar*, p. 179).[32]

The street and, primarily, the square are the places where the main characters in the Israeli stories are swallowed up in the anonymity of the masses. Here for transitory and illusory moments they are stripped of themselves, their memories, and their attachments—from all that is hidden in their cellars:

> There are many places in this city that awaken the melody of loneliness, but only in the square does its virtue reach perfection. In the square a person can forget who he is, what he has undergone, how sick he is: only in the square can a person emerge from his small and depressing isolation into the expanse of the great isolation. ("Hakikar," *Adnei Hanahar*, p. 174)

However, the transition from the cellar space to the open public space involves a grave danger. A breach in the partition between the two spaces always results in the annihilation of the cellar life. The main characters, who expose the secondary, cellar characters to the light of the world and to life in the ordinary course of (historical) time condemn them and, indirectly, themselves as well, to loss. Max takes Bertha from her sealed dwelling to open space, thereby causing her to leave her biological and emotional stagnation and to fall sick and die. After her death he stands in the street, holding her clothing in his hands: "He did not dare to open [the package], or perhaps these were no longer his hands, but rather iron hoops" ("Bertha," *Ashan,* p. 76). The young boys in "Bekomat Hakarka" cause the ceiling of the ruin in which they had lived to collapse on the head of their old uncle so as to free themselves once and for all from him and from the memory of the past that he represents. However, just as the ceiling collapses, the light of day penetrates the dark space and "the voice of the old man was heard [from within], flashing like a spark, and thus through the open ceiling they met face to face" ("Bekomat Hakarka," *Ashan,* p. 203). Those living in cellars are doomed to die, even when the main characters do not intend it. The collapse of the cellar space, which preserves the memory of the self and that of the tribe, is certain.

Centrifugal forces—those that impel the characters to leave their cellars (the desire to integrate into the new surroundings and to form new ties)—always overcome the centripetal forces (the connection with the tribal heritage and ties formed among the characters during the war), those that preserve the cellar existence. Thus it is only "natural" that many of the early stories from the Israeli region end with the metaphorical invasion of polluting factors from the surrounding space (the changes wrought by time and the forces of nature) into the inner space and the destruction of the memory shelters. Thus, for example, "the house, which was once called the [Yiddish] theater, slowly peeled, and the wind settled in its entry" ("Halahaka" [The Troupe], *Adnei Hanahar,* p. 190); Zinger's cellar, which had been a pilgrimage center "for the scattered remnants of Soloctin," was now vacant, and only "foreign ghosts [knock] on the windows" ("Akhsanya," *Adnei Hanahar,* pp. 34, 38). Similarly, the office of Ehrlich, a lawyer "who had devoted his life to the matter of compensation," was crammed of late with "sharp spirits" and "dark barrenness" ("Orekh Hadin Shelanu" [Our Attorney], *Adnei Hanahar,* pp. 186–87). Furthermore, the powers that invade the cellar space are always forces of nature, universal forces independent of social and historical context.

The Good, the Sturdy, and the Industrious Work Outside.
The Weaklings Are Sent to the Laundry

In his first Israeli stories, and also in his first Israeli novella, *Haor Vehakutonet,* and the last Israeli novella, *The Immortal Bartfuss,* Appelfeld almost completely ignores the social and ideological context in which the

Holocaust survivors find themselves upon their arrival in Israel. But in the novella *Mikhvat Haor,* Appelfeld adopts a different approach. This work tells the story of a group of teenage boys, Holocaust survivors, who live on a farm where they are supposed to undergo Zionist training. The encounter of these young new immigrants with Zionist ideology triggers complex emotional and cognitive processes that the central protagonists in the other Israeli stories were spared. Collectively, the boys view the new ideology, which encourages them to erase their past and turn over a healthy new leaf, simple and more heroic, with ambivalence. On the one hand, they are tempted to integrate into the new, conquering essence and to relinquish their past completely. On the other hand, they sense that to integrate and give up their past endangers their existence as individuals. To defend themselves, they make an extreme effort to preserve the isolated scraps of memory that remain with them from their childhood in the Land of the Cattails.[33]

The boys' emotional and cognitive struggle with their past is portrayed within a well-defined cultural climate—one such as Appelfeld created only in his late Land of the Cattails stories—and is reflected, conspicuously, in the topographical arrangement of *Mikhvat Haor.* This novella is structured on a topographical pattern that combines two complementary spatial patterns. The first pattern—similar to the spatial pattern of most of the Israeli short stories that were later reprinted in collections—is built on the conflict between closed, dark spaces and open, bright ones. The second pattern, which encompasses the first one, is in the form of a triangle whose features represent the author's emotional and cognitive map. One vertex of the triangle serves as the central location of the action, and the basic existential possibilities are combined within it. The other two vertices serve as secondary settings for the action; there the main existential possibilities are portrayed in extreme and unequivocal guise.

The central setting for the action in *Mikhvat Haor* is the agricultural training farm—a fictional amalgam of the three farms where Appelfeld lived[34]—that embraces all the boys' responses to the predominant ideology. Some cruelly repress any shadow of consciousness and memory through "positive activity." The most extreme case is Yanko, who devotes all his time to productive work and athletics. The other boys, such as Bloch, the dwarf, and Blum, resolutely refuse to fit into the life of the farm and the ideological framework that seeks to knead and shape them, and they cling obsessively to images of the past. Unlike those who demonstrate these two extreme responses, both of which produce dismal failures, the

narrator and Shapira take a middle way that permits them to survive in
the complex situation. Both cooperate, at least ostensibly, with the mechanism of Zionist indoctrination, and at the same time they secretly nur-
ture precious scraps of their memory.

The scope of existential possibilities offered by the farm has a manifest topographical expression. The farm is divided into secondary expanses of two types: closed and dark places where "cellar characters"
act, those who do not wish to change or cannot do so; and open, illuminated spaces, where "positive characters" act, those who wish to change.
The secondary spaces of the first type are the laundry and the clothing
storeroom. Those of the second type are the orchards, the orange groves,
and the decorative garden. One of the women workers sums up the difference between the two types of secondary spaces, according to the
ideological hierarchy of the farm authorities: "the good, the sturdy, and
the industrious work outside. The weaklings are sent to the laundry" (p.
71). One of those weaklings is Druck, who refuses to forget the past, to
strengthen his muscles, and get a suntan. Hence a "moral failing" clings
to him, and he is judged before the "Old Maid" (pp. 72–73). Another
character who refuses to change is the dwarf. This boy's "frozen" physical being—which is, not coincidentally, very reminiscent of Bertha in
"Bertha"—represents in metonymic-metaphoric fashion the essence of
the "cellar character." He "digs into" the remembered past and refuses
obsessively to become attached to the "new life." Thus it is no surprise
that the "Old Maid" orders the boy's removal from the training farm;
nor is it any surprise that the hiding place his friends find for him, to save
him from expulsion, is a "bunker."

Various combinations of the two main existential options represented
in the training farm are also represented—in a more extreme and unequivocal fashion—in the marginal vertices of the fictional triangle. The
first option, the main feature of which is to forget the past and change ab-
solutely in accordance with Zionist ideology, is represented first of all by
the "kibbutzim in the valley" and the closed farms in the interior of the
country. There the "hard cases," the boys who have not reformed properly within the framework of the farm, are exiled. The boys learn about
the nature of those places, among other things, from rumors about their
future that circulate on the farm:

> They said that the Old Maid is going to send us to the interior of the coun-
> try, to the mountains where they clear stones, make walls, build terraces,

and do hard labor without any vacations or recreation. Another rumor said that it wouldn't be the mountains but corrective facilities that would uproot bad traits from us. (*Mikhvat Haor,* p. 123)

The second option, whose main feature is clinging to precious scraps of memory, is represented primarily by the "cafes on the outskirts of the city [Jaffa]," which the boy who narrates the story discovers with his friend Shapira in their wanderings beyond the boundaries of the farm. The character of these cafes, which call forth fragmented images from the boys' childhood, emerges in the following passage:

> I went out to the seashore and immediately my feet pulled me to our secret cafe. A few people sat around the tables, and a woman served them coffee and omelettes. A light aroma of baked cheese stood in the air. Now I saw the woman who owned the place for the first time. A few delicate lines were traced on her figure. Her voice was clear. She served the coffee without a tray.
>
> It turned out that everyone in the cafe spoke German, one with a Hungarian accent, one with a Czech accent. Something of the frivolity of the Viennese old-timers was present here, even in the curved cane of an old man who never stopped puffing on his pipe. The woman sitting by his side took pleasure in every word that left his mouth. The man, it seems, had once been a tobacco merchant of the rare sort.
>
> "Why don't you sit down?" the owner of the place turned to me the way people once addressed cousins who had grown up from one summer to the next. I sat down next to the window. Spots of afternoon shade were scattered on the floor. The people spoke quietly, but their voices were clear. For some reason I imagined I was seeing yellow grains of wheat pouring from a narrow funnel.[35] (*Mikhvat Haor,* p. 117)

Mikhvat Haor, which is Appelfeld's Israeli novella *par excellence,* is built on the same topographical pattern as his Austro-Hungarian stories. Hence the extremely dramatic transition from the Land of the Cattails to Israel did not cause an essential change in the architectonic pattern. In other words, with Appelfeld—as with other skeptical authors who immigrated to Israel before and after the Holocaust, from Y. H. Brenner, S. Y. Agnon, and L. A. Arieli-Orlov through Haim Hazaz and Yitzhak Shenhar to David Schuetz—the change in place does not produce a change in fortune, and the new skies do not change people.

In both regions the characters hesitate between essentially the same existential alternatives: self-abnegation and integration within the "alien" space versus the effort to cling to personal and tribal roots. This similarity between the spatial patterns of the two large regions in Appelfeld's realm necessitates at least two comments: First, it is impossible to ignore the fact that the Zionist option in *Mikhvat Haor* occupies a place parallel to that of the option of assimilation in the stories of the Land of the Cattails, which is to say that it symbolizes a clear tendency to unwitting suicide.[36] Second, and these matters are interrelated, it is impossible not to notice that assimilated Jewish life in Central Europe is viewed differently in the stories of the Land of the Cattails from the way it is viewed in stories of the Land of Israel. In both regions this way of life is viewed through a double prism—sympathy and understanding versus a sober and critical view. However, in the stories of the Land of the Cattails the sober and critical view is dominant, while in the Israeli stories sympathy and understanding are more prevalent. This difference is shown in that in the Israeli stories in general, and in *Mikhvat Haor* in particular, the assimilated Jewish way of life of Central Europe—represented here mainly by the forgotten cafes on the outskirts of Jerusalem and Tel Aviv—are given the place reserved in the stories of the Land of the Cattails for rooted existence— the Jewish way of life in remote villages in Bukovina and or the small hasidic centers in the Carpathians—and for the new life in Israel.

It is interesting to examine the portrayal of existential space in all the stories of the Land of the Cattails and in the long stories of the Land of Searing Light against the background of the principal ways in which existential space is portrayed in the corpus of modern Hebrew literature. Such an examination reveals that Appelfeld is far more closely tied to classical and postclassical Hebrew and Yiddish writers, who depicted the life of Jewish villages in Eastern Europe (the shtetl), than to writers of the Land of Israel.

According to sociologists Mark Zborowski and Elizabeth Herzog, life in the Eastern European shtetl revolved around three centers: the home, the synagogue, and the market. The home represented people's intimate and secure space; the synagogue (and also the *heder* [boys' elementary school] and the *yeshiva*) represented the connection between Jews and their God and the tribal heritage; and the market or the street represented the connection between Jews and the secular world—the world of difficulties in making a living and of physical dangers in encounters with gentiles.[37]

The classical authors of the shtetl—first of all Mendele Mokher Sefarim (Shalom Yaakov Abramovitch) and Shalom Aleichem—created similar if not identical existential triangles. In their writing, too, life revolved around the home, the synagogue, and the market. There, however, unlike historical reality, in the market and the street there is hardly any mention of the encounter with non-Jews either as individuals or as representatives of an ethnic and religious community. This distortion apparently derived, as Dan Miron argues, from the desire of these authors to represent the shtetl as "a pure unit of existence, a kind of enclave of undiluted *yiddish-kait* [Jewishness], . . . a tiny and weak 'realm,' exposed to every peril, but also autonomous and complete unto itself."[38] The postclassical authors—H. N. Bialik, Y. D. Berkowitz, and others—relied upon the classical authors, but they changed the image of the shtetl from the ground up. Here the Jewish existential triangle is no longer autonomous and self-sufficient. One of its vertices, the market or street, is almost always related to the trials of economic existence and also to real physical danger—phenomena that are always connected to the encounter between Jews and non-Jews, who represent hostile and violent forces. Rather than an idyllic picture of "a pure unit of existence," the postclassical authors presented a picture embodying an ethnic and ethical dichotomy: on the one hand, humble and peace-loving Jews, and on the other hand, violent non-Jews who trample the Jews' liberty and honor and steal their property. In this corpus the Jews are portrayed mainly as passive victims of gentile violence and incitement[39] or as innocent and honest people who are always injured by the negative forces of history, which are embodied in the eccentric ways of hostile, non-Jewish authorities.[40]

The picture of reality in Appelfeld's stories of the large regions is an interesting and surprising development of the portrayal of Jewish town life, with a shift in time and place. As in the classical literature of the shtetl, the setting here is portrayed as "a tiny and weak 'realm,' exposed to every peril," but unlike the classical portrayal of the shtetl, it is not "autonomous and complete unto itself." Life is not at all autonomous in the isolated estates in "Bimlo Hastav" and *Keishon Haayin,* in the health resorts in *The Retreat, Badenheim,* and *Ritzpat Esh,* in the villages in *The Age of Wonders, The Conversion, Ad Sheyaaleh Amud Hashahar,* and others, and also in the cellars and ground floors in the Israeli short stories and in the enclosed areas of existence in *Hakutonet Vehapasim* (trans. 1983 as *Tzili: The Story of a Life), Mikhvat Haor,* and *The Immortal Bartfuss.* Life is always buffeted by powerful "winds of the times." These "winds of the times" are sometimes rooted in the social and cultural context (in the long stories of the Land of the Cattails and in *Mikhvat Haor),* and sometimes they have a universal character, as though more objective (in the short Israeli stories and in *Tzili* and *The Immortal Bartfuss*). These winds penetrate the places where the stories are set and destroy them along with their inhabitants. Unlike the Jews of the classical shtetl, Appelfeld is not at peace with the tribal heritage.

The relations between Jews and non-Jews in Appelfeld's stories of the Land of the Cattails are similar to the relations in postclassical fiction, but at the same time different from them. As in many stories by Bialik, Berkowitz, and their contemporaries, a dichotomy is presented. However, that dichotomy is based on another principle: a talent for life. The non-Jews are connected to their tribal roots and to the natural world, and for that reason they survive and will continue to survive like the strong plants, whereas the Jews are severed from their tribal roots and from nature and therefore they, like pampered plants, lose their grip on the world.[41]

As noted, the marginal regions of the existential space of Appelfeld's main characters represent the existential possibilities in their most extreme forms: assimilation versus clinging to family and tribal roots. In the stories of the Land of the Cattails, the former extreme is represented by Vienna, Prague, Budapest, or a Ruthenian village; in Israel it is represented by Tel Aviv (the new Hebrew city), the *kibbutzim* in the interior of the country, or an army camp. The latter extreme, the possibility of clinging to family and tribal roots, is represented in the Land of the Cattails by trips to villages and hasidic shtetls in the Carpathians or in romantic visions of journeys to Palestine. The attachment of Appelfeld's characters to these marginal existential regions is similar to that of the deracinated main characters (*telushim* in Hebrew) of M. Z. Feierberg and M. Y. Berdyczewski, and those of Y. H. Brenner, Uri Nissan Gnessin, Gershon Shofman, S. Y. Agnon, and other writers of that generation. One extreme of these areas for them was the shtetl, the provincial Jewish town where they were born and which they abandoned with the aim of developing and of acquiring secular education. The other extreme was the large city in Eastern or Western Europe, representing the "wide world" into which they wished to integrate or assimilate. This arrangement of existential space derives, of course, from the similarity in the fundamentally ambivalent attitude of all these writers, in their respective generations, to their personal past and cultural heritage.[42]

This basic similarity implies a kind of declaration of allegiance by Appelfeld to a certain segment of Hebrew literature, which can be called the Jewish-historical segment. At the same time it implies that he does not belong to another segment, which can be called the Israeli-regional segment. It also permits us to discern a central trait that distinguishes the uprooted characters of Appelfeld's Land of the Cattails from the uprooted characters whom he portrays against the background of life in Israel. Appelfeld's deracinated Austro-Hungarians express their basic attitude toward their past—like the *telushim* of Brenner and Gnessin—in conversations and arguments and mainly in abundant reflections and inner monologues. These expressions indicate an impressive introspective ability. In contrast, the uprooted characters who arrive in Israel after the Holocaust are largely inarticulate, devoid of introspective ability, expressing their distress primarily in rich body language and inscrutable silences.

The Italian Region: An Intermediary Region

> For someone who has lost his home, any place is home.
> —"BEMAKOM AHER"
> (IN ANOTHER PLACE, *Kefor al Haaretz*)

Appelfeld's imaginary realm includes, as we noted earlier in this part, two other regions: the Italian region and the Penal Colony.[43] The Italian region constitutes a kind of intermediary area between the Land of the Cattails and the Land of Israel. The Penal Colony, a region of evil decrees, is viewed, at least on the topographical level, as decidedly extraterritorial.

The Italian region, where quite a few stories are set,[44] is arranged according to a topographical pattern similar to that of the long stories in the Land of the Cattails and in the Land of Israel. This arrangement is especially prominent in the novella *1946*, the longest and most detailed Italian story. This novella is built on a triangular spatial arrangement whose specific traits are no different in essence from those of the parallel arrangement in *Badenheim,* the novella with which it was first published in 1978 in the Hebrew volume, *Shanim Veshaot*.

The main actions in *1946* are set in the transit camp of Holocaust survivors who are on their way from various places in Europe to places that will take them in: Israel, the United States, Australia, New Zealand, and even Alaska. In the transit camp, as in all the main locations of the long Austro-Hungarian and Israeli stories, the central existential possibilities are presented, with their most extreme and unequivocal forms located on the marginal vertices. Among the buildings in and near the transit camp, the most prominent is a rickety shed that serves as a synagogue, where a sick and depressed rabbi dwells. When he is lucid, he tries to prepare hearts for repentance and/or immigration to Israel. On the door of another shed, the word "Headquarters" is written in German. There the self-hating Jew Frank tries to transform a group of boy survivors into a "storm squadron." Another shed belongs to Lucy and Hermina, two prostitutes who dream of a life of luxury in a large city. In a shack near the sea live Lump and his gentile wife, Stella, who try (at least at the beginning of the story) to forget the past and "return to nature," in the non-Jewish, rural manner.

These structures and the action that takes place inside them represent the refugees' range of existential possibilities. They start with the effort to reestablish contact with the national and tribal roots (the rabbi's shed) and extend to the effort to assimilate into the non-Jewish surroundings, either rural (Lump and Stella's shack) or urban (Lucy and Hermina's shed). These existential possibilities are marked, in a more extreme and unequivocal way, in places outside the camp. The effort to forget the past and assimilate into the non-Jewish surroundings is identified with Naples, because "everything is possible in Naples" (p. 162). The effort to reunite with tribal-national roots is identified with "the warm, magical land" (p. 149), for at least in appearance, "all roads lead to Palestine" (p. 160).

These two existential possibilities, which Appelfeld ironically sets up as parallels by "correcting" the proverb about all roads leading to Rome, are of course vain, an outcome hinted by the collapse of the buildings that represent them. Sea winds penetrate the rabbi's shed, and he is transferred to the shed of Lucy and Hermina (p. 161); Lump falls ill with typhus and is transferred from his seaside shack to the "quarantine" (p. 171); and the kiosk, where the various existential possibilities were discussed vociferously, "was completely eaten up by the winds by now, and all the expensive summer equipment was scattered over the sands" (p. 173). The ridiculous and horrid gap between the promising possibilities that the characters contemplate and what the future has in store for them—portrayed here, as in all of Appelfeld's stories, as heavily overshadowed by the past—is clearly suggested by the difference between the images with which Hermina the prostitute and the omniscient narrator describe the transit camp. Hermina compares the camp, with the frenetic activity that takes place in its sheds, to a "resort city" (p. 121), whereas the narrator compares those very sheds, swaying and teetering in the wind, to "muddy freight cars, shunted pointlessly along barren railways" (p. 169).

The similarity between the stories of the Italian region and those of the two large regions, in the topographical context, is also expressed by the character of the relation between the fictional map and the geographical-historical map. The transit camp, the center of the fictional map of Italy, is a marginal place on the geographical-historical map, whereas central places on that map—Naples, Vienna, and Jerusalem—are marginal places on the fictional map. This reversal in degree of centrality and importance of the places here, as in the stories of the large regions, serves two main functions: thematically it represents Appelfeld's unique picture of the world; and poetically it creates an effect of restraint by portraying emotional situations in a gray and remote environment.

The status of the Italian region as an intermediary link between the large regions is derived primarily from its position as a junction for the major directions of movement in the fictional realm. Through this region pass many of the Holocaust survivors on their way to various places of refuge in Europe (for example, in *Mesilat Barzel* [The Iron Tracks, 1991; trans. 1998]) and outside it (as in *Tzili* and *Mikhvat Haor*). Other refugees do not fulfill their intention of moving on to another destination and settle here (for example, in "Hashayara" [The Convoy], *Bagai Haporeh*]). Still other refugees who reach Israel do not find their place there and dream of returning here (for example, in *Tzili* and *The Immortal Bartfuss*), and one even fulfills that dream (Chokhovsky in "Beei Sant George" [In the Isles of St. George, *Kefor al Haaretz;* trans. 1983 in *Jerusalem Quarterly*]).

The emphatic desire of the Holocaust survivors for the Italian region is always connected to two factors. First, in their minds, this region signifies being "open to possibilities" ("Al Yad Hahof," *Ashan,* p. 163). Here everyone receives temporary respite after the persecution of the Holocaust and before the traumatic encounter with Israel.[45] "There were no days lovelier than these," declares the narrator in *1946*. "Success, like the sun and the sea, shone upon everything. Whoever didn't smuggle, dealt, and whoever didn't exchange money opened a kiosk. The girls bought lots of dresses in Naples, dreamt about a career, and the men learned to drink Turkish coffee" (p. 118). "People said in astonishment, this is a rest home" (p. 111).

Second, the principal characteristics of the Italian region are portrayed as a comfortable mixture of the principal characteristics of the large regions. This mixture is marked, for example, by the struggle between forgetting and remembering. As noted, in their extreme guise, these are always embodied in the cold and snow of Europe versus the glaring heat of Israel, which allows no refuge. Here, on the Italian coast or in the islands to the south of it, which are characterized by warm and pleasant sun and clear but not searing light as a comfortable mixture of the principal characteristics of the large regions, memory is aroused for the first time. Though the process is oppressive and demanding, it is not accompanied by destructive qualities that always accompany the parallel awakening of memories in the stories of the Israeli region.

The character of the struggle between remembering and forgetting is reflected in the stories of the Italian region—as in all of Appelfeld's other stories—in the portrayal of the topographical dimension. The Italian stories are always set in remote places and ruins with a checkered history. They include episodes imbued with a glow of significance, splendor, and sanctity and chapters replete with historical evils and crimes. For example, the refugees in "Bagova Hakar" are housed in the tower of Larma:

> Originally, as the ruins show, it served as a watchtower for one of the princes. Later, due to its rare qualities, it was made into a castle. . . . In time the place became a dwelling for monks; there is even a notion that during the eighteenth century people used to attribute curative powers to it. For reasons that cannot be explained now, the monks left the mountain, and prisoners with life sentences were brought to the tower, for the place could also serve that low purpose. It is far from any settlement, a natural barrier to all flight. From here on the chronicles tend to break down. Some maintain that the castle became a monastery again, and, in contrast, others maintain that it was a prison("Bagova Hakar," *Bagai Haporeh,* p. 135). [46]

The vicissitudes of the tower of Larma, which combine sanctity and sin, destructive and curative forces, a history that contains more rumor and conjecture than proven fact—a phenomenon that the narrator reinforces by his vague formulation—are a faithful reflection of the state of consciousness of the refugees from history who arrive in the tower. They apprehend their personal and tribal past as a faint combination of reality and imagination. They seek to flee the few scraps of memory, which arouse in them feelings of dread and guilt, and at the same time they try to cling to them, the way survivors of a shipwreck cling to flotsam from their ship.

The survivors' relation to the past in "Bagova Hakar" and the other Italian stories is different from the relation to the past of the refugees depicted in the Israeli stories. Those in the Italian stories are described shortly after the end of the war, and they are in a state of cognitive shock in relation to the near and more distant past. While they are already beyond pursuit and persecution, they have not yet succeeded in fortifying themselves in cellars and ground floors—the spaces so typical of refugees in Israel. The spaces typical of the refugees in Italy are barren places where signs of the Holocaust, which has just ended—at least historically—are evident.[47] A place like this is revealed to Chokhovsky, the main character of "In the Isles of St. George":

> When he reached the top of the hill a startling sight greeted his eyes. The plain was covered with huge clumps of disembowelled earth, testimony to a holocaust not long past. Upturned rocks leant unsteady on each other, suspended in thin air. A force not of this world seemed to have ripped them out of the earth. The silence was more absolute than any he had ever known, as if this was its true home. The recently unearthed rocks did not look like inanimate objects. They looked different, raw, as if they had not yet had time to die. ("In the Isles of St. George," *Jerusalem Quarterly,* p. 57)

The state of matter in the expanse that Chokhovsky contemplates is a clear projection of his conscious state. The world here is no longer in the chaotic stage—the stage depicted in the Penal Colony stories, as we shall see below—but it has not yet been organized in its ordinary manifestations.

This state leaves Chokhovsky "openings . . . as small as antholes" (p. 60) to the more distant past—the period of his childhood in the Land of the Cattails. However, these entries are blocked. Chokhovsky's efforts to make contact with his childhood memories ultimately end in dismal failure. This failure, it must be said, was expected, hinted at by means of an architectural-spatial metaphor: the drilling that had been done on the island at various times produced no result. This spatial metaphor appears, in very similar fashion, in the other Italian stories as well.[48]

The Penal Colony: Primeval, Formless Space

> I remember one boy, whose movements had been made flexible and rounded like those of an attentive animal by the war years. He would not touch an object before examining it at length. This was certainly the way people behaved on the earth after the flood.
>
> —"EDUT" (*Masot Beguf Rishon*)

Several of the stories in Appelfeld's first two collections, *Ashan* and *Bagai Haporeh,* depict the region of the Penal Colony, as do most of the stories in the fourth collection, *Bekomat Hakarka,* and several of those in the fifth collection, *Adnei Hanahar*.[49] This region is doubtless unusual in Appelfeld's realm, at least with respect to its topography. Its exceptional nature is evident as soon as we seek to define its extent and its geographical and historical boundaries. It is possible to identify it by combining two elements: temporal signs, which are few and blurred; and allusions to the special character of the fauna and flora. Principally, however, it must be defined in relation to our knowledge of the author's life. The area in question is probably the fertile and savage expanse of Transnistria in the Ukraine. This region is huge and at the same time very monotonous; it is here that Aharon Appelfeld wandered as a child for many months during the Second World War and immediately after it was over.[50]

The exceptional and strange character of this region also emerges when we try in vain to map out what appear to be its extent and features. Unlike the stories of other regions, topographical centers are not indicated in the stories of the Penal Colony, nor are their secondary and marginal areas delineated. The action of the plot is always set on the broad plains. Sometimes they are dry, sometimes they are flooded with water, sometimes they are covered with snow, and sometimes they are swampy. In any event, it is a "plain without variation; the same view is seen on all sides" ("Bamidbar" [In the Desert], *Bagai Haporeh,* p. 102), and it is "a monotonous, exposed plain" ("Hagilui Haaharon" [The Last Revelation], *Adnei Hanahar,* p. 96). Similarly, in "Beyahad" (Together):

> Now they were in an open field. It was exposed like the autumn itself, that sheds skin after skin, and only the thin branches are like transparent fingers. Nothing will disappear. Transparency through another transparency; smell and sound as though in competition across plains that are joined to other plains. A leaf will fall, and the sound of its separation will fill space with a rustle. ("Beyahad," *Bekomat Hakarka,* p. 48)

The gigantic, monotonous plains do not create a feeling of free and open space because they are portrayed as infinite and hermetically sealed at the same time. The characters feel as though they are in an enormous trap. Although they have a large expanse in which to move, they can also be easily discerned from a distance:

> They were exposed. The valley gleamed like a brass vessel: light broke in other light and joined together again. There was no escape. The bushes

were too low to provide cover, and the shepherds around them were like
sentinels at their posts. . . . They had no hiding place, the ringing of the
bells crossed the clear space as though it were not a space. ("Beyahad,"
Bekomat Hakarka, p. 52)

Some of the Penal Colony stories are set in regions with dense vegetation
("Shlosha," "Shohet" [Ritual Slaughterer, *Bagai Haporeh*], "Habriha"
[The Escape, *Bekomat Hakarka*], "Hamatzod" [The Hunt, *Adnei Hanahar*], and "Hahishtanut" [Transmutation, *Bekomet Hakarka*]), and some
against a background of the inner space of the monastery ("Kittie" and
"Hamahaseh Haaharon" [The Last Refuge, *Bagai Haporeh*]). In these
stories, too, the pursued characters find no refuge.

The characters in all the Penal Colony stories set in this region are
aware that they have no sanctuary. This knowledge or feeling is always indicated by reference to the distant landscape that cannot be traversed:
high mountains, broad lakes, quicksand marshes, and the like. These features shut in the setting of the action on all sides and make it into a "natural" valley of slaughter. Thus it is no surprise that nature, which is apparently neutral, is described in many of these stories as lustful and predatory.
The final passage in "Hagilui Haaharon" is one of dozens of examples:

Later the sharp autumn winds came. Birds filled the air with a deafening
tweeting. . . . The horizon polished its redness and the nights were cold. . . .
The trees grew barer, and the winds chopped like sharp scythes. Everything
about sought to exhaust itself completely. In the distant villages thin smoke
curled up. The horizon turned red like the mouth of an oven. The distance
hid nothing. The cold made his skin turn the color of metal. ("Hagilui Haaharon," *Adnei Hanahar*, pp. 90–100)

The unique character of the Penal Colony region in the topographical
dimension of Appelfeld's fiction is also expressed in the vertical plane. In
most of these stories there is no real separation between sky and earth:
"The sky lowered, the greenery rose wildly, and there was a kind of ceremonial conversation between sky and earth" ("Shlosha," *Ashan*, p. 13];
"Now they were blocked by the rain . . . only sky and earth in some harsh
conversation" ("Beyahad," *Bekomat Hakarka*, p. 51). Nor is there separation between water and land ("Beyahad," *Bekomat Hakarka*, p. 51),
or between roots and trunks ("Shlosha," *Ashan*, pp. 10, 12), or between
buildings and the vegetation around them ("Hamahaseh Haaharon,"
Bagai Haporeh, p. 29; "Rushka," *Bekomat Hakarka*, p. 92). The difficulty in distinguishing between high and low—and at the same time

between near and far—is often connected to a blurring of the boundaries between darkness and light. In many stories inanimate objects, animals, and people are viewed in twilight hours, just before sunset or dawn, or in a fog or through a veil of blackening swamp mists.

The lack of distinction in relations on the horizontal and vertical planes in the Penal Colony region is consistent with the protean quality of all the materials that compose it. Everything is in constant flux: the abstract becomes concrete, the concrete becomes abstract, flora changes to fauna, the inanimate comes to life, the living becomes inanimate.

This constant change in form gives the Penal Colony a quality of formless space. Because the materials that compose it are in a chaotic state, they are always at a precategorical stage. People move about in this space as though "after the deluge"; everything is seen as though for the first time, every bit of ground must be examined before it is stepped on, and every object must be scrutinized before it is handled. The only beings who find their way in this threatening commotion are, it seems, horses:[51]

It was the first spring sun: cold rose from its beams. Sometimes the mired wagon wheels announced contact with gravel, a tree trunk, crusting soil. You still couldn't put your foot down on the earth. Black rocks rose from the water, floating, it appeared, on the stream, detached from past years. The twists in them would recall a familiar human movement: a woman's head, the stretching of a spring, forms sometimes embedded in an inanimate thing. They appeared to be carved, turned toward you with a primal, angry gaze.

A wide lake. You had to keep away from the mountains, because like water-soaked walls, churned by heat and cold, they would heedlessly eject big rocks that sank without an echo. The sediment was soft, but at a certain depth the strata of the earth still remained stable. The horse could tread upon them, and the wheels could turn. The horse would raise its head, survey the surroundings, look for a bit of ground where it could lay its body, but since no earth like that could be seen, it would pull us where its legs led it. ("Bamidbar," *Bagai Haporeh*, pp. 101–2)

People in the Penal Colony stories also frequently change their essence. There are several versions of this phenomenon. One version is the change from a Jewish way of life to a gentile peasant way of life. Many of the Jewish characters in these stories become gentile peasant figures, sometimes in a very short time. We must emphasize that this change is both mental and physical, and it also passes the test of the non-Jews.

The ruse worked. After a month his earlier face was no longer recognizable. A new, whiskery face was cast upon him, molded so well that you wouldn't suspect it, as though nature itself had done it. And the smell came along as though on its own, the smell of peasants who are with animals. A relaxed gait, feet that know the earth and paths. He had a horse, not particularly well kept, a common horse that could be used for various purposes. Together they were a pair, without any separation of strangeness between them. He walked through the villages, greeted, cursed, as called for by the moment and opportunity.[52] ("Habriha," *Bekomat Hakarka*, p. 5)

This first version of transformation takes place within the human sphere. By contrast, the second version of transformation joins the human and animal spheres. Many characters in the Penal Colony stories are depicted as animals. A characteristic of Holocaust literature,[53] here this depiction has two particular features: first, the ones who undergo a process of dehumanization are in fact the victims and not—as is always the case in classic Holocaust literature—the executioners; and second, the "animals" are of a different kind. They belong to a defined "zoological" group ("black Jews") and are always described as a rare and artificial species—a combination of insect (beetle, grasshopper) and bird.[54] This species cannot blend into the environment, just like the artificial species of plants mentioned in the Austro-Hungarian village stories in "Bimlo Hastav" and *Keishon Haayin*.

The third version of transformation connects the human and transcendent realms. In several Penal Colony stories the persecuted characters pass from the human realm, or even from the animal realm, to that of the superhuman: in "Kittie" ("Now they were not people. Angels grasped her arms," *Bagai Haporeh*, p. 58); in "Hamatzod" ("He still saw their eyes swaying on antennae, and they themselves were too thin to be real, and only the looks, as though all of their being was in their glowing gazes," *Adnei Hanahar*, p. 73); and in "Matzod" (Hunt) ("They strode in the open air, removing the fetters from themselves. Now there was nothing binding them to the earth," *Bagai Haporeh*, p. 82).[55]

The world depicted in the Penal Colony stories is thus marked by constant changes in form on both the material and the human level. Everything here "changes and is transformed and changes and is transformed again" ("Hagilgul" [Metamorphosis], *Adnei Hanahar*, p. 91). The fictional space is depicted as governed by an inexorable force. The materials that constitute it overlap and cannot be defined categorically. This, in short, is "the world of chaos" ("Hagilgul," *Adnei Hanahar*, p. 88).

This "world of chaos" is portrayed according to certain rules that, not coincidentally, are reminiscent of the laws of depiction governing space in Greek adventure novellas.[56] Here the plot is always built on tension between disintegration and unification and between escape and submission or willing surrender. The effort of the main characters to evade the trap laid for them requires detachment from Jewish identity (transformation into gentile peasant figures). Their renewed or belated unification with that identity is accompanied by submission or willing surrender to the pursuers.

It must be stated clearly that the transition between these two stages of the plot—disintegration and unification—does not occur as a result of the characters' choice but rather as a result of fateful encounters. Those persecuted people who have already become, apparently, thoroughgoing non-Jews happen to meet Jews who are unable to change ("black Jews"), and following this encounter they themselves change back.

The coincidental nature of this decisive but chance encounter is typical of the Penal Colony. In this region everything is ruled by a single force: chance or fate. The decisive encounter, like any other event in this twilight realm, results from the intervention of outside forces. These forces, which are called "the hidden powers" or the "supreme powers," are irrational, entirely blind, and indifferent to human fate.

Section 2
The Chronotopic Dimension of the Realm

> Most of the day I am jostled by travel, every path is known to me, every hill greets me. I am condemned to constant motion, I shall make the horses run back and forth.
> —"MASA" (*Bagai Haporeh*)

Appelfeld's fictional realm is thus divided, in the topographical dimension, into two sections. One section includes the two large regions and the Italian middle ground, which are portrayed through solid, categorical distinctions, permitting the reconstruction of lifelike locations. The second section, which includes the region of the Penal Colony, is represented through precategorical components, which do not permit the reconstruction of a lifelike location.

The differences between these two sections on the level of topographical organization can also be formulated in cognitive terms. The first section, the stable one, reflects a situation in which human understanding appears to comprehend existence. In contrast, the second section, which is driven by an inexorable force, reflects a situation in which existence seems to baffle human understanding.[57] Indeed, the division between the stable and inexorable regions is not hard and fast. This characteristic, which is of decisive importance in relation to Appelfeld's narrative art, becomes clear when we carefully examine his portrayal of other dimensions of spatial arrangement—the chronotopic and the textual—in the regions that are topographically stable.

Condemned to Constant Motion

The chronotopic dimension deals with the organizational principles that are imposed on space by events and movement or, in other words, by the action of the plot. In this action one must distinguish between diachronic and synchronic relations. Diachronic relations refer to directions, axes, and the force field created from the connections among them. Synchronic relations refer to the reciprocal connections between states of motion and states of rest. Between these two types of chronotopic relations there is always—as shown by several central studies in this field[58]—mutual conditioning.

The diachronic relations within the boundaries of Appelfeld's fictional realm suggest a force field based on inner contradiction. The source of this contradiction is the conspicuous lack of correlation between the declared direction of motion and the motion that actually occurs. The ostensible direction of movement is not consistent with the pattern of coordinates underlying the topographical maps of the large regions. Many isolated characters and large and small groups of people are drawn to the central points. All the forces are concentrated along the axes of motion that extend between the various points of departure and those central points, especially Jerusalem, Bukovina, and the Carpathians. In many stories, however, both short and long, these axes, which are so central, are ultimately conceived as unreal directions of motion, just as the road leading toward the castle is conceived as an unreal direction of movement in Kafka's *Castle,* though this is the axis upon which all the powers of this somnambulistic novel are focused.

This chronotopic pattern is formed in Appelfeld's fiction in two principal versions. In the first version, the characters set out on their way, but they do not reach their destination, at least not within the framework of the fictional world. This version, which already serves as an organizing pattern in some of the early short stories (for example, "Haredifa" [The Pursuit], "Hashayara," and "Sibir" in *Bagai Haporeh;* "Batahana," "Habesora" [The Tidings], and "Hagerush" in *Kefor al Haaretz;* and "Baderekh" [On the Way] in *Bekomat Hakarka*), is transmitted in several versions and receives marked development and improvement in some of Appelfeld's later novellas.

Tzili ends with a scene in which Holocaust survivors are described as finding themselves—"by chance" and almost against their will—on a ship headed for Israel. The fact that the final scene of the book does not take place in an Israeli destination such as Atlit, Jaffa, or a kibbutz is no coincidence. It shows that even if those refugees reached Israel (like the boys in *Mikhvat Haor,* who, in a similar scene, also board a ship that will take them to Israel), they will remain "on the way" for the rest of their lives.

Rita, the protagonist of *Ritzpat Esh,* and the people riding in the wagons in *Layish* (1994) do not even reach the ship that, according to their plans, is to carry them to the Land of Israel. In both these novellas, the Land of Israel is viewed by the protagonists (unlike those in *Tzili* and *Mikhat Haor)* as a desired destination, a place where their hopes will be fulfilled. However, their path to the desired destination is blocked by stubborn obstacles, most of which derive—as in many of Rabbi Nahman of Bratslav's travel stories—from flaws in the characters' inner intentions.[59]

Thus Appelfeld's stories about journeys to Israel are based on an anti-teleological pattern, as several scholars have noted.[60] However, contrary to the opinion of some of these scholars, this pattern is not peculiar to this corpus alone. Other travel stories by Appelfeld, where the destination is in the Land of the Cattails, are based on the same pattern. We see this pattern most conspicuously in the novel *Ad Sheyaaleh Amud Hashahar* and the novella "Al Kol Hapeshaim" (1987; trans. 1989 as *For Every Sin*).

Ad Sheyaaleh Amud Hashahar, published in 1995, describes the journey of a Jewish woman named Blanca who has murdered her gentile husband, Adolph. She makes her way, first accompanied by her son Otto and then alone, to the hasidic center of Vizhnitz. However, like the main characters in *The Retreat* and *Layish,* Blanca does not reach her destination where, "it appeared to her, . . . the snarl of her life would be untangled, and she would be free" (p. 187). The book concludes with a scene in which Blanca, just a few hours' walk from her destination, is either captured or allows herself to be caught by gendarmes.[61]

The novella, *For Every Sin,* revolves entirely around the unbridgeable gap between the desire or apparent desire to reach a destination and the possibility of attaining it. This gap is well illustrated by explicit references to that destination in the opening and closing passages of the story. The book, whose protagonist is a Holocaust survivor named Theo, begins with the following passage:

> When the war ended Theo resolved that he would make his way back home alone, in a straight line, without twists or turns. The distance to his home was great, hundreds of miles. Nevertheless it seemed to him he could see the route clearly. He knew that this would separate him from people, and that he would have to remain in uninhabited places for many days, but he was firm in his resolve: only following a straight course, without deviation. Thus, without saying good-bye to anyone, he set out. (*For Every Sin,* p. 3)

Theo is determined to reach his home. However, as we find at the end of the story, he comes no closer to it, nor does he succeed in keeping a distance from people who hinder him. Instead of staying the course, which is plotted in great detail on a military map, he joins a band of refugees, which has gathered in a deep ravine. In this cellarlike and womblike place, which recalls the bunker where the refugees gather in "Aviv Kar" (*Ashan,* pp. 49–51), the pit where Tzili and Mark hide in *Tzili,* and the fortified basement in *The Iron Tracks* (pp. 109–11), "it became clear to Theo beyond any doubt that he would never return to his hometown. From now on he would advance with the refugees" (p. 167).

In the second version of Appelfeld's journey stories, the protagonists reach their destinations, but this plot development brings no resolution. Sometimes the protagonists are incapable of identifying the destination

they have reached; occasionally they find the place in shambles; or they
feel that the yearned-for place "rejects" them; or they do not manage to
reconcile the place as it is in reality with the place of their dreams; or
they may reach that destination only in a dream or vision. To this formula belong, among others, the early stories such as "Kefor al Haaretz"
(Frost on the Earth, *Kefor al Haaretz*), "Hashiva" (The Return) and
"Haaliya Lekatzansk" (The Ascent to Katszansk) in *Bekomat Hakarka,*
and the novella *To the Land of the Cattails.* The story, "Haderekh ben
Drovna Ledrovitz," which opens *Kefor al Haaretz,* is especially interesting in this regard, as is the second part of *The Age of Wonders,* entitled
"Many Years Later When Everything Was Over."

"Haderekh ben Drovna Ledrovitz" describes the journey of a band of
hasidim from their hometown, Drovna, to Drovicz, the holy city of the
"joyful congregation," which is termed "the center of the world" ("Haderekh ben Drovna Ledrovitz," *Kefor al Haaretz,* p. 12). The road
between the two cities is not an easy one, "and more than once our effort
to traverse it has failed" (p. 10), but the company overcomes all impedi-
ments and reaches its destination, which is described as follows:

> And when they reached Drovicz it was already morning. The city was
> empty and the houses stood as though planted in slumber. No one was to
> be seen. This was Drovicz. Our eyes saw the houses and paths. And when
> we called Rabbi Barish's name and the name of his sons and the name of
> the great retinue, the space soaked up our voices without returning an
> echo. And we walked in the narrow streets, walking after the horses and
> after the creak of the wheels. Though we had never been there, we recog-
> nized the houses, and we saw that they were our houses. Breath flew out of
> them, and darkness glowed in the windows. The Rebbe's court, too,
> stood, a house surrounded by a fence. We were afraid to approach, be-
> cause everything was silent and empty, so that the hand of the wind alone
> could have knocked it over. ("Haderekh ben Drovna Ledrovitz," *Kefor al
> Haaretz,* p. 13)

Thus Drovicz was an entirely alien place ("we had never been there"),
and at the same time a familiar and intimate one ("we saw that they were
our houses"). These combinations of opposites are typical of the destination, and the combinations that complement them[62] endow it with the
status of a place that is both realistic and visionary, worthy of the name
given to it by the narrator, "the lost center point" (p. 12).

The city of Knospen, Bruno's birthplace, has similar status in "Many

Years Later When Everything Was Over." Bruno, the protagonist, who returns to "the town of his birth" (p. 177) after about twenty years, is described as someone who keeps having the same strange experience dozens of times. Its main quality is a combination of the familiar and the strange. On the one hand he "realiz[es] again that nothing has changed here . . . as if the scenes of his childhood have been embalmed in all their subtlest nuances of light and shade" (*The Age of Wonders*, p. 216). On the other hand, he says, "'Everything has changed in the years I was away'" (p. 235). This strange experience of space, also characterized by oxymorons here—"familiar exile" (p. 216) and "familiar strangeness" (p. 219)—reminds Bruno of a childhood nightmare in which "he had come back to his town and no one knew him. He would wander from place to place, panic-stricken because of the silent, conspiratorial refusal to acknowledge his existence" (p. 233).

The main characters in some of Appelfeld's journey stories do not reach their destination, while in others they do but fail to recognize it or connect with it. Both types of story are versions of a single basic plot structure based on a confrontation between two contradictory trends: on the one hand, a desperate effort to find once again "the lost center point" and, on the other hand, the desire, no less desperate, to be freed once and for all from that effort. These two trends can be called, respectively, the circular, cyclical trend and the linear trend.[63] The contradiction between them sets up a pendulumlike system that underlies the chronotopical dimension of all Appelfeld's fiction. Every event in the plot has a dual status here: it belongs to a linear, nonrepeating movement, which has a beginning, a middle, and an end, and it belongs to a circular movement in which every "end" marks the start of another cycle. In this respect, there is no difference in principle between Appelfeld's short stories and his novellas, aside from an increase in the range of the pendulum's swing or, in other words, aside from the extent of space in which a certain plot takes place.

The characters within Appelfeld's imaginary realm are caught, like those in the Penal Colony, in a repetitive, circular movement around "the lost center point." The eternal cyclical nature of this movement, which is explicitly described in some of the stories as "constant movement," blurs the chronotopical distinctions in the stable realms on both the diachronic and synchronic relations. For, viewed from above, the points of departure are also seen as end points. Accordingly the dynamic plot events are constantly repeated and essentially static.[64]

Against this background, several important phenomena in Appelfeld's writing can be explained. The first phenomenon is the frequency of journey stories of various kinds throughout the author's work.[65] The second phenomenon is the way in which many of the stories typically end. Appelfeld concludes a considerable number of his stories, especially the novellas, with a description of the way Jews are swallowed up in various vehicles. These scenes of being swallowed up can be comprehended—quite horribly—as the desired conclusion of the life stories of people who are constantly tossed between the effort to find "the lost center point" and the wish to be freed from that obsessive effort. Among other examples, there are the family in *Keishon Haayin,* who, "at the place and time that were decreed," report for deportation in a train to an "unknown destination" (p. 270); the Jews in *Badenheim,* who willingly board the death train, and were "sucked in as easily as grains of wheat poured into a funnel" (p. 148); the Jews who happily board a similar train in *To the Land of the Cattails* (p. 120); of course the refugees, who escaped extermination, whom the Joint Distribution Committee representatives placed on board the ship (*Tzili,* p. 182); and the boys in *Mikhvat Haor,* whose "bodies are poured one after the other into the back of the truck" that was to bring them from the training farm to the army camp for basic training (p. 155). The characters who are most thoroughly swallowed up are the father in *The Age of Wonders,* who gradually succumbs to the rhythmic, swaying motion of the train, and Erwin in *The Iron Tracks,* who defines himself as "a creature of the tracks," addicted to their intoxicating rhythm (p. 30).[66]

The almost unending, cyclical character of the movement of Appelfeld's characters through narrative space explains another phenomenon: the parallel that is drawn between the journeys of the characters and those of the Israelites in the desert, on their way to the Land of Canaan, which is described as an infinite journey.[67] This parallel is meant to emphasize what was latent in the chronotopical structure of the stories: Appelfeld's characters belong to the generation of the desert, those who have left one place but will never arrive at their destination or return to their place of origin. These characters are involved in a journey that represents a damaged spiritual and cultural condition that can never be repaired. This is a journey to eternal exile. It takes place in a region that, it appears, is suitable for such a journey: a twilight region between myth and history.

Bolted: The Model of the Closed Camp

"Imagine that you're in a camp. You can do that."
"What do you mean? I was in seven camps. I remember their names."
"If you've been in seven camps, you can also be in an eighth."
—MIKHVAT HAOR

The topographical map of the stable regions in Appelfeld's realm—a soothing, pseudorealistic map—is often dislocated by a different manner of chronotopic organization.

Most of Appelfeld's stories take place in an enclosed area. However, these stories also contain various directional signs that give guidance to a broader surrounding space as well, a space that is much more extensive than the arena in which the action occurs. Nevertheless, the division between the surrounding space and the arena of action is almost absolute. The surrounding space serves as a static background, and the story takes place in an almost autonomous setting and according to an almost independent inner logic. Thus, for example, *The Iron Tracks* refers to an enormous surrounding space that includes the United States, Argentina, and Uruguay; Siberia, Copenhagen, and Naples; Australia, New Zealand, and Israel. Yet not a single plot event takes place in that enormous area; all events occur within a limited space bounded with precision by the oval course of the railroad stations Erwin traverses year after year. Erwin's only departure from this course, to which he is attached ("I am compelled to return here every year," p. 14), takes place when he leaves the train in the town of Steinberg and walks to the village of Weinberg, where Nachtigal lives, the man who murdered his parents and whom he wishes to kill. This exception, like exceptions in other stories, only serves to emphasize the vacuumlike quality of the space in which Appelfeld's protagonists wander.

Several versions of this vacuumlike, closed space are portrayed in Appelfeld's fiction. The most prominent version appears in the stories set in enclosed spaces where the characters are confined against their will. To this group belong all the monastery stories ("Hamahaseh Haaharon" and "Kittie" from *Bagai Haporeh* and "Baeven" and "Habehira" [The

Choice], from *Kefor al Haaretz*); "Keshet Hakimron" (The Arch of the Vault, 1964), which tells the story of a group of Jews trapped during the Second World War in the cellar of the palace of an anonymous prince; "Bagova Hakar" from *Bagai Haporeh,* which describes the transfer of a group of Holocaust survivors to the land of the living in an isolated and enclosed place; the stories whose plots are set in educational institutions in Israel ("Mukar" [Known] from *Bagai Haporeh,* and *Mikhvat Haor*); the novella set in a resort that is made into a detention camp (*Badenheim*); the novella part of which is set in a prison (*Katerina*); and the play that takes place entirely in a synagogue that has been locked from the outside, *Al Bariah* (Bolted In, 1992).

The second version of the vacuumlike, closed space appears against the background of small and isolated places where the characters have lived for a long time or where they have arrived either by chance or by intention. To this group belong several stories of the Austro-Hungarian provinces ("Bimlo Hastav," *Keishon Haayin,* and *The Conversion*), the stories about recluses with sacred missions ("Gonev Marot" and "Mimrom Hadumiya" [From the Height of Silence, *Kefor al Haaretz*]), and the stories of the isolation of characters who try to flee from their past and/or to reconnect with it ("In the Isles of St. George" and "Bemakom Aher").

The third version of this spatial pattern appears against the background of resorts and spas. To this group belong "Bamekomot Hanemukhim," which is set in Israel; the Austro-Hungarian novellas *Badenheim* (which has already been mentioned in connection with the first version of the closed space), *The Retreat,* and *Ritzpat Esh,* and also the novella, *The Healer,* which is set in an isolated village in the Carpathians.

In all these stories, in their respective groups, isolated scraps of information are inserted about events that took place within the historical period that serves as background for the plots. In *To the Land of the Cattails,* for example, one explicit reference to the calendar appears. This is also true of the first part of *The Age of Wonders.* The logic behind the scant reference to historical dates in these two relatively long works becomes clear when we closely examine the sentences in which Appelfeld chose to insert them:

> It was the end of summer 1938, but here everything was as it should be, quiet and idle. As if the plains held out as much time as you please on the palms of their hands. (*To the Land of the Cattails,* p. 6)

> It was the summer of 1938. I was twelve years old and Father was forty-

three. Nobody knew what the future held in store and what experiences awaited us." (*The Age of Wonders*, p. 87)

In both cases sharp tension is implied between what takes place in the fictional space according to the understanding of the characters and what takes place in extrafictional space according to the understanding of the two narrators and their readers. The narrators and readers examine the fictional space retrospectively. From that perspective it is easy to discern signs of the impending catastrophe. By contrast, the characters are enclosed in a "spatial bubble." They cling to the illusion "that here everything is still in its place" (*To the Land of the Cattails*, p. 13), and they repeatedly ignore any evil augury—of which there are dozens. Thus they detach themselves, with their own faulty consciousnesses, from the historical arena.

In the Israeli stories, too, scant scraps of information appear regarding events that take place in the historical period that is background for the fiction. "Bronda" is in fact the only Israeli story in which a truly local event is staged (Independence Day), and with emphatic economy of description, without any indication of the exact time or place. In *Haor Vehakutonet* there is a single reference to a date, and only one mention, quick and vague, to a historical event. In *The Immortal Bartfuss* there are no references to dates; the historical context is represented by means of three vague and indirect references, nothing more.

The ignoring of the historical context is particularly conspicuous in *Mikhvat Haor*. This novella, the only Israeli story in which Appelfeld refers to the social and ideological context, contains just one reference to the historical context. That reference, which is intentionally made to appear coincidental, occurs halfway through the novella. It reveals that around the training farm, where the fictional events take place, the War of Independence is being fought in all its ferocity.[68]

This emphatic separation of the arena of action of the Israeli stories from their historical context is not typical of fiction by other authors who portray the absorption of Holocaust survivors in Israel.[69] The function of this separation is different from that of the parallel separation in the Austro-Hungarian stories. Here this phenomenon indicates that the characters are turned inward as in a cellar, and it expresses their feeling of absolute alienation from the "historical homeland."

The cognitive fixity of Appelfeld's characters in their various regions is projected very powerfully upon the structure of the fictional space. The transitions between the secondary spaces in the arenas of action are not explained by causal and substantial connections. For example, there is no ideological justification such as "ascent" to Israel or "descent" from it. Nor is there a psychological justification such as maturation or falling in love and the like. Rather the explanations for the transitions are external, such as changes in time and weather. This weak form of connection invites Appelfeld's reader to attempt to tighten connections by means of spatial parallels.[70] After completing this structural process, the reader realizes that all or most of the secondary spaces are constructed on a single model, which reflects one cognitive state.

The novella *Mikhvat Haor* is a prime example of this phenomenon. It is divided into seventeen chapters that are overtly linked to each other by external ties such as references to the calendar: Chapter 2 takes place "in late February"; Chapter 9 takes place in July; Chapter 15 is set in December. Changes in weather are also indicated: in Chapter 10, "The sun did not leave its course. The heat was oppressive, uniform, and in the evening the water was pale blue as though heated" (p. 78); and in Chapter 12, "The heat subsided and moderate sea breezes swept along the seashore" (p. 98).

The prominence of these external ties between the chapters of the novella emphasizes the absence of substantial, causal connections. The narrator makes us aware of this absence explicitly or indirectly at each of the three central junctures in the story. The first juncture is the opening scene on the Italian coast. "We arrived there by chance" (p. 7). The second juncture is the laconic account of the arrival in Israel: "And thus we reached Palestine. We arrived in the month of Adar, with the terrible feeling that we had arrived by chance" (p. 27). The third juncture is the scene of conscription in the Israeli army that concludes the book. It begins with the sentence: "Late at night a [military] truck arrived"; and it ends with the sentence: "Bodies are poured one after the other into the back of the truck" (p. 155). Thus the narrator invites us to seek the common denominator among all the secondary spaces into which the characters of the novel move or are moved. That common denominator can be called Model of the Closed Camp, which has its own organizational logic and particular traits.

The organizational logic here is expressed as "a violent caprice" ("El Meever Latragi" [Beyond the Tragic], *Masot Beguf Rishon*, p. 46), which is epitomized in arbitrary yet precise mechanisms. One of the central mechanisms of this type is that of reeducation, which is applied to all the

Holocaust survivors in *Mikhvat Haor,* in Italy, on the way to Israel, and also in Israel.

The mechanism of reeducation is always portrayed according to a rigid, graduated model: a group of pupils without status and a kind of authoritarian commander or commissar, who may be soft and seductive or occasionally threatening and cruel. For example, in Chapter 2, still set on the Italian coast, three somewhat older brothers try to transform the group of young boys from "parasites" and "worthless people" to "working men who live from their handiwork" (p. 18). In Chapter 3, the Swedish captain, a Christian imbued with messianic faith, tries to convince the miserable and embittered refugees that they are "the chosen people of God" (p. 23). As the sarcastic narrator puts it, "he tries to convert us from our faith" (p. 20). In Chapter 6, Rakosh the dentist, who is reminiscent of the Great Balaban in *The Retreat* and the Great Frank in *1946,* tries to extract the damaged teeth of the boys who have arrived in Israel "by chance," and at the same time to remove "their softness and Jewish twitches" (p. 47). In other chapters the "Old Maid"—the commander or commissar of the training farm where the group of boys has ended up— tries to "help" them forget their scraps of childhood memory and the events of the Holocaust, and she "encourages them"—with the help of her staff—to become accustomed to pioneering Zionist life. In the last chapter, the "Old Maid" is replaced by the army recruiting officer.

As the Holocaust survivors in the story move from one secondary unit to another, the ideologies that they are supposed to absorb change, and, accordingly, the identity of the character serving as commander or commissar changes. However, the reeducation mechanism remains in force, as does the psychological model from which it is derived and which it reflects: the Model of the Closed Camp.[71]

The Fictional Space as a Laboratory

The bubble in space, which is so typical of Appelfeld's stories, undoubtedly serves, to use T. S. Eliot's terminology for a moment, as an objective correlative for the mental and cultural state of the characters. However, this typical structural component has an additional function, which is no less important. It creates an imaginary space similar to a laboratory within which, under isolated conditions, the author observes the disintegration of Jewish organisms (deracinated individuals, couples, families, bands of

refugees, whole communities) from the mid-nineteenth century until the
1960s. The process of disintegration of Jewish organisms—sometimes including signs of reintegration[72]—is observed in Appelfeld's laboratory in
an almost scientific manner. The central method here is prolonged observation of the behavior of "objects" who are investigated by gradually
limiting their living space.

In all Appelfeld's stories the arena of action is described as a narrowing or gradually blocked space, until such time as the characters no
longer have any way out except for the threatening surroundings, into
which they are ejected at the end of the stories. This process is conspicuous in the resort novellas, especially in *Badenheim,* which describes a
group of Jews who arrive at a famous resort town, as they do every year.
However, in earlier years it was possible to enter and leave the town, but
this year one can only enter it. What was a resort town slowly becomes a
detention camp under the supervision of the "Sanitation Department,"
whose authority expands from chapter to chapter. At first it is not felt at
all, but then it is "authorized to conduct independent investigations" (p.
11). At a later stage inspectors are "now spread all over the town. They
took measurements, put up fences, and planted flags" (p. 15). Somewhat
later we find that "The Sanitation Department now resembled a travel
agency festooned with posters: "LABOR IS OUR LIFE," "THE AIR IN PO-
LAND IS FRESHER," "SAIL ON THE VISTULA" (p. 29). As the jurisdiction of
the Sanitation Department expands, the living space of the vacationers
constricts. First the post office is closed, then the spring and the pastry
shop, the veranda of the hotel, the tennis court, and so on. Horribly, the
only living space that remains open is that of "Jewish Poland," where
the vacationers are sent at the end of the book, as though of their own
free will.

Of course Appelfeld is not the only author who isolates his characters
in sealed and enclosed spaces, permitting precise observation of the processes they undergo in laboratorylike conditions. Each version of the
bubble in space that is portrayed in his writing has many parallels in
both European and Hebrew fiction, including the corpus known as Holocaust literature. Appelfeld's stories that take place on a desert island or
somewhere similar are related to an extensive tradition going back to
Daniel Defoe's *Robinson Crusoe* and beyond. This tradition has been reworked many times in various contexts, as in William Golding's *Lord of
the Flies* and in Holocaust literature, such as *W ou le souvenir d'enfance*
by Georges Perec and *Hai Birhov Hatziporim* (The Island on Bird Street)

by Uri Orlev. Those of Appelfeld's stories that take place in closed educational institutions are related to the genre of coming-of-age fiction that is set in educational frameworks. A masterpiece of that genre, which Appelfeld said that he has read many times, is Robert Musil's *Die Verwirrungen des Zoeglings Toerless* (*Young Toerless*).[73] This genre, too, was reworked in the literature of the Holocaust, as in the books by David Schuetz, *Haesev Vehahol* (The Weed and the Sand), *Shoshan Lavan, Shoshan Adom* (White Rose, Red Rose), and *Yoman Hazahav* (The Golden Diary). Appelfeld's resort novellas are also related to a rich tradition or subgenre of resort and spa stories,[74] that includes such masterpieces as Thomas Mann's *Magic Mountain* and *Death in Venice*. Fascinating works in this tradition were written by Austro-Hungarian Jews in German and in Hebrew, such as Arthur Schnitzler's *Fraulein Elsa* and *Beit Hamirpeh* (The Sanitorium) and *Nokhah Hayam* (Before the Sea) by David Fogel. Holocaust literature also includes new examples of this subgenre, as in *Adam ben Kelev* (Man Son of Dog) by Yoram Kaniuk. In addition to these, dozens of Holocaust stories take place wholly or in part in various detention camps, beginning with *Salamandra, Beit Habubot* (The Dolls' House) and *Pipel* by K. Tzetnik, and *Se questo e un uomo* by Primo Levi and *Sorstalansag* by Imre Kertesz, and including long passages from David Grossman's *See under Love* and *Avimelekh Oleh Besaara Hashamayma* (Avimelekh Ascends to Heaven in a Storm) by Ami Dvir. To these, of course, we must add the thousands of autobiographies and recorded testimonies whose background is the detention camps. In these camps, as Primo Levi wrote, vast biological and sociological experiments took place, under the most rigorous laboratory conditions.

Thus Appelfeld is not unique in using the bubble in space as a laboratory. His uniqueness is expressed in the essence of the process that he examines in his laboratory. This uniqueness emerges more conspicuously when one compares his stories to those of other Jewish writers, including Holocaust writers. This comparison clearly shows that Appelfeld concentrates time and again on one issue: the identity crisis of the modern Jew.

This matter warrants clarification. Appelfeld touches upon many "big" subjects in his writing. Thus, for example, in his Austro-Hungarian novellas, as in works by Thomas Mann and, following him, Peter Altenberg, Arthur Schnitzler, Stefan Zweig, Joseph Roth, and David Fogel, there is great concern with the tension between love and death and between nature and culture. In his Penal Colony stories, as in many Holocaust stories, Appelfeld is intensely concerned with relations between

Jews and non-Jews, and between people and animals. Needless to say, the question of "Is this man?" also arises in its universal sense—as it is posed, for example in the works of Primo Levi, Ida Fink, Imre Kertesz, and Elsa Morante—and occupies an important place in his work. Nevertheless, and I wish to emphasize this here, with Appelfeld these subjects are generally subordinate to the issues of Jewish identity.

Furthermore, with regard to the chronotopical character of the depicted space, there is no essential difference between Appelfeld's journey stories and those of the enclosed spaces. These two subgenres (which, in fact, are combined in several stories)[75] are represented in the literary corpus under discussion as various elaborations of the same intellectual and artistic pattern—the pattern that prevents or hinders the full and stable reconstruction of a lifelike space.

Section 3
The Textual Dimension of the Realm

> Everything was so familiar, lit only by a thin darkness that removes the domesticity of ordinary objects.
> —HAOR VEHAKUTONET

The topographical map that emerges from Appelfeld's fictional realm is based on a sharp dichotomy: three "normal," lifelike regions, on the one hand, and one exceptional region, the so-called Penal Colony, which is extraterritorial and chaotic, on the other. This dichotomy loses its sharpness, however, as we have seen, upon close inspection of the chronotopical manner in which the three "normal" regions are portrayed. A similar phenomenon takes place upon close inspection of the textual portrayal of those regions.

To be sure, essential changes in style are notable in various groups of Appelfeld's stories.[76] However, generally speaking, in all his writings Appelfeld adheres to the same stylistic line: an effort to retain the process of perceiving space at the precognitive level. In other words, Appelfeld's descriptive language guides us to experience the fictional world as a primal and amorphous space, strange and threatening.

Here I shall try to bring out the special character of the linguistic portrayal of space in Appelfeld's work by studying in detail the opening chapter of the Israeli novel, *Haor Vehakutonet*. For the reader's convenience I shall begin by presenting the entire chapter:

A nocturnal winter's end flows in the streets, as slowly as in a transparent bell. A man with an umbrella in his hand, a woman in a summer dress, a car parked on the side of the street, a scrap of fog that has stuck to the wall. Nothing, nothing, were it not for the slow pace.

And perhaps the looks, as though they stood, lightly frozen, and perhaps the light that throbs beneath the sparkling patch of water, that reminds one's heart of an animal's breathing, whose blood circulation is covered by a thin layer of skin, and its heartbeats leap silently. And perhaps Gruzman, whom the winter evening has found in this ordinary street, which for some reason stopped flowing for a moment. Perhaps he recalled something, perhaps he heard. Perhaps the roof or, rather, the eaves, which had been attached to the gray stone building years ago.

Nothing, nothing. Only a winter evening whose flow has slowed, in this street, lit by few signs, has almost stopped flowing. The man leans on the umbrella, his head slightly bent, as though he had heard something, but it wasn't a sound at all. His head did not straighten quickly but remained as it was, inclined. The woman put on her coat.

Now they all stood still. They seemed to be listening to music, but it could not be heard. The silence rose to the banks of the buildings. Darkness flowed from the windows and poured into the courtyards like bright and sparkling coal. The owner of the umbrella raised it, as though swaying to the beat of music. The woman buttoned her coat.

"Evening," said Gruzman.

The street was abandoned. Its residents were sleeping indoors now, inside the windows of darkness. The shop owners turned off the lights, leaving them on in only two stores. The signs now illuminated the silence all around. A distant bell roused the street slightly from its wonder. The woman recoiled, and her neck leaned back, as though she were fearful. No one but them could be seen in the street, just the silence that was doubled.

The man raised his umbrella, and it seemed to Gruzman that he was addressing him. He wanted to approach him but remained where he was. The side streets were plunged in thin darkness. A car stood half on the sidewalk. Its right headlight was crushed and not bandaged, a dim hollow was in its pupil.

He approached the woman. She stood all wrapped up, as though belonging only to herself. She's certainly waiting, he said to himself, though it didn't appear so.

It was a strange winter. The rain didn't stop. There was little work in the warehouse. He met almost no one. He went through the whole winter in a prolonged sleep, with thoughts that weren't thoughts, some discomfort before a far-reaching change.

This was the first night, blue, not oppressively humid, a light that reminds your heart of the days after the war, after the heavy snows, an intense desire to find someone in the street, to awaken some slumbering tongue.

He walked from street to street as though under a veil of clear liquids, the city withdrew behind its doors, the shutters were closed, though it was still early everything was abandoned to the darkness, loneliness clung to him, his years now peered up around him, as though from behind bars. He felt: the houses were attached to each other; now darkness flowed in the veins of stone and nourished their permanence.

He remembered the first nights in Jerusalem, the first walks that seemed like deep breaths. Even then someone said: It isn't air, it's too fresh to be air. In freshness like that a person can smother. The stones, too, were like inanimate things slowly growing. Then he did not know their stoniness, their nakedness, their eternal isolation.

Now he felt it: the years in Jerusalem had removed everything from him. He remained without attachment.

"Good evening," he called to the woman in a whisper. The woman withdrew somewhat into the darkness, and the man with the umbrella straightened up like a watchman, and his jaw stiffened. He took a few steps and stood still, "Good evening," unable to control his voice any longer. The woman withdrew into the corridor, and the man with the umbrella stepped down from the sidewalk and called out: Quiet.

The lights in the two stores went out by themselves and other shadows spread out and crawled among the nearby buildings. Now the darkness flowed patch by patch and covered the street with a thick cloak. The man mounted the sidewalk as though emerging from liquid. He muttered something.

The woman was not to be seen, but her presence was felt. She was obscured by the corridor. Now he noticed: the place was not entirely vacant. In a doorway across from him was a woman pressed in the arms of a tall man, sunk so deeply in the darkness that they weren't noticeable. It seemed he was trying to bring her inside, into the thick darkness of the courtyards. In another doorway as well a noise was heard, a vapor.

For some reason he recalled the days of the liberation after the war. People delivered themselves to each other with some hard physical love. Women, girls, men, and boys who had come of age in the bunkers. An improper mixture of ages, they spread out from the forests and fell upon each other with sensual madness; and when day broke they would hit each other, curse, and shout. No one could have stopped the intoxicating flow that swept women, girls, and men into the blossoming nights of the first spring after the war. Some other death.

Later there was that panicked flight: not to be heard and not to meet. But the paths that separated brought them together again, like a bitter, spiteful fate; and so it was for many days, separately and together, like drugged animals. These were infinite planes, the coast was distant.

All of this now arose in Gruzman's memory and flooded him. The slow evening lost its moderation and became populated. As if the people were afraid of the darkness of the street and plunged into another, thicker darkness. Now he felt the dim phosphorous in their gazes, a bare arm, a struggle beneath the liquid, without rescuing, without being rescued.

The man with the umbrella approached the doorway where the woman was hiding and called inside into the corridor. The woman whispered an answer to him. They spoke in some incomprehensible language like birds.

"Evening," said Gruzman without knowing what he was saying. The hopes of the blue night vanished, again he was within his expanded life, isolation now crawled beneath his thin coat.

Distant bells were roused. Their sound was soft, like the raised voice of music whose instruments suddenly arise from within it. Gruzman raised his eyes and looked for the sound. Nothing could be seen. The darkness poured into the windows and piled up at the doors. The sounds were lost. The blue heights turned gray and descended to the street. Now the layers of the darkness were evident. The neon lights only lit their upper parts. Below the darkness was complete.

Suddenly, from an unexpected direction a unified pounding of bells poured down. One after another the imprisoned bells were aroused, and the sounds flowed with the hot darkness like a cascade.

Now motion was evident in the doorways. A man in a short coat with a woman hanging onto him. They stood still, and their eyes glowed in the darkness. "What's this?" said the man. The woman didn't loosen her hold on him. She was small next to him, as though trying to negate herself entirely. The sounds of the bells buzzed in circle after circle and sank to the bottom, to the damp street, shattering.

One after another the people crawled out of the doorways, a kind of improper mixture of ages, bald spots and young hair. They seemed frightened in the naked darkness. Though they clung to each other, the seal of loneliness was stamped in their stance.

A window opened on the top floor. An old man stuck out his head and shouted: Quiet.

"We'll go away from here," one said.

"Nothing," said another.

Now the bells reached their full tempo and would not let up. Like the village church bells calling to prayer. It was evident that they were cut off from their nocturnal chorus. With a shout they fell from on high.

How miserable the women looked now. Sorrow stuck to their faces like skin. They were small. Their lipstick glowed like smeared fire. "Nothing," someone tried to calm them. Someone lit a cigarette and threw the match onto the road. "Let's go," said another. They walked away stooped over. Gruzman withdrew under the narrow awning of a shop.

There were some tidings in the bound metal, hitting with all its power, like shouting mutes. Thus the church bells of his childhood would rouse at night and spread out over the village houses; or sometimes in a dry year, when the priest tried to awaken the mercy of heaven. Those alarms did not end well. The peasants would break into Jewish houses and loot them.

The man with the umbrella was now leading the woman under his coat, not as a lover, but like her father.

We strike, we strike, trumpeted the metal. As though after a confining winter: the ice shakes free of the mountains, the river is flooded, the cows break out of their pens, the peasants stand at the doors of their houses with a harsh and dim look in their eyes.

The area looked like the sides of a worn copper boiler, and the clapper strikes and makes its skin quiver. No one was there any longer, and even when all was silent, and night fell, as at first, blue as at first and also stars, maybe quieter than before. He could not stand without covering his head.

In this short chapter we become aware of the arena of action as it is observed through the eyes of Gruzman, one of the novel's two protagonists, with the help of an omniscient narrator. Gruzman wanders through the streets of Jerusalem one night in late winter. Those streets, where a few other people (mainly, and not by coincidence, couples) are also wandering, are lined by residences, most of them dark, and shops, several of which advertise themselves with illuminated signs. Up to this point everything is fine—a normal evening in a familiar season, in the ordinary streets of a well-known city. However, the particular means of description employed in this sample passage undermine the routine, familiar, and ordinary character of the quasi-realistic space.

The undermining of the fictional space is produced by literary devices that can be classified into three groups: (1) devices that bring out the nonspecificity of the materials that construct the space; (2) devices that bring out the indistinguishability of the materials that construct the space; and (3) devices that bring out the unconnectedness of the materials that construct the space.[77] These devices, in their various groupings, function on several levels: the structural and plot level, the syntactical level, the figurative level, the level of narration, the level of focalization, and others.

Nonspecificity

In this chapter from *Haor Vehakutonet* the arena of action is characterized by a conspicuous lack of specificity, making it difficult to construct a clear cognitive framework for the events of the plot. While we know that the plot deals with a man named Gruzman in a city named Jerusalem, we are deprived of many identifying details. We do not know the names of the streets where Gruzman is wandering, we do not know what is written on the illuminated signs of the shops, we have no notion of the form of the houses, whether they are surrounded by foliage, for example.

The lack of specificity of the details of the space stands out especially in relation to people. All the people whom Gruzman meets are called "someone," "another," "the man," "a man in a short coat," and the like. We are not given real information about the outer aspect of the people who walk about in the street, not even about the outer aspect of Gruzman. The only traits attributed to this group are collective, as, for example, in the following sentences: "Sorrow stuck to their [the women's] faces like skin. They were small. Their lipstick glowed like smeared fire."[78]

Nor are there any verbal expressions characteristic of a specific person. Most of the dialogue is anonymous: "'We'll go away from here,' one said. 'Nothing,' said another." Similarly: "'Nothing,' someone tried to calm them. . . . 'Let's go,'" said another."

This lack of specificity in portraying physical space is typical of the entire novel as well as of Appelfeld's other Israeli novels. All the main characters in this region move through a world full of objects—streets, crossroads, coffeehouses, trees, plants, and animals. Some of these have names, primarily a few streets and coffeehouses, but the vast majority remain anonymous. Most of the trees are simply "a tree" and "another tree," and most of the flowers are "a flower" and "another flower." On rare occasions there is a blue or yellow flower. Most of the dogs (of which there are few in any event) are just "a dog" and "another dog." The prominence of this lack of specificity in Appelfeld's Israeli fiction is notable when contrasted with the specificity of animals, trees, and flowers in the works of the Palmach generation (Moshe Shamir, Benyamin Tammuz, and especially S. Yizhar) and the generation of the state (mainly in some works by Ruth Almog, Yitzhak Ben-Ner, and Yehoshua Kenaz). Ironically, this lack of specificity is even true of the novel *Mikhvat Haor,* which takes place mainly on an agricultural training farm. The scarce references to specific trees, plants, and animals in Appelfeld's Israeli stories (as well as in those of the Land of the Cattails) are almost always related to states of cognitive shock.[79]

The lack of specificity in the physical space of Appelfeld's Israeli fiction is also apparent in the living quarters of most of the main characters. Thus, Bartfuss's room is described in *The Immortal Bartfuss:*

> His room is practically bare; just a bed, a chair, and a cupboard. When he does his accounts he sits on the bed and uses the chair as a desk. Once Rosa tried to dress up the walls a little. She even brought in a table and chairs. That was years ago, when they still talked. Bartfuss cleared them right out, with his own hands.
>
> Since then the room has stood bereft of any garment. If not for the few shadows that creep in through the shutters, white glare would cover everything. (*The Immortal Bartfuss,* p. 4)

Bartfuss, Gruzman, and their like leave no mark on physical space, and Appelfeld does not conquer the land with words. The result is a strange and alien space, nearly devoid of reality.

Indistinguishability

The difficulty in reconstructing a realistic fictional space in the opening chapter of *Haor Vehakutonet* also results from Appelfeld's frequent use of linguistic expressions that combine areas, materials, and qualities we are used to comprehending as fundamentally distinct. The two areas that Appelfeld frequently mingles here are the abstract and concrete. Especially typical are sentences in this context that touch upon the feelings of sorrow and isolation of Gruzman and of the figures that surround him: "isolation now crawled beneath his thin coat"; "loneliness clung to him"; "the seal of loneliness was stamped in their stance"; "sorrow stuck to their faces like skin."

A similar blurring of distinctions occurs in several sentences in which a unit of time is give concreteness. For example: "A nocturnal winter's

end flows in the streets"; "only a winter evening whose flow has slowed
. . . has almost stopped flowing" (as though time were a gas or liquid).
Elsewhere Appelfeld writes: "His years now popped up around him, as
though from behind bars" (as though the units of time were people in
prison).

Another mingling of areas occurs through the incursion of the world
of animals, the human world, and the world of plants and minerals into
one another: "a car stood half on the sidewalk. Its right headlight was
crushed and not bandaged, a dim hollow was in its pupil." The bells are
"imprisoned," the metal is "bound," and "inanimate things slowly growing." Similarly, people continually meet like "like drugged animals" and
speak "like birds."

These descriptions blur the conventional boundaries between defined
areas, and they are accompanied by descriptions of transitions between
distinct physical states. Conspicuous examples are: "Darkness flowed
from the windows and poured into the courtyards like bright and sparkling coal" (a transition from light of a certain color to a liquid to a solid
that preserves the original color); "the sounds flowed with the hot darkness like a cascade" (transition from a sound, which is mingled with light
with a thermal quality, to a liquid); "The sounds of the bells buzzed in
circle after circle and sank to the bottom, to the damp street, shattering"
(transition from a sound to a solid to a liquid and back to a solid). Here
one transition is made by means of the verb "buzz," which translates the
Hebrew *nisru,* derived from the Hebrew root, *nun-samekh-resh,* which
means "to saw" and also "to make a sawing sound."

The conventional boundaries between areas, materials, and qualities
are also burst by use of language that mingles the senses ("light . . .
throbs"; "thick darkness") and of language that applies a defined form or
measurement to materials that cannot in reality, be delimited that way:
"the silence that was doubled"; "smeared fire." Other expressions combine opposite or seemingly opposite elements ("shouting mutes"; "naked
darkness"), or they subvert the point of view of ordinary directions of
movement, as when darkness is described as invading the realm of light.
Other expressions contain statements that are inconsistent with our
awareness of the nature of the animal, vegetable, and mineral world, as
when the darkness nourishes the durability of the stones and the freshness of the air stifles people. Expressions of this type blur the outlines
between experiences that we normally regard as separate. To use termi-

nology borrowed from Gestalt psychology, it can be said that the "good patterns," those that permit a clear distinction between various descriptive categories and inspire a sense of order and security, are replaced by "weak patterns," which do not permit such a clear distinction and inspire a feeling of uncertainty and dread.

Unconnectedness

This chapter from *Haor Vehakutonet* is also replete with devices through which adjacent details are perceived as connected in a seemingly arbitrary way or in a way fundamentally different from the expected or familiar connection. The phenomenon of "unnatural" connection characterizes here, among other things, the fabric of the plot—a fabric that of course has a central role in structuring the fictional space.

The plot fabric in the arena of action of the chapter is organized by a clear chronotopical pattern: a solitary man wanders through the streets with the purpose of finding someone willing to converse with him. This pattern is hard to grasp in the continuum of reading because its elements —Gruzman's efforts to approach people and the responses of those people—are dismantled and scattered in separate graphic units at a distance from one another. Thus, for example, Gruzman's efforts to approach the man with the umbrella and the woman in the summer dress, using bodily gestures and words, all of which takes place within a short time, are portrayed in ten separate and distant phrases that extend over a relatively long reading period. Moreover, the sentences that separate those that deal with this minor plot contain other minor plots, which are conveyed in the same fragmentary, skipping, and delayed manner. Some of these minor plots belong to the present time, while others belong to the past; and some are based on the movements of people while others are based on the movements of atmospheric elements—the various auditory paths of the bells and the many chiaroscuro effects—which add to the difficulty of constructing the physical setting. Apparently arbitrary connections also typify the fabric of many of the paragraphs. Thus, for example, the first paragraph of the story is composed of three sentences that include several subordinate units, each of which relates to a different spatial or linguistic-emotional element. This fabric of syntax and content is diffusing (as opposed to focusing), preventing the construction of a clear spatial framework.

We are also prevented from constructing a spatial framework because of a large group of devices based on "unnatural" connections. One device of this kind, which is very common in Appelfeld's writing, is based on granting autonomy to parts of the whole. This device appears here in two interesting variants: one variant is the treatment of parts of the body as if they were independent organic units ("the woman recoiled, and her neck leaned back"). The second variant is treatment of spatial elements as though they were bodies acting under their own power ("the ice shakes free of the mountains"). These two variants, and there are many more like them, project a world where every part acts according to an independent logic, or else this world is guided, like the "reeducation mechanism" in *Mikhvat Haor* or the "Sanitation Department" in *Badenheim,* by a kind of violent caprice. In this world we cannot take the nature of anything for granted, and therefore nothing can be comprehended.

Idioms, Semantic and Syntactic Patterns, and the Indefinite Pronoun "Some"

The feeling that the fictional space is uncertain and unstable also results from the author's way of using language. In the sample passage under discussion, Appelfeld's narrator often uses words, combinations of words, and syntactic patterns that reflect his lack of faith in the existence of solid facts. One typical device of this stylistic and cognitive tendency, which recalls the stylistic and cognitive hesitance of Franz Kafka in all his writings and that of S. Y. Agnon in *Sefer Hamaasim* (The Book of Tales),[80] is Appelfeld's use of a series of speculations of equal status that relate to one context, whose structure, for lack of data, is elusive. Such a series of speculations organizes the second paragraph: "And perhaps the looks, . . . and perhaps the light. . . . And perhaps Gruzman. . . . Perhaps he recalled something, perhaps he heard. Perhaps the roof. . . ." This series of speculations creates an atmosphere of hesitation, doubt, or uncertainty, made thicker by the lack of question marks, giving the sentences an undefined status. They may be either questions or declarative sentences, or, alternatively, they may have the status of pseudo-rhetorical questions, yet still they lack answers.[81]

The narrator's lack of confidence in facts, and even more so in unequivocal positions, is also presented by the frequent use of words that express doubt or that limit the validity of his viewpoint and that of the main protagonist. Phrases such as "it seemed" or "they appeared," "as though" and "for some reason" are attached to several statements. Other statements are accompanied by phrases that express reservations or even negations: "perhaps the roof or, rather"; "She's certainly waiting, he said to himself, though it didn't appear so"; "'Evening,' said Gruzman without knowing what he was saying."

The narrator's reluctance to use complete forms and unequivocal statements is evident in the frequency with which he uses the indefinite pronoun "some," usually in connection with abstract nouns: "some discomfort"; "some hard physical love"; "some other death." This usage compresses the obscure, opaque, and mysterious atmosphere that prevails.

Appelfeld's great repertoire of devices that disintegrate and blur in this short chapter from *Haor Vehakutonet* denies the reader the possibility of reconstructing a lifelike, orderly, and soothing physical space. Instead the reader is called upon to reconstruct a precategorical, chaotic, and threatening space. The tension between these two types of reconstruction, between which the reader vacillates in the course of the reading, is the focus of the first chapter of *Haor Vehakutonet* on the thematic level as well.

The entire chapter is marked by the struggle between blind forces, signified by verbs of movement and flow, and conscious forces, which seek to halt the flow with categorical distinctions and/or recapitulative words or phrases. However, here the inexorable forces, as in all of Appelfeld's work, are at a clear advantage. Gruzman and the narrator try to stop the erosion by means of soothing expressions such as "nothing, nothing," or by means of the word "evening," which is intended to imprison within it the explosive chaos, but their weak efforts fail. Thus the darkness, which was thin at first, now "flow[s] piece by piece," and Gruzman's memory is "flooded." The sound of the church bells "poured down . . . like a cascade." The river in his memory is "flooded," and "the cows break out of their pens." Thus, not surprisingly, the chapter ends with a report that "night fell, as at first, blue as at first and also stars, maybe quieter than before." Despite all of these soothing signs, and even though "all was silent," Gruzman "could not stand without covering his head." Gruzman was well aware—and we, too, are expected to sense this—that the sky above him is not a shelter or protection, and he must hurry back to his cellar space.

Conclusion

The large regions of Appelfeld's fictional realm are portrayed through a perspective composed of two contradictory secondary perspectives. The first of these, which is identified here with the topographical dimension, leads us to construct in our mind's eye an orderly and stable expanse that is consistent, aside from certain differences deriving from the author's intellectual positions, with realistic space. The secondary perspective, which is identified here with the chronotopical and textual dimension, leads us to construct an entirely different space in our mind's eye, a precategorical, chaotic, and threatening space. The combination of these two secondary perspectives is marked by an extremely tense equilibrium. The physical space that Appelfeld portrays in the stories located in his three large regions is ultimately grasped as a visionary space, where everything appears to be in its place but at the same time strange and uncertain.

To whom does this dual-focus perspective belong? How was it created and consolidated, and against what background?

The answer to these questions is suggested by the character of the mutual relations among the regions of Appelfeld's realm. All of Appelfeld's fictional empire, which was built laboriously and with great talent over many years—all of that vast kingdom—is viewed through the eyes of someone whose vision was formed in the Penal Colony, that chaotic and amorphic extraterritorial region.

This conclusion is not in keeping with the common assumption regarding the character and intention of Appelfeld's work. Appelfeld does not touch upon the Holocaust, as is generally thought, via the margins, by means of plots set in frameworks of time and space that preceded the Holocaust or came afterward. On the contrary: Appelfeld continually touches upon the margins through his unique prism, which was shaped during his wanderings through the simultaneously infinite and hermetic expanses of his own Penal Colony, and which was greatly enhanced later on.

Let us conclude this discussion with Appelfeld's own words, taken from an essay that is entirely devoted to the issue of artistic responses to the trial of the Holocaust.[82]

93

The new [artistic] form, if one may say so, was brought by the children. These were child survivors, whose faces and expressions were shaped by the war years spent in forests and monasteries. Some of them sang well. I say they sang "well," though their voices were mainly scorched, a mixture of the remnants of melodies from the Jewish home and organ songs from the monastery. Everything was mingled in them into some new melody. Something sad, inarticulate, and grotesque. These were blind melodies, which only children in their blindness could create. . . .

There were also girls. I remember one well. Her name was Amalia. A girl of about ten, she would appear every evening. In her repertoire Jewish folksongs were mingled with forest sounds. Her body was thin and bird-like, and it seemed as if she were about to fly off.

There were also child acrobats, who wondrously walked on tight ropes. In the forests they had learned how to climb on branches and thin treetops. Among them was a pair of twins, boys of about ten, who juggled wooden balls marvelously. Among the others were also child mimics, who imitated animals and birds. These children used to wander through the camps by the dozen. While the adults tried to forget and be forgotten, and tried to become rooted in the soil of life, the children distilled suffering the way perhaps only a folk song can do it.

The children retained no concrete memory, only dread itself that was absorbed darkly in every cell of their body, dread with no name. Since it was not concrete, the children were incapable of forgetting it. It was part of their essence, like hands and feet. When they came to sing, to mimic, or to toss balls, suffering was latent in all of their movements, even in their laughter. . . .

I was a boy, but I remember clearly the long conversations until the middle of the night. Even then we understood that it was not enough to scream. A form for that scream had to be found. Otherwise it would sound mad, or, even worse, counterfeit. The wandering children unwittingly gave shape to the poetics of suffering. There was nothing in their voices except what there was: suffering and blindness. ("El Meever Latragi," *Masot Beguf Rishon,* pp. 47–49)

III

In God's Image, or Dust and Ashes:

Literature and Religious Anguish

Section 1
A Culture in Confusion

> Among the Jews we see that there is no religiosity or nonreligiosity, relation or lack of relation to other worlds. Among the Jews all religion is devoid of relationship. The Jews aren't a religious nation, rather they are people who observe a creed.
> —YOSEF HAYIM BRENNER

Prelude

Appelfeld's first collection of stories, *Ashan,* was greeted by most literary critics with great respect. In various ways, commentators agreed that the stories reveal a mature author who manages to portray, in convincing artistic manner, the psychological and moral consequences of the Holocaust upon its survivors.[1] But, as Dan Miron pointed out nearly two decades later, Appelfeld's early and justified success exacted a very heavy price: "His readership, including critics and other literary taste-makers, pinned a label on him and placed him in a well-defined cubbyhole in their minds: that of a writer who writes refined stories about the Holocaust. That static image soon became an obstacle to understanding the author's artistic endeavors."[2]

Over time the image established during the 1960s and 1970s was replaced by a new one. From the late 1970s on, Appelfeld was repeatedly presented as an author who seeks to grapple with the human condition of the Jew in a hundred years of solitude in the modern European world.[3] The new image, like its predecessor, has a valid basis in Appelfeld's literary oeuvre. Moreover, the change in image reflects, though considerably after the fact, real change. Appelfeld's second collection of stories, *Bagai Haporeh* and, even more, his third volume, *Kefor al Haaretz,* show an evident tendency to connect the "syndromes" that came to light during the Holocaust to the period that preceded it. Eliezer Schweid and Gershon Shaked both pointed out early signs of this tendency, which grew stronger in Appelfeld's fiction beginning in the 1970s.[4]

97

Thus the problem is not actually the label that was pinned on Appelfeld, but rather the critical stasis that resulted from it, which has two complementary aspects. The first aspect, according to Miron, is that critics ignored the changes that took place in Appelfeld's work, or at best they responded to them conspicuously late.[5] The second aspect, which is graver in my opinion, is "comfortable contentment" with an identifying label. This contentment is more conspicuous with respect to the second characterization of Appelfeld's work. Although as early as the 1960s, and especially in recent years, the author's poetical style has received significant critical attention and has been the object of several studies that have gained academic recognition,[6] the second subject—the human condition of the Jew's hundred years of solitude in the modern European world—has not received extensive scholarly attention.[7]

Here I attempt in some degree to fill that scholarly gap by systematically examining the central junctures in Appelfeld's "religious journey." I say "religious journey" and not "journey of faith" or "Jewish religious journey" because I refer here, following Appelfeld's sharp words in his essay on Yosef Hayim Brenner ("Sfat Mahalato Usfat Kisufav: Mashehu al Yosef Hayim Brenner" [The Language of His Illness and the Language of His Longing], *Masot Beguf Rishon,* pp. 67–77), to the author's unwearying endeavor, as an individual, to achieve "a primary and fundamental attitude of 'who am I and what am I?'" (p. 70). Appelfeld seeks to go beyond an individual's wonder at the mystery of life to "his search for the meaning of life, not as something useful or comfortable, or a matter of spiritual richness, but as anguish. For so long as there is no flicker of hope in reality—all craving, beauty, and pleasure seem stale" (p. 70).

The Kingdom of the Cheated

Appelfeld began his literary career as a poet. During the second half of the 1950s and the first years of the 1960s he published about sixty poems that have never been collected in a book. The poems can be classified into two large thematic groups. The first group, containing about twenty poems, deals with efforts to recreate the lost and smoky regions of childhood and with the acute feelings of guilt that were bound up with that act of creative imagination. The second group, which also contains about twenty poems, deals with relations between the poet and his God.[8]

The speaker in this second, large group of poems conceives himself as a poetical emissary of God. He is called upon to accomplish an extremely difficult poetical mission, and he pays for it with heart and soul:[9]

> Not a single word remains
> That has not been smelted in the forge of pains
> The volcano is shut within me
> Behind bolt and double doors.
>
> Silence has fanned the flames
> All is molten white hot
> My words were of red metal
> Bound in the living flesh.
>
> I worshiped you with this fire, my God,
> Unto embers and ash
> The volcano is locked within me
> And it cries out in the flames.
> ("Gaash" [Volcano])

The speaker within whom a volcano seethes is yearning for a burst of revelation that will redeem him from his torments:

> Now the blood speaks
> The caves expand and the dams collapse
> . . . .
> Now . . .
> Everything awaits revelation
> In trembling.
> ("Akhshav" [Now, 1957])

But the revelation does not occur. Instead there is an opaque silence that stifles and oppresses the creative volcano:[10]

> Lord of storms who gave us this silence
> For torments
> Upon which our soul-birds knock
> And chirp silence.
> Father of storms who has so silenced our hearts
> Who casts stones of muteness at us
> Until we have been stoned to death.

> The thoughts swoop down like a cloud laden with fury
> And thunder is not released here
> And no lightning is kindled
> Only the silence of those laden with a heavy burden
> Who flee, scored
> And strangled.
>
>   ("Ribon Hasaarot" [Lord of the Storms, 1956])

Nor is the tense yearning for revelation answered in more serene times ("Meever Lapargod" [Beyond the Curtain, 1958], "Hine Bati Kimaat" [Here I Have Almost Arrived, 1958], "Kolot Lohashim" [Whispering Voices, 1958]), and the speaker feels cheated:

> I know
> That today, too, you do not call me
> Just my heedful, bristling limbs
> Will tremble within me
> Will wait even for the imaginary sign from my soul
> That leads me far from here
> Far
> To the kingdom of the deceived.
>
>   ("El Malkhut Hamerumim"
>   [To the Kingdom of the Deceived, 1959])

The speaker feels like a rejected and cheated son, and a fierce struggle between faith and heresy is waged in his soul. He tries to flee, but he knows that he has nowhere to go:

> By seven paths they will return
> And by the eighth they will flee from you
> Whither shall they flee?
> You shall not pursue them
> You know,
> By themselves they shall return
> To captivity.
>
>   ("Beshiva Derakhim"
>   [By Seven Paths, 1958])

The speaker feels like the accused, like someone unworthy of his mission, and at the same time like someone with a reckoning to make, complaining and accusing:

That you bound sadness around my neck
So that I cannot stand in prayer
That you called me from every side
To mount me upon lying melodies
And you knew that all the rhythms
Pace within me toward you
With steps that I cannot attain. And why
  do you whisper heretic to me every day?
     ("Yadata" [You Knew, 1958])

A Rabbi in a Wheelchair

This group of poems raises crucial questions. What became of the fervent religious energy that is reflected in them? Where did Appelfeld channel his unwearying yearning for some revelation that would answer his religious distress? The pertinence of these questions also emerges from the examination of the author's early essays, which were devoted to poets with missions,[11] and it grows in intensity when one examines the status of established, traditional Judaism and its official representatives in the totality of Aharon Appelfeld's literary work.

Appelfeld has stated on several occasions that he has great respect for the institutional, traditional form of Judaism, but that it is beyond his own existential and emotional limits.[12] These statements are consistent with the implications of the plot and thematic structure of his stories. In dozens of his stories the main characters consciously or unconsciously confront a dilemma. On the one hand, they can (at least seemingly) choose the traditional, religious way of life and survive or at least maintain their human dignity. On the other hand, they can choose other paths (rejection, assimilation, or ways of life that are not traditionally Jewish or at least apparently not traditionally Jewish), paths that lead them, sooner or later, to their tragic end or at least to the loss of human dignity. This dilemma in theme and plot is always resolved the same way: choice of the destructive path. It emerges clearly in the longer of Appelfeld's early stories, as, for example, in "Nisayon Retzini" from his first collection, Ashan.

Zimmer, the main character in this story, is a Holocaust survivor who works as a hired driver for the Sadir taxi company. The taxi drivers are divided into two groups: those who drive on "short routes" and those who have "long routes." The "short routes" are reserved for "strong-armed men" ("Nisayon Retsini," Ashan, p. 90), headed by Lipa the "zhlob" (boor) (p. 122). The "long routes" are given to the "weak" drivers: Drimer, Mendel, and Zimmer himself.

Zimmer's "weak" colleagues have very different attitudes toward their status in the company rosters. Drimer repeatedly tries "to attach himself to the short line" (p. 107), whose workers, especially Lipa, are characterized by a rapacious, gentilelike way of living. All Drimer's efforts fail, and ultimately he finds his death in an "unexpected" automobile accident (p. 107). Mendel, by contrast, does not try to overcome his "natural" situation. The expressions of that rapacious, gentilelike way of living in the story arouse revulsion in him or leave him indifferent (pp. 111, 119, and elsewhere). He cares mainly for religious books and Hebrew literature that is anchored in the traditional Jewish world ("the stories of Agnon, [and the] poem about the House of Study by Bialik [p. 97]). Mendel's religious faith saves him and provides him with tranquility just like his hero, Reb Yudel Hasid of S. Y. Agnon's *Hakhnasat Kala* (The Bridal Canopy), whose "faith [brings him] to find a treasure" (p. 121).

Drimer and Mendel represent two existential possibilities of equal status (at least so it seems) that are available to Zimmer. Zimmer chooses the one represented by Drimer, and he, like Drimer before him, finds his death in an "unexpected" traffic accident (p. 124). The question asked here is, of course, why Zimmer rejects the possibility represented by Mendel, the way of religious faith that would permit him to survive. A flashback at the end of the story provides the answer to this question. On the last night of his life Zimmer finds himself taken by Mendel to evening prayers. As soon as Zimmer enters the synagogue he feels uncomfortable: "Strange, and, to a degree, repulsive the room seemed to him, like the purification room in the cemetery of his town, that he had peeked into once on Lag B'Omer and fled" (p. 121). Later "the worshipers crowded into the eastern corner, and the evening lights broke on their heads," but Zimmer, "who sat in the last row . . . reckoned up the overtime he had worked in the past week and added in four hours from earlier weeks, calculating that altogether he had accrued seventeen hours, and he tried to multiply it" (p. 121).

Zimmer thus feels revulsion for the way of life that could have served him as an existential refuge. Similar reactions to traditional Jewish life typify other Holocaust survivor protagonists in Appelfeld's stories. These responses are frequently connected to early memories and/or to early memories as they have been recast during the Holocaust.[13]

However, it is not only Holocaust survivors who are depicted as people for whom the traditional Jewish way of life does not fall within the range

Michael Appelfeld, father. Born in Vizhnitz, 1898.

Boniah Appelfeld (Sternberg), mother. Born in Sadigorah, 1905.

Aharon Appelfeld. Tchernovitz. End
1936–beginning 1937.

Aharon Appelfeld.
Tchernovitz. End
1936–beginning 1937.

Boniah Appelfeld, mother (center) with two of her nieces, Sally and Bondia.

Aharon Appelfeld.
During training in
the Zionist Youth
School, Ein Karem
1946–1947.

Aharon Appelfeld. During training in the Zionist Youth School, Ein Karem
1946–1947.

Aharon Appelfeld. During service in the Israel Defense Forces, 1950–1951.

Aharon Appelfeld. Student ID picture taken at the beginning of his studies at the Hebrew University of Jerusalem, 1952.

Aharon Appelfeld. On his first trip to Europe, Switzerland (after immigrating to Israel), 1955.

Aharon Appelfeld.
Jerusalem, 1954.

Aharon and Yehudit Appelfeld with their 3-week-old son, Meir. Jerusalem, 1965.

Aharon Appelfeld with sons Meir (age 6) and Itzhak (age 3). Jerusalem, 1971.

Aharon Appelfeld with sons
Meir (age 8) and Itzhak (age
5). Yom Kippur War, 1973.

Aharon Appelfeld with daughter, Batya (age 6). Boston, 1981.

of their existential possibilities. The other main characters in the dozens of stories that take place before the Holocaust exemplify the same condition. Prominent among these are the main characters in Appelfeld's Austro-Hungarian stories, who suffer in particular from the phenomenon that Appelfeld has called in various places, "the auto-antisemitic malady."[14] Among others, there is the young narrator of *Keishon Haayin*, a sensitive and intelligent young man who describes a group of his religious relatives as "a flock of black Jews, short, thin, and the look suspended in their eyes scurries about restlessly" (p. 217). This description is almost identical to the "standard" depiction, in other stories, of religious Jews by antisemitic peasants.[15] The father in *The Age of Wonders* suffers from the same malady of antisemitism, as he tries to prevent his friend the sculptor, Stark, the son of a Jewish mother and an Austrian father, from "return[ing] to the crucible of his origins" (p. 103). That father, an artist himself, argues to Stark that this action will bring personal disaster: "Why take this trouble on yourself, Kurt? You're a free man. Even your posture speaks of freedom. Your artistic heritage speaks of freedom. Your father, an Austrian by birth, left you land, health, hands fit to carve stone, and you want to exchange this health, freedom, for an old, sick faith"(p. 120). The rhetoric used by the father—that Judaism equals illness while Austrianism equals health—serves, ironically and horribly, his antisemitic and auto-antisemitic critics, who argue that he and those like him must be expelled from "healthy" Austrian society (p. 72).[16]

The status of traditional, established Judaism in the existential space of Appelfeld's stories can also be learned from the way its official and nonofficial representatives are presented: the rabbis, the middlemen, and the preachers. These always appear as powerless people, as representatives who have lost their status among their flock (Rabbi Leibush in "Mota shel Hashtadlanut," Rabbi Yisrael in "Tzel Harim," Rabbi Hershel in "Hagerush" [all in *Kefor al Haaretz*], Rabbi Siedendorf in "Hayom" [*Adnei Hanahar*], Rabbi Mueller in the play *Al Bariah,* the rabbi in four chapters of a novel in progress that have been published in various places—"Haminyan Haavud" [The Lost Minyan, 1985], "Hafrada" [Separation, 1985], "Hatzar Hamatara" [Courtyard of the Gaôl, 1987], and "Shefatim" [Blows], and the rabbi in the chapter that concludes the first part of *The Age of Wonders*).

The spiritual helplessness that characterizes the representatives of established religion is often accompanied by a physical handicap, a serious disease, and death. Thus, for example, the rabbi in *Badenheim* is described as follows: [17]

Suddenly the old rabbi appeared in the street. Many years ago they had brought him to Badenheim from the East. For a few years he had officiated in the local synagogue—or to tell the truth, the old-age home. When the old men died, the place was left empty. The rabbi had a paralytic stroke. In the town they were sure that he had died along with the other old men.

The hotel owner stood in the doorway and said, "Come in, sir." . . . The rabbi shaded his eyes, and a blue vein throbbed on his white forehead.

"Jews?" asked the rabbi.

"Jews," said the hotel owner.

"And who is your rabbi?" asked the rabbi.

"You, you are our rabbi."

The rabbi's face expressed a grim astonishment. His old memory tried to discover whether they were making fun of him.

"Perhaps you will allow us to offer you something to drink?"

The rabbi frowned. "Kosher?" he asked.

The hotel owner lowered his eyes and did not reply. . . .

The next day the mystery cleared up a little. A Christian woman, a good woman, had looked after him all these years, but suddenly she had abandoned him. The rabbi spent a few days trying to move the wheelchair, and in the end he succeeded. (*Badenheim,* pp. 100–101)

Section 2
To the Simplicity of Life

Waldeinsamkeit,
Wie liegst du weit!
Oh, dir gereut
Einst mit der Zeit.
Ach, einz'ge Freud,
Waldeinsamkeit!

Forest loneliness,
How far you lie!
Oh, you shall regret
Once in time.
Ah, only joy,
Forest loneliness.

—LUDWIG TIECK, *Der Blonde Eckbert*

Prelude

In Appelfeld's work, established Judaism is viewed as anachronistic and petrified. Therefore, he certainly could not look to it for a suitable solution to his religious distress, the force of which is evident in so many of his poems and early essays.

The place of the established Jewish religion and of any other established religion is taken in Appelfeld's work by a poignant yearning for what can tentatively be called "religious fundamentalism." By a yearning for "religious fundamentalism" I mean, following Appelfeld's own definition in his important essay on Yosef Hayim Brenner, "the effort to descend from the peaks of a culture that has become complex, distorted, or that has depleted itself—the simplicity of life" ("Sfat Mahalato Usfat Kisufav," *Masot Beguf Rishon*, p. 73). Appelfeld's version of the yearning for religious fundamentalism is very reminiscent—and not by chance—of the desire for natural life, as it appears in the authors of the so-called primordial romantic myth. I refer to a group of thinkers and artists (mainly German) who called for the rejection of the established religion and Western rationalism, which, in their view, had become complex and distorted, and for the return to "basic values."[18] These values were a sense of nature, tribal affiliation, ties of blood, a direct attachment to nature, and the like. This primordial romantic myth underwent various transformations. One of them, of course—and this is a pertinent and thought-provoking fact—was the myth upon which the Nazi movement was based in Germany and its satellites.

Appelfeld's longing for religious fundamentalism, as influenced by the primordial romantic myth, is expressed in two major directions taken in his work. The first involves the extensive connections that link many of his stories to "underground Judaism"—that is to say, to use a diagnosis made by Martin Buber[19] to the Jewish way of life as expressed in the "esoteric" movements of Judaism, in the Kabbalah and mainly in Hasidism. The second direction is expressed in the yearning, repeatedly appearing in Appelfeld's work, for a "strange" mingling of the basic components of Jewish faith and of the "primitive" gentile Christian faith. The yearning for this strange mixture, which could perhaps be described as pagan-Christian Judaism, is the deepest expression of what I believe to be Appelfeld's religious attitude.

From the foregoing it might be concluded that Appelfeld's religious fundamentalism, with its two connected and interwoven central paths, is simple and clear. But the opposite is the case. While in most of his fiction (and especially in the latest works), it is easy to identify the primitive and the naive in both content and form, nevertheless the yearning for religious fundamentalism is always portrayed from an ironic perspective. Thus we have a dual tendency. On the one hand, we discern a yearning for the simplicity of life that reflects a critical attitude toward "a culture that has become complex, distorted, or that has depleted itself" (Sfat Mahalato Usfat Kisufav,"*Masot Beguf Rishon*, p. 73). On the other hand, we discern a powerful affinity with that "culture that has become complex," modern culture with its humanistic, rationalistic, and universal values. This affinity is reflected, among other things, in the ironic illumination of the yearning for fundamentalism. This dual tendency is expressed in every stratum of Appelfeld's stories: the cast of characters, their typical linguistic expressions, the structure of the plot, the narrator's point of view, and the like. Similarly, this tendency is expressed in the generic character of most of Appelfeld's works published from the early 1980s on.

The First Path:
The Jews of the Carpathians as Industrious Dwarfs

Appelfeld's relation to Hasidism, which, as he reports, began to develop under the influence of Dov Sadan and Leib Rochman,[20] should be investigated by an expert in Hasidism. I shall content myself with a general survey of the stories in which the influence of Hasidism is evident, in the order of their publication, and I shall try to address the attitude implicit in them toward that important cultural tradition.

The first of Appelfeld's stories in which his connections to the hasidic world are evident is "Haderekh ben Drovna Ledrovitz." Here Appelfeld tells the tale of a band of pilgrims on their way to a holy man who lives in the hasidic village of Drovicz. This journey, which is focused through the eyes of a boy but presented to us in the first person plural, is a ritual journey undertaken every year for the High Holy Days with the declared aim of purifying and sanctifying both the congregation and the individual. In the course of the journey the travelers, especially the most vulnerable among them ("the boy" and "the penitent") are exposed to grave spiritual dangers. Indeed, toward the journey's end, all the travelers have an unforgettable religious experience.[21] Drovicz seems to the pilgrims who approach it, "in this mixture of darkness and light" like "the lost central point" ("Haderekh ben Drovna Ledrovitz, *Kefor al Haaretz*, p. 12). The boy knows "with a palpable, unsurpassed certainty, that the world has a center, that everything is drawn to Drovicz, that even the twilight longs for it. A person who travels to greet the High Holy Days in the court suddenly feels that he was distant and disavowed during the year" (p. 12). The relation with the hasidic world is also evident on the stylistic level, for the story is studded with many hasidic expressions. This relation is also notable in the stories "Hashiva" and "Haaliya Lekatzansk" (both in *Bekomat Hakarka*), and in "Ahar Hahupa" (After the Wedding, *Adnei Hanahar*).[22]

The novella *The Healer* is also based on a journey to repair the soul. This is the story of a family making a pilgrimage to a holy man in a remote village in the Carpathians. The declared aim of the trip is to try to heal the daughter Helga's illness. Like many of the young assimilated Jewish women in Appelfeld's work, Helga suffers from the loss of the will to live.[23] The only hope for curing her depends upon return to a simple, rooted Jewish life. This, at least, is her mother's belief. Her father, Felix, disagrees. He "had opposed this caprice with all his soul" (p. 6), and he rationalizes his opposition: "He would no longer chase moonbeams. The local pagan doctors were more than enough. 'We won't go to the old sorcerers'" (p. 9). But in the end he submits to his wife's will and sets off on the journey "against his will" (p. 6).

The simple, rooted Jewish way of life is exemplified in this novella by the Jews of the Carpathian village. As always in Appelfeld's fiction, they and their like are perceived as existing on an island of tranquil and innocent religiosity.[24] Naturally the old village holy man himself, described at length here, is representative of this way of life.[25]

Many components of the novella *Layish* link it to the world of Hasidism. It tells the story of a group of Jewish wanderers, instructed before his death by a holy man to go to Jerusalem. This motley band—including murderers, religiously observant old men, compulsive thieves, merchants, and visionaries—makes its way along the Prut River, stopping over in several towns, in most of which famous holy men once lived. In its structure and style and with respect to what is conceived as its teleology, *Layish* is similar to legendary hasidic novellas. Using Martin Buber's familiar definition of the legendary novella, the story of this band of wanderers can be defined as the "story of fate represented as a single process."[26] Like the earlier pilgrim stories in *Bagai Haporeh*,[27] the wanderings of the Jews in *Layish* are meant to represent the existential condition of the Jewish people as a whole.

Clear lines of similarity can be drawn between the plot structure of *Layish* and that of the story "Seder Hanesiya shel Rabi Nahman Mibratslav Leeretz Israel" (The Order of the Journey of Rabbi Nahman of Bratslav to the Land of Israel). Both stories are modeled on a plot idea that involves descent and humiliation for the purpose of elevation and purification of the soul. Descent and humiliation are expressed in deviations from the straight way (literally and figuratively) and in long delays of the plot, whereas elevation and purification of the soul are expressed in clinging to the straight way, which is meant to lead to Jerusalem, the holy city. In both stories this model symbolizes the effort to free oneself of the worldliness and degradation of the heart's exile.[28]

The plot of Appelfeld's *Ad Sheyaaleh Amud Hashahar* is also essentially one of decline and humiliation and then an effort at self-liberation in a journey to repair the soul. The main character of the novel, a young Jewish woman named Blanca, has married a violent gentile who torments her and violates her honor and freedom. Blanca finally takes her fate into her own hands. She murders her husband and flees to the Carpathians with her son, for she imagines that this region is the precious domain of "a simple life, country life" (p. 98). The exact place toward which she sets her course is the town of Vizhnitz, the residence of the famous holy man. Blanca's thoughts as she makes her way toward Vizhnitz show what that town signifies to her:

> For some reason she pictured the road to Vizhnitz to herself as a long, illuminated tunnel. In the front part of it was a ritual bath, where one immerses oneself and is purified. Afterward, those purifying themselves put on linen garments and advance to the next stage. At the next stage they sit in a gallery until the soul is rid of its dross and no longer remembers anything. Henceforth the tunnel twists and turns, but it is not difficult to walk in it. (*Ad Sheyaaleh Amud Hashahar*, p. 187)

As noted, in Appelfeld's later writing, the small hasidic towns and villages of the Carpathians and of Poland (as emerges mainly from *Badenheim*) are portrayed as a precious realm of Jewish life full of true, simple, and innocent religiosity. From the perspective of that precious realm, the life of the assimilated Jews of the big cities and provincial towns of the Austro-Hungarian Empire seems corrupt and distorted.

Nevertheless, careful reading reveals that the Carpathians and their Polish parallel are not described as real places but rather as utopias. Thus it is no surprise that the various efforts to return and renew contact with them are always cast in an ironic light, as in the efforts to fulfill the Zionist ideology or the romantic ethos in S. Y. Agnon's fiction. The irony results because the return is presented as late or illusory, shown in various ways. Sometimes there is no longer anywhere to return to. Sometimes the return itself is grasped as fundamentally artificial, or the returnees are unable or unwilling to sever completely the ties of the "culture that has become complex, distorted, or that has depleted itself" ("Sfat Mahalato Usfat Kisufav," *Masot Beguf Rishon*, p. 73) Occasionally, set against a background of imminent historical catastrophe that will obliterate everything, the entire effort of return seems ridiculous. One way or another (and in most of the stories, both one way and the other), every effort to return is a dream—or a nightmarish illusion.

"Haderekh ben Drovna Ledrovitz" begins with the sentence: "Again we are about to undergo the nighttime journey from Drovna to Drovicz" (*Kefor al Haaretz*, p. 7). This sentence defines the experiential and conscious context in the light of which, so it seems, we must read the entire story. The narrator announces that we have before us an account of a sequence of events that repeats a similar sequence of events that took place in the past or, at least, a conscious reconstruction of that sequence of events. As the story continues, it gradually becomes clear to us that we have here neither a repeated journey nor yet the re-creation of an earlier trip, but rather an effort to create and imagine a reconstruction of such a trip. This realization implies that the unforgettable religious experience around which the entire story is built is not an authentic remembered experience but rather longing for such an experience. There is neither a true return nor even a belated return, but an illusory, dreamlike, and nightmarish journey. This realization is consistent with the last lines of the story, which paints a surrealistic picture:

Though we had never been there, we recognized the houses, and we saw that they were our houses. Breath flew out of them, and darkness glowed in the windows. The Rebbe's court, too, stood, a house surrounded by a fence. We were afraid to approach, because everything was so silent and empty, so that the hand of the wind alone could knock it over. ("Haderekh ben Drovna Ledrovitz," *Kefor al Haaretz*, p. 13)

The illusory character of the family's return journey in *The Healer* is no less unmistakable. As one reads the novella, the illusion is revealed through several ironic perspectives. Appelfeld uses Felix, the father of the family, to create one of them. Felix is endowed with the characteristic features of the *eiron*, a man capable of sharp perception, suspicious, and a confirmed skeptic. Through his inquisitive eyes his wife's and daughter's efforts to return to religion appear in all their falsity. He sometimes even identifies tinges of a Christian-monastic sanctimony in them.

The holy man, the village healer, also serves as an *eiron*. In his heart he harbors fondness and mercy toward people, even toward the arrogant and sanctimonious among them, and thus he is very different from Felix and also, significantly, from the "petrified" establishment rabbis. However, he knows very well that the illness is incurable, and in fact fatal, and that he is unable to bring redemption. This recognition is already clear in his first meeting with Henrietta, Felix, and their daughter Helga:

> The old man closed his eyes. Not many people came to him from the capital, and the few who did were desperate and came unwillingly. The winds of despair bore them to him. When he was young contention had renewed his zeal, but in recent years the struggle had become hard for him. He hadn't the strength to sail out of his body and cleave to people's despair. His ulcer too, in the cold season the pains became sharper. They no longer let him take leave of himself. They locked him into his sickly body.
>
> If only he could shut himself off, cling to his books, no longer see anyone, return his soul to the Creator in serenity, without rushing. Haste was unseemly. But what could he do? The world knew no mercy: give us advice, give us cure, give us blessing. And those attendants, flushed with greed. If he could, he would send them all away from him. He shook himself free of his thoughts, angry that he had let them take control, and turned to those sitting before him. (*The Healer*, p. 38)

Felix and the holy man, each in his own way, shed ironic light on those who try to return and attach themselves again to the pure and primordial world, and also those who try to help them in that effort. However, their irony is dwarfed in comparison to the satanic irony of the angel of history.[29] For the efforts to return and take refuge in the warm

bosom of innocent faith, like their ironic illumination, seem pale and de-
risory in the face of the storm that threatens to sweep all of them from
the halls of history.

Blanca's efforts, too, in *Ad Sheyaaleh Amud Hashahar*, to return to
"her origins" is portrayed through several ironic perspectives. One of
them is created by her conversations with her little son Otto. These conversations take place after Blanca tries to captivate Otto's imagination
with stories about the simplicity and beauty of the Jewish villages in the
Carpathians, and about their gentle and hospitable inhabitants. Otto's
sensitive queries and Blanca's ridiculous responses reveal the character of
these stories, which are based, as the narrator takes pains to inform us,
on descriptions "that she read in Buber" and on "everything that her
imagination embroidered" (p. 169). For example: "In Otto's imagination, for some reason, the Jews of the Carpathians were pictured as industrious dwarfs. Blanca corrected the impression: their height is the
same as ordinary people. Maybe even a bit taller, but by no means were
they dwarfs" (p. 169).

Another conversation tinged with acute irony reveals the tragi-pathetic
character of the return journey for Blanca, from beginning to end. That
conversation takes place in the concluding scene of the book. Blanca,
who is only three kilometers from Vizhnitz, enters a tavern to have a
drink and doze off. While she is conversing with the innkeeper, two gendarmes from her native town enter the place. They have been pursuing
her for months because of the murder she committed. Rather than make
herself inconspicuous—for, "had she closed her eyes and curled up in a
corner, as she intended, they would not have noticed her" (p. 192)—
Blanca begins a lively conversation with the two gendarmes, revealing her
identity to them and telling them fervently of her intention "to receive the
holy man's blessing" (p. 193). She tries to interest them "in the faith of
holy men" (p. 193) and in the greatness and importance of Buber's book,
The Hidden Light. While the gendarmes place handcuffs on her and lead
her to the police station, Blanca neither complains nor begs for mercy.
"She said only this: I used to go to 'My Corner' with my father almost
every week. It was an excellent coffeehouse and its cheesecake was worthy of all renown. If there is one thing that I long for now, it is for a cup of
coffee and their cheesecake. That's all, nothing more" (p. 194). Thus we
find—and this is the focus of the irony here—that in one impulsive moment, longing for a cup of coffee and cheesecake (which represent, of
course, the urban, assimilated life that Blanca had decided to abandon),

can overcome all longings for repair of the soul, which are symbolized by "the simple life" in the Carpathians and "the faith of holy men."[30]

The Second Path: Guardians of the Flame

Prelude

In reading Appelfeld's writings, one also notes a yearning for a strange mixture of the basic Jewish components of faith and "primitive," gentile, Christian components. I intend to examine the manifestations of this yearning, which become more acute in Appelfeld's later works, by examining two novellas: *Tzili* and *Katerina*. The choice of these two novellas is almost self-evident, because in both the mixture of components of Jewish and Christian faith occupies a prominent position and also because this strange mixture is dramatized in them from opposing points of view. Tzili Kraus, the protagonist in *Tzili*, is a Jewish girl, whereas Katerina, the protagonist in the novella of that name, is an old Christian woman.

The attitude toward the "Jewish-gentile-pagan" mixture implied in these two novellas is fundamentally ambivalent. It is similar, but not identical, to the ambivalent attitude toward "simple Jewish life" that emerges from Appelfeld's hasidic stories. Here the ambivalence is produced by a violent clash between two very different cultural conceptions. The first, the Jewish-gentile-pagan amalgam, is portrayed in a quasi-mythological time scheme, and it includes—at least from the perspective of the main characters—supernatural events. The second, a European, humanistic, rational liberalism, is portrayed in a realistic time scheme, and it includes events that orient the reader toward major historical events.

Exactly like the parallel clash in the hasidic stories, the clash between the two cultural conceptions in *Tzili* and *Katerina* represents the author's religious anguish, an anguish from which one can never be freed because escape from it is blocked. On the one hand, efforts to connect with the naive—the simple life—are presented as impossible, for the tribe and/or the characters are no longer capable of ridding themselves of the plague of modern doubt. On the other hand, efforts to renounce the naive are presented as destructive. The result is morbid addiction to the dying tremors of "a culture that has become complex, distorted" ("Sfat Mahalato Usfat Kisufav," *Masot Beguf Rishon*, p. 73). I believe that this unavoidable clash between the naive and the modern is the central subject of all of Appelfeld's later stories, and I wish to study it here mainly by means of a partial but detailed examination of the generic character of these two novellas.

A Cruel Fate, Without Glory

Tzili tells the story of a Jewish girl who was abandoned by her family "when the war broke out" (p. 7). During the entire period of the Holocaust she wanders alone through expanses inhabited by "primitive" gentile peasants. After the liberation, Tzili joins a group of refugees that reaches Zagreb and then the Italian coast, and from there continues to the Land of Israel. Tzili's wanderings follow a course very similar to those of Appelfeld himself [31] and of other Jewish children who were exiled to Transnistria.[32] Hence *Tzili* seems to invite a reading that is biographical and historical. Indeed, this connection is underscored by the subtitle of the English translation, *Tzili: The Story of a Life,* and by the opening lines of the book, which are unique in the author's work: "Perhaps it would be better to leave the story of Tzili Kraus' life untold. Her fate was a cruel and inglorious one, and but for the fact that it actually happened we would never have been able to tell her story" (p. 1). Apparently, at least, this opening implies an anti-Aristotelian approach, suggesting that the story should be told not because it could have happened but rather "since it did happen."

However, *Tzili* contains other reading instructions, distancing us from the biographical-historical and/or the realistic-mimetic context, guiding us to an "other" context. Various critics, mainly in the United States,[33] have argued that the "natural corpus" of the novella is not mimetic, realistic literature, but rather naive literature, in particular German folk tales. Indeed, there is a decided similarity in structure and motif between the story of Tzili and some of the fairy tales collected by the Grimm brothers. I refer to the stories of growing up, whose heroes, boys and girls or princes and princesses are exiled or flee from their homes to the forest, or they are held there either by some hostile force or their own uncontrollable curiosity.[34] There is also a similarity between the story of Tzili and German romantic fiction written in the folk style.[35]

The validity of relating *Tzili* to naive literature is supported by Appelfeld's own comments in his wide-ranging and significant conversation with Philip Roth.

When I wrote *Tzili,* I was about forty. At that time I was interested in the possibilities of *naiveness* in art. Can there be a naive modern art? It seemed to me that without naiveté still found among children and old people, and, to some extent, in ourselves, the work of art would be flawed. [In *Tzili*] I tried to correct that flaw.[36]

The relation to the naive—in the sense given to that term by Friedrich Schiller and Heinrich von Kleist[37]—is reflected both in coming-of-age folk stories and in Appelfeld's novella, primarily in the plot topos upon which they depend. I refer to the topos of the rite of passage from childhood to maturity as it has been described in primitive societies. In coming-of-age folk tales and in *Tzili,* just as in rites of passage from childhood to maturity, children advance along an elaborate, complex course that is inspiring and exalting and also humiliating and cruel. In the process they are expelled from their communities and undergo a series of tests, after which they once again are absorbed into their society.[38]

The fact that *Tzili,* like coming-of-age folk tales, depends on a primitive plot topos, permits us to associate it, at least so it would seem, with naive literature. I say "so it would seem" because such an act of association does not take into account the cultural context within which this primitive topos is formed. Indeed, in coming-of-age folk tales there is full correlation between the (naive) character of the rite of transition from childhood to maturity and the (naive) character of the cultural context within which it takes place. By contrast, in *Tzili* there is only a partial correlation between these two central variables. Indeed a significant portion of the book is constructed as a primitive rite of passage within a cultural context with decidedly primitive characteristics: the Holocaust. However, in other sections of the book, aspects of the very same rite are structured within modern contexts. In those sections, which relate to periods before and after the Holocaust, there is an acute lack of correlation between the naive plot and the modern social context. The consequence of this lack of correlation is the utter failure of the rite of passage itself.

The failure of the primitive rite of passage reflects the author's failure to write a naive story. This failure, it must be emphasized, is intentional. Its purpose is to present us with the tragic inability of modern man in general, and of the modern Jewish person in particular, to experience the world naively, and, according to Aharon Appelfeld, to exist in a state of religiosity.

In his classic work, *The Rites of Passage,* Arnold Van Gennep shows that all rites of passage, including ritual transitions from childhood to maturity, are marked by three stages. First is the "stage of separation," which includes a variety of activities that symbolize the individual's separation from a previously defined point in the social structure, or from a system of determined social conditions, or from both. This is followed by the stage of marginality, the "liminal stage," in which the traits of the subject of the ceremony, the initiate, are ambivalent. The initiate loses all the marks of affiliation that characterized him or her in the period before the separation, but still lacks the marks of affiliation that will characterize him in the stage following the liminal stage. At the same time the initiate displays a strange mixture of traits from both periods. In other words, the initiate is no longer categorized with his or her former clarity but is not yet marked by distinct, new traits. In the final "stage of reintegration," the subject of the rite, the initiate, is placed once again in a stable social system with responsibilities and rights that are defined within an established structure. At this stage, the initiate is expected to behave according to the social, moral, and religious norms that are obligatory within the tribal tradition.[39]

Victor Turner and Mircea Eliade adopted and elaborated upon the model developed by Gennep. These two scholars focus mainly on the liminal stage. They identify its typical components and discuss the decisive function it fills in the texture of both individual life and social life. Turner and Eliade emphasize that at this stage, marked doubly by chaos and sanctity, the initiate is exposed to the roots of the tribe's religious existence. These primary elements always appear in strange mixtures of symbols.[40]

At least in two of its three stages, the course followed by Tzili is very similar to that traversed by adolescents in primitive rites of passage. The novella is divided into three parts. The first (chapters 1–2) presents the background of Tzili's separation from her home, her family, her people, and the scene of the separation itself. This part closes with a powerful event that symbolizes the stages and purpose of the entire rite of passage. The second part (chapters 3–20), dealing with the liminal stage, includes two large sections. The first section (chapters 3–9) describes Tzili's wanderings through the fertile and wild expanses and her meetings with several representative figures. In the second section (chapters 10–20), a long ritual ceremony is described, one that is supposed to symbolize Tzili's transition to the stage of renewed affiliation, upon which the third part (chapters 21–31) focuses. Tzili departs from "existential limbo" and joins a group of Jewish refugees, ultimately boarding a ship whose destination is the Land of Israel.

The similarity between the novella and primitive rites of passage can also be traced in the portrayal of the temporal and spatial realms. The stages of separation and reintegration take place in *Tzili* exactly like rites of maturation, at specific and defined places and times (first in a small village somewhere in the former Austro-Hungarian Empire about October 1941, just at the onset of World War II there, and finally in various places, some of which are mentioned by name, along the route of the Jewish refugees, near the end of the war). Similarly, in *Tzili,* as in a coming-of-age ceremony, the liminal stage takes place in a temporal realm that has hardly any concreteness at all.[41]

The Stage of Separation: They All Ran Away, Leaving Tzili To Look after the House

The stage of separation in Tzili's rite of passage takes place, as noted, in the first chapter of the novella and at the beginning of the second chapter. It is announced as early as the following lines, which conclude the opening paragraph: "Tzili was not an only child; she had older brothers and sisters. The family was large, poor, and harassed, and Tzili grew up neglected among the abandoned objects in the yard" (p. 1).

The sentence, "Tzili was not an only child," informs us that Tzili belongs to a group that includes several individuals identical in their formal social status: the siblings within the family. This formal identity later brings out her otherness. Tzili is the little sister, and she grew up—unlike her elder siblings—"neglected among the abandoned objects in the yard." The adjective "neglected" indicates Tzili's isolation within the family. Her belonging to the objects in the yard signifies her isolation from human society in general.

Tzili's otherness also becomes clear in the context of the ethnic system: "Unlike other the members of her race, Tzili did not shine at school. . . . Even the gentile children knew more than she did. . . . A Jewish girl without any brains! They delighted in her misfortune" (p. 2). These sentences implicitly express clear and sharp ethnic symmetry. The Jews are outstanding in studies, and the gentiles are "without any brains." Tzili shatters that symmetry just as she shatters the validity of the faith that "united" everyone in her home: "if you want to you can" (p. 3). Tzili very much wanted to: "for hours she sat and studied. But all her efforts didn't help her. In the fourth grade she hadn't mastered the multiplication table and her handwriting was vague and confused" (pp. 2–3). While her "brothers and sisters all . . . prepared for external examinations, registered for crash courses, devoured supplementary material, Tzili cooked, washed dishes, and weeded the garden" (p. 3). Even her appearance was different from the members of her family and people. "She was small and thin, and kneeling in the garden she looked like a servant girl" (p. 3).

Another decisive difference that expresses the separation between Tzili and her primary associative group, the family, is that "it had fallen to the lot of this dull child to keep the spark alive" (p. 5). "The family no longer observed the rituals of the Jewish religion" (p. 4). "But her mother for some reason got it into her head that religious study would be good for Tzili" (p. 4). Once a week an old teacher from the village would come to Tzili's house. "For the first hour he would tell her stories from the Bible and for the second he would read the prayer book with her" (pp. 4–5).

At the end of the reading in the prayer book he would ask Tzili, in the traditional, unvarying formula:

> "What is man?"
> And Tzili would reply: "Dust and ashes."
> "And before whom is he destined to stand in judgment?"
> "Before the King of Kings, the Holy One, blessed be He."
> "And what must he do?"
> "Pray and observe the commandments of the Torah."
> "And where are the commandments of the Torah written?"
> "In the Torah." (*Tzili*, pp. 5–6)

The traits that distinguish Tzili from the members of her family anticipate her physical separation from them:

> When the war broke out they all ran away, leaving Tzili to look after the house. They thought that nobody would harm a feeble-minded little girl, and until the storm had spent itself, she would take care of the property for them. Tzili heard their verdict without protest. They left in a panic, without time for second thoughts. "We'll come back for you later," said her brothers as they lifted their father onto the stretcher. (*Tzili*, p. 7)

It is difficult to ignore the narrator's sarcastic tone in reporting the excuses offered for Tzili's final separation from her family. We see clearly that concern for Tzili did not motivate the family, but rather denial of her value and importance. The rationale that "nobody would harm a feeble-minded little girl" is ridiculous. No less ridiculous is the thought that Tzili was abandoned for fear she would be a burden, for the family did not abandon the sick father.

At the same time, it must be remembered that "it had fallen to the lot of this dull child to keep the spark alive" (p. 5). She in particular was chosen "to look after the house" and "the property" (p. 7). Tzili is thus described from the start as a mixture of contradictory elements. She is the despised and rejected daughter, but at the same time the chosen one. She is "feeble-minded" (p. 7), "small and thin, and kneeling in the garden she looked like a servant girl" (p. 3), yet at the same time she was the only one who knew how to pray.

The Liminal Stage (A): The Heat and the Cape Swathed Her

The second stage in Tzili's rite of passage is the most important one because, as with the parallel stage in primitive rites of passage and in coming-of-age folk tales, the roots of religious experience, upon which the fictional world is based, are laid bare. These roots are revealed in a series of symbolic, ritual scenes. The first marks the entry of Tzili the initiate into the liminal realm:

> She slept for a long time. When she woke it was night and everything was completely still. She poked her head out of the sacking, and the night sky appeared through the cracks in the roof of the shed. She lifted the upper half of her body, propping herself up on her elbows. Her feet were numb with cold. She passed both hands over the round columns of her legs and rubbed them. A pain shot through her feet.
>
> For a long while she lay supporting herself on her elbows, looking at the sky. . . .
>
> But in the meantime the numbness left her legs, and she kicked away the sacking. She said to herself: "I must get up," and she stood up. The shed was much higher than she was. It was made of rough planks and used to store wood, barrels, an old bathtub, and a few earthenware pots. No one but Tzili paid any attention to this old shed, but for her it was a hiding place. Now she felt a kind of intimacy with the abandoned objects lying in it.
>
> For the first time she found herself under the open night sky. When she was a baby they would close the shutters very early, and later on, when she grew up, they never let her go outside in the dark. For the first time she touched the darkness with her fingers. (*Tzili*, pp. 8–9)

Tzili enters the liminal realm under the sign of the "cosmic night," a chaotic, primordial realm where, as is characteristic of "the other world," the world of death and that of the embryonic state, new life, are mingled.[42] The shed, like the night, symbolizes that mixture. As in similar temporary dwellings in rites of passage,[43] the shed is conceived simultaneously as a grave and a womb; it serves as a grave for the "abandoned objects," and it could also have been Tzili's grave, had the soldiers found her there. But it also serves as a womb, from which Tzili emerges into the world as though for the first time: "For the first time she touched the darkness with her fingers" (p. 9).

Tzili's emergence into the world is described as an accelerated evolutionary process in three stages. She passes from the state of a "thing" (the objects in the shed to which she feels "intimacy"), to that of an animal on all fours, and then to the stage of a human (the first one?), standing on both legs. These three stages, combined together, symbolize the life story of the entire human race, including, at least as a promise, Tzili's "life story."

After the opening scene of the second stage, Tzili is characterized as a liminal personage. In the existential limbo where she is stuck, she undergoes, like all initiates in the second stage of the initiation ceremony, physical and psychic processes that represent antitheses: death and life, illness and health, growth and disintegration, cleanliness and impurity, memory and oblivion, and the like. Similarly, she loses all the ethnic attributes with which she was characterized in the first stage (the stage of separation) and by means of which she is supposed to be characterized in the third stage (that of reaffiliation). At the same time she is linked to all those components in wild and threatening mixtures.

The ambivalent character of the physical processes that Tzili experiences is reflected prominently in two contexts: her first menstrual cycle, and the skin inflammation that afflicts her. Tzili's first menstrual period occurs after a symbolic meeting with the mysteries of sex (a blind peasant tries to rape her),[44] and her responses to it are dramatized in the following passage:

> When dawn broke she saw that her dress was stained with a number of bright spots of blood. She lifted up her dress. There were a couple of spots on the ground too. "I'm going to die." The words escaped her lips. . . .
>   "I'm going to die," she said and all at once she rose to her feet. The sudden movement alarmed her even more. A chill ran down her spine, and she

shivered. The thought that soon she would be lying dead became more concrete to her than her own feet. She began to whimper like an animal. . . .
    "Mother, mother!" she wailed. She went on screaming for a long time.
Her voice grew weaker and weaker and she fell to the ground with her
arms spread out, as she imagined her body would lie in death. (*Tzili*, p. 22)

Her first secretion of menstrual blood, which symbolizes, biologically
speaking, fertility and health, is accompanied here with a death rite, as in
all rites of passage for girls in primitive societies.[45] A similar binding of
life and death in a single phenomenon emerges from the description of
her skin inflammation:

Her clothes gave off a bad, moldy smell and her face was covered with a
rash of little pimples.
    She did not know how repulsive she looked. She roamed the outskirts of
the forest and the peasants who crossed her path averted their eyes. When
she approached the farmhouses to beg for bread the housewives would
chase her away as if she were a mangy dog. . . . Her ugly existence became
a byword and a cautionary tale in the mouths of the local peasants, but the
passing days were kind to her, molding her in secret, at first deadening and
then quickening her with new life. The sick blood poured out of her. She
learned to walk barefoot, to bathe in icy water, to tell the edible berries
from the poisonous ones, to climb the trees. The sun worked wonders with
her. . . .
    Her life seemed to fall away from her, she coiled in on herself like a co-
coon. And at night she fell unconscious onto the straw. (*Tzili*, pp. 29–30)

The abscesses that afflict Tzili give her a monstrous appearance, a
symbolic condition common in the liminal stage of rites of passage.[46] Her
appearance is what keeps her alive. During her revolting illness, Tzili is
immune to the assaults of the gentile peasants and entirely given over to
the experience of adaptation. These are the days that, as the narrator explicitly tells us, pass under the sign of death and life together.
    Tzili's ambivalent situation in the liminal period is also notable in terms
of identity. The third chapter begins with the sentence, "When she awoke
her memory was empty and weightless" (p. 13). That sentence marks the
end of her separation from the social system from which she has been sent
and from all its characteristics. First of all, the sharp dichotomy between
gentiles and Jews has disappeared. Indeed, immediately afterward Tzili is
described as a creature freed from all attributes of belonging:

She saw what was before her eyes: a thin forest and the golden calm of summer. All she had endured in the past days lost its terror. She was borne forward unthinkingly on a stream of light. Even when she washed her face in the river she felt no strangeness. As if it had always been her habit to do so. (*Tzili*, pp. 13–14)

However, the basic dichotomy between Jews and gentiles does not disappear completely. In that very same chapter it appears again, though in a new form, similar to that which was signaled in the stage of separation but also different from it. The blind man who tries to rape Tzili addresses her and asks, "You're Maria's daughter, aren't you?" (p. 15). Tzili, knowing full well that he is referring to a disreputable gentile whore, answers in the affirmative. Later Tzili again uses that dubious attribute of belonging, first as a successful stratagem to disguise and conceal her Jewish origin, but later also out of choice and identification.

Tzili's adoption of Maria the whore as her mother has several important meanings. First, she loses her first and family name and becomes an anonymous member of a large, egalitarian group: "[Maria] had many daughters, all bastards" (p. 15). Second, her new status is a mixture of the sacred (the "obligatory" name of Maria) and the impure ("you were born in sin," says the old woman who employs her in her home as a servant, p. 57). Third, and principally, as the daughter of Maria, Tzili is bound to two contradictory ways of life: gentile and Jewish. Maria appears in Tzili's mind as a proud gentile woman, bold and daring, but also as a woman who had a special relation with Jews, for she bore bastard daughters to some of them.

The place of Maria, whom Tzili adopts as an imaginary mother, is taken by an adoptive mother of flesh and blood. This is Katerina, another gentile prostitute. She herself (and of course her "business"), the house where she lives, and the area where it is located all create a most decidedly liminal setting:

It was a poor house with a dilapidated stable beside it. And in the yard: a few pieces of wood, a gaping fence, and a neglected vegetable patch. These were the houses outside the village, where the lepers and the lunatics, the horse thieves and the prostitutes lived. For generations one had replaced the other here, without repairing the houses or cultivating the plots. The passing seasons would knead such places in their hands until they could not be told apart from abandoned forest clearings. (*Tzili*, p. 33)

As Katerina's "daughter," Tzili is linked ever more strongly to that strange mixture of identity that she had adopted when she chose Maria as a mother. This connection, with its contradictory components, becomes clear in the very first meeting between the two, a meeting that has an evident ritual and symbolic character. Katerina orders Tzili, immediately after taking her into her house, to remove her moldy clothing and wear instead "a fancy city gown, flowered and soaked in perfume" (p. 30).

The ceremony of changing clothes symbolizes the strange state of identity in which Tzili finds herself. The act of removing her clothing, the only thing Tzili has taken from home, symbolizes detachment from the attributes of her former world. In contrast, the act of putting on the frock symbolizes attachment to the same attributes, but—and this is the main point —in a strange new mixture. That old frock is a metonymy for an entire way of life that characterizes gentile peasant whores, on the one hand, and dissolute urban Jewish men, on the other. This mixed way of life, represented by Katerina and Maria, "who had a lot of good times together in the city, especially with the Jews" (p. 31), enchants Tzili.

The Liminal Stage (B): The Magic Mountain and the Enchanted Bunker

The second stage in Tzili's rite of passage ends, just as it began, with an impressive ritual event. All the incidents included in this event are etched in Tzili's memory like "vivid ritual tableaus" (p. 144). It takes place on a high and isolated mountain, a decidedly ritualistic place.[47] From a structural point of view, this event includes three acts that are supposed to symbolize Tzili's life story, like the three stages of the entry into the liminal period. The principal purpose of this event is to serve as a bridge to the third stage, the stage of reintegration, in which Tzili is supposed to rejoin her tribe as an adult in every respect.

The first act of the rite concluding the second stage again confronts Tzili with her previous identity, the Jewish identity that she had sloughed off in the course of her wanderings. That confrontation takes place by chance, in an accidental way, like all the other encounters in the story:

> When she woke it was daylight. Scented vapors rose from the fields. And while she was sitting there a man seemed to come floating up from the depths of the earth. For a moment they measured each other with their eyes. She saw immediately: he was not a peasant. His city suit was faded and his face exhausted. . . . She smelled the stale odor of his mildewed

clothes. . . . Tzili rose to her feet. The man's appearance revolted her, but it did not frighten her. His soft flabbiness. (*Tzili,* pp. 59–60)

The rite of entry into the second stage takes place under the sign of the cosmic night, a primordial, chaotic realm always identified with the unconscious. The rite concluding that stage, which constitutes a bridge to the stage of reintegration, is marked by broad daylight, decidedly a symbol of consciousness. The man who "seemed to come floating up from the depths of the earth" (from the depths of the unconscious) is Mark, a Jew who fled from a concentration camp. Tzili's first meeting with him and his characteristics (which are a "copy" of her characteristics at the beginning of her journey, especially the musty clothing from home) repel her. But the repulsion quickly fades, to be replaced by renewed acquaintance with her Jewish identity. At first Tzili is "reaccepted" by her tribe. Mark asks her if she has parents. She says no, and then he declares, "So you're one of us" (p. 60). Later she identifies herself by name ("My name is Tzili," p. 61) and this is after many months of identifying herself as Maria's daughter and even, as I have already pointed out, feeling full identification with that name. As the story continues Tzili is opened up to her "mother tongue, a mixture of German and Yiddish, and with the very same accent" (p. 61), to "the smell of home" (p. 62), and at the end of the first act of the rite, also to the memory of her mother. "For the first time in many days she saw the face of her mother, a face no longer young. Worn with work and suffering" (p. 72). She knows: "The stranger had done something to her" (p. 71).

In the second act of the "concluding ceremony," Tzili again experiences liminality, this time not in isolation but together with Mark, after he himself passes through the stage of separation: "Mark stopped speaking of the camp and its horrors" (p. 85); he is opened up to nature: "Summer on the mountain charmed him. Sometimes he would pluck a flower and whisper: "How lovely, how modest'" (p. 86); and also, of prime importance, he digs a bunker for them to live in, "backbreaking work," because of which his arms "were full and firm," and "it gave him the look of a simple laborer" (p. 89). Afterward, exactly like Tzili before him, he becomes a liminal personage: "His face grew lean. There was a kind of strength in his leanness. His days became confused with his nights" (p. 91).

The shared liminal experience of Tzili and Mark takes place in a decidedly liminal realm, the bunker that Mark had dug with his own hands. That bunker is described simultaneously as a womb and a grave.

It defends them against the ravages of nature and serves as a hiding place from the gentile peasants. Of course, it also serves as the metaphorical womb of new life, the fruit of the union between Tzili and Mark. However, that very bunker is also the dwelling of ghosts who threaten to take control of the living:

> Distant sights, hungry malevolent shadows invaded the bunker in dense crowds. Tzili did not know the bitter, emaciated people. Mark went outside and cut branches with his kitchen knife to block up the openings, hurling curses in all directions. For a moment or two it seemed that he had succeeded in chasing them off. But the harder the rain fell the more bitter the struggle became, and from day to day the shadows prevailed. In vain Tzili tried to calm him. His happiness was being attacked from every quarter. (*Tzili*, pp. 98–99)

The third act of Tzili's concluding ceremony is marked by separation and then renewed affiliation. Tzili's and Mark's "small happiness" in the "wonderful bunker" (p. 101) does not last long. "The many shadows besieging their temporary shelter" (p. 101) give Mark no rest. He is incapable of forgiving himself for fleeing the camp without his wife and children. In the end he descends from their ceremonial mountain to scout the area (p. 103), never to return. Tzili waits for Mark for many days. She passes this time by remaining in the "dark and warm" bunker (p. 105). She sorts and dries the clothing of Mark's family that he had tied in a bundle and taken from the camp, and she prays to God to return her beloved. Finally, when she understands that he will not return, she loads the bundle of clothes on her back and leaves the only place that is connected in her mind to happiness.

The third act, and with it the concluding ceremony of the entire liminal stage, is sealed with Tzili's reunification with Mark, this time in her mind, by internalizing him. Tzili notices "that her belly [has] changed, and it [is] slightly swollen" (p. 114). First she does not attribute great importance to this change, but "it did not take long for her to understood: Mark was inside her" (p. 114). That discovery causes Tzili to feel close to Mark once again, "even closer than in the days when they had slept together in the bunker" (p. 116). Moreover, at this stage Tzili, who had adopted various mothers during the previous stage, becomes a mother who adopts herself. In one of her "conversations" with Mark, she declares, "I love your children as if they were my own" (p. 116). The psychological maturity that characterizes Tzili at this time is expressed in another way. For the first time in her life she is aware of her human and female identity and defends it. In a break with the past, she refuses to accept blows from her employers. At first she is beaten mercilessly by a peasant woman who hires her, and, "as if she knew that this was her lot in life," she does not respond (p. 116). But "one night she snatched the rope from the woman and said: 'No you won't. I'm not an animal. I'm a woman" (p. 116).

The Stage of Reintegration: The Visible Edge of the Garden of Eden

Thus Tzili's rite of passage is successful. She has been exposed to her religious roots, engaged in ceremonial sexual relations, become pregnant, and discovered her identity as a human and a woman. Now it would be possible to expect her to rejoin her tribe as an adult, the expected course of action after the conclusion of the liminal stage in primitive rites of passage and in coming-of-age folk tales.

However, as soon becomes clear, Tzili is to have another fate. Instead of rejoining the tribe, a series of events occurs that repeats the ritual events Tzili has undergone during the liminal stage, but empty and void of content, though with enormous intensity. At the end of this astounding course of events, Tzili is presented as someone who has returned to her point of origin, the place from which she began the journey of coming of age and self-awareness; once again she resembles an object in the yard of her house.

The opening paragraph of the section devoted to the stage of reintegration does not deviate from the pattern of rites of passage. On the contrary, it heralds a full return to the bosom of the tribe: "At that time the great battlefronts were collapsing, and the first refugees were groping their way across the broad fields of snow. Tzili was drawn toward them as if she realized that her fate was no different from theirs" (p. 119). Tzili's return to her tribe takes place concurrently with its return to historical time. Her liminal stage, which took place during the Holocaust, an ahistorical, mythological time, has ended, and now that she has matured in the forests, her individual fate is correlated with that of her tribe.

However, as early as the second paragraph, a sharp deviation from that model occurs: "Strange, precisely now, at the hour of her new freedom, Mark stopped speaking to her. 'Where are you and why don't you speak to me?' she would ask in despair" (p. 119). Immediately afterward comes a scene that repeats but parodies her first meeting with Mark, for it is devoid of content.

"Who are you?" [ask the three refugees who are sitting in a ditch.]

"My name is Tzili."

"So, you're one of us. Where have you left everyone?"

"I," said Tzili, "have lost everyone."

"In that case why don't you come with us. What do you have in that haversack?"

"Clothes."

"And haven't you got any bread?" one of them said in an unpleasant voice.

"Who are you?" she asked.

"Can't you see? We're partisans. Haven't you got any bread in that haversack?"

"No I haven't," she said and turned to go.

"Where are you going?"

"I'm going to Mark."

"We know this whole area. There's no one here. You'd better stay with us. We'll keep you amused." (*Tzili*, pp. 119–20)

Again the components of the ritual and religious event that Tzili had undergone with Mark are depreciated and deprived of meaning. The lofty, enchanted mountain now appears to her as "undistinguished and not particularly lofty" (p. 121). The marvelous bunker inspires her with "only a thin stream of longing" (p. 128). And Tzili loses Mark's bundle of clothes, which she and Mark had sold to support themselves during their stay in the bunker, clothing that had belonged to the dead members of his family. It was probably burned, for, as the medic in the hospital where she is admitted explains to her, "There's disinfection here. We burn everything" (p. 176).

This regressive process reaches its peak after the fetus is removed from Tzili's womb. She grasps her loss with clouded consciousness, as a barren reprise of the cosmic night:

Then it was night. A long night, carved out of stone, which lasted three days. Several times they tried to wake her. Medics and soldiers rushed frantically about carrying stretchers. Tzili wandered in a dark stone tunnel, strangers and acquaintances passing before her eyes, clear and unblurred. I'm going back, she said to herself. (*Tzili*, p. 173)

After the "uprooting," Tzili "floated on the surface of a vacant sleep for a few days, and when she awoke, her memory was emptier than ever. . . . Of all her scattered life it seemed to her that nothing was left. Even her body was no longer hers. A jumble of sounds and shapes flowed into her without touching her" (p. 175).

Tzili thus returns to her situation of long ago, to the status of an object. That regression is alluded to at an earlier stage, when vitality still throbbed within Tzili:

> The night was warm and fine and Tzili remembered the little yard at home, where she had spent so many hours. Every now and then her mother would call, "Tzili," and Tzili would reply, "Here I am." Of her entire childhood, only this was left. . . . She was seized by longing for that little yard. As if it were the misty edge of the Garden of Eden. (*Tzili*, p. 158)

The last scene of the novel testifies to the nature of that Garden of Eden. There Linda is described, Tzili's new adoptive mother, as she hugs a bottle of cognac to her breast and sings Hungarian lullabies to it (p. 185).

Tzili's failure to rejoin her tribe as an adult, although she successfully underwent the complex rite of passage from childhood to maturity, sheds light upon the problematic opening paragraph of the novella and also upon the connection between Appelfeld's story and both naive and modern literature—matters that are mutually interrelated.

Tzili was destined to have "a cruel fate, without glory," because at a critical time in her life, her formative period, she experienced an enormous rupture between two different and hostile cultural systems. The cultural environment in which Tzili was born and to which she returned after the Holocaust is a modern one. Tzili's assimilated Jewish family, the refugees she joined after the war, and the pioneering settlement in the Land of Israel where she is supposed to fit in after her long journey—all these indeed represent separate existential experiences, but they share a common denominator: separation from the primordial, mythological roots of the tribe. During the Holocaust, whose very existence is conceived here as the result of a cosmic accident, Tzili was caught in a different cultural environment, a primitive one. There she underwent an emotional and cognitive journey, in the course of which she was exposed to those primordial, mythological roots and became attached to them. Tragically for Tzili—and in this she stands as the representative of all modern, secular Jews—her attachment to her roots, a momentary revelation, takes place (extremely ironically) during the Holocaust. After the Holocaust, with her return to the modern cultural context, the religious tie is once again severed.

The fate overhanging Tzili's life explains or is explained by the generic character of her story. Perhaps it is forbidden to tell the story of her life, *Tzili,* because the story embodies, at most of its stages, an impossible conjuncture of two very different cultural conceptions: the plot topos of the primitive rite of passage guides us toward naive literature, and the general historical and cultural context guides us toward modern literature. The fact that the harmony between the plot topos and the cultural context was created only during the Holocaust, which is presented here, as in all of Appelfeld's books, as a kind of extraterritorial domain,[48] emphasizes the hybrid character of the novella. Its presentation of an intentional failure to correlate two of its central compositional elements indicates an existential and cultural dead end.

In Shutting the Eyes There Is a Great Wonder

Identifying the genre of *Katerina* was a central issue in the studies of two scholars: Sara Halprin and Avidov Lipsker.[49] Both agreed with the author, who defined his book as a "novella" in the subtitle. However, they disagreed with each other by assigning the novella to two literary traditions that gave rise to two different literary forms, both of which, to make matters complex, go under the same name. Halprin placed *Katerina* within the realistic, mimetic tradition, basing her argument on its general compositional character and realistic approach. Lipsker maintained that this classification was erroneous. In his opinion *Katerina* belongs to an entirely different tradition: the medieval exemplary tradition, in which a semihistorical hero's deeds represent a moral or philosophical ideal. In these exemplary tales, the main character acts on the strength of ritual or following a tradition of the suffering of exemplary figures. According to Lipsker, both Christian and Jewish legendary novellas are especially important links in that tradition.

In my opinion, both scholars are right and wrong at the same time. They are right because *Katerina* contains many components that permit it to be read in the light of these literary traditions. They are wrong because each attempts to place the novella in one tradition exclusively.

Katerina, just like *Tzili,* is a generic hybrid, related to two literary traditions that represent very different cultural conceptions. In *Katerina* the medieval exemplary tradition and, especially, late Christian and Jewish legendary novellas represent a naive cultural conception in which the connections between people and the world surrounding them are based on ethical and mythical bonds, whereas the realistic tradition represents a modern cultural conception in which the connections between people and the world surrounding them are based on secular, social conventions. The fact that *Katerina* channels us at the same time in these two distinct conceptions, which relate to the issue of faith from such different, not to say opposing points of departure, again expresses, like *Tzili,* Aharon Appelfeld's acute religious distress.

The connection with the naive is reflected in *Katerina,* as in early exemplary and later legendary novellas, in the plot topos upon which the novella is based. This topos is the same topos that underlies the novella *Tzili* and the folk tales mentioned earlier—that of the primitive coming-of-age ritual.[50]

The essential difference between *Tzili* and *Katerina* in this context derives from the fact that the two novellas relate to two separate versions of that plot topos. Tzili's path, as we have seen, follows rites of passage from childhood to adulthood. The path of Katerina relates to mystical initiation ceremonies.[51]

We have seen that the initiation ceremony portrayed in *Tzili* is an utter failure. Although Tzili successfully negotiates the rite of passage to the stage of reintegration, at that stage she undergoes a fearful process of regression. By contrast, Katerina's initiation rite concludes with full success. At the end of the novella she becomes a mystical personage in every respect. However, that success is illuminated, as we shall see, in a sharply ironic light, because of which the reader of *Katerina,* like the reader of *Tzili,* is exposed to the tragic inability of modern man in general and of the modern Jew in particular to experience the world in naive fashion.

Katerina is without doubt a naive figure. That is, basing ourselves again upon Schiller and Kleist, she, just like Tzili, experiences the world with no ironic barrier. I refer to the naiveté about which Appelfeld spoke in his conversation with Philip Roth, which is "still found among children and old people."[52] Katerina's naiveté is expressed, among other things, in a direct connection with nature, a decidedly gentile trait in all of Appelfeld's fiction.[53]

Katerina, again like Tzili, can be defined as basically a liminal personage. This definition or a parallel one—in an interview with Orli Toren, Appelfeld called her "a bohemian soul"[54]—is called for, among other things, because of her social and cultural "intermediate situation," which has been pointed out by most of the critics and scholars who have dealt

with the book.[55] She does not belong to the gentile world, but neither has
she been taken into the Jewish world. She appears at the same time as
both a gentile and a Jew.

All these traits make Katerina fit for her role as "guardian of the flame"
of Judaism. She has been charged with a mission that is carried out by
many elderly gentile village women in Appelfeld's fiction,[56] as well as by
Tzili, who grows up as a kind of gentile Jew. This mission is to remember
and preserve the elements of the Jews' faith, for the Jews themselves, Katerina assumes, have been completely destroyed. In the final chapter the
elderly Katerina is seated, compulsively writing down every word and
concept connected in her mind with the faith of the "hidden tribe" (p.
202) that she believes has been exterminated. She writes, for example,
"*Rosheshone* and *yonkiper* and *sukes* and *khanike* and *purim* and *tubish-
vas* and *peysekh* and on and on" (p. 205). Then she goes on to list "*treyf,
tume, orel,* Sabbath candles, Yom Kippur candles, *nile, kharoyses, tkin-
khatsos, slikhes, shabesnakhmu, sude-hamafsekes*" (p. 205), and so on.

But Katerina's task is not limited to guarding "property." She has
taken on a graver task: to try and experience the primordial covenant
between man and God. That effort is expressed in the mystical reconstruction of two sacred events: one from the Old Testament, the burning
bush, and the other from the New Testament, the crucifixion and resurrection of Jesus.

First Katerina experiences the ceremony of the crucifixion and resurrection. She imagines her dead son Benjamin, the fruit of her love affair
with a Jew named Sammy, to be the savior who was crucified and who returned to life. Later Katerina experiences the burning bush through
ruined Jewish houses that become, in her imagination, "a temple" (p.
202). Benjamin's "return" and the ceremony of sanctifying the Jewish
ruin constitute, for Katerina, the fulfillment of a double mythical cycle.
The conclusion of that cycle, combining covenantal ceremonies from
both the Jewish and Christian religion, symbolizes for her a renewed connection with her religious roots.

The task Katerina has taken upon herself also has a pagan aspect, for
both in official, established Judaism and in established Christianity, covenantal ceremonies between man and God are historical events that occur
only once.[57] To perform her task, she passes through a long and complex
preparation, at the end of which she becomes a mystical personage. This
path she follows is a three-stage pattern similar to that of Tzili's coming
of age.

The Stage of Separation: The Way You Abandon a Sick Animal

In the separation stage, both Katerina and Tzili abandon their houses in response to being abandoned by their families. Although the members of Katerina's family do not flee and leave her behind, they abandon her in other ways. Her mother dies very young. The stepmother, who takes her place, rejects her. Her father ignores her completely. Later he tries to sleep with her, and in the end "he abandoned [her] the way you abandon a sick animal that you don't want to put down right away" (p. 21). The only creature with whom Katerina has a common language is her beloved dog Zimbi, of whom she says, "If there is any warmth in my body, it is the warmth I absorbed from him" (p. 10).

Katerina's separation from her primary environment is foreshadowed and explained by her otherness, again, just like Tzili's separation from her primary environment. This otherness is expressed through her seeming to deviate from the natural dichotomies. Tzili, as noted, is seen as an abandoned object. Katerina is conceived as an "animal" (p. 5). Unlike other Jewish children, Tzili does not do well in school. Unlike other gentiles, Katerina was fearful in her childhood: "I was afraid of every shadow and listened for every sound; at night, even the crickets would alarm me" (pp. 15–16). Similarly, Tzili as a girl was the only member of her family who learned to pray, and Katerina, unlike the members of her family who were believers, "had no desire [in her youth] either for prayer or for the Holy Scriptures. The words of prayers that [she] intoned were not [her] own" (p. 6). At the same time, even in her early childhood, Katerina underwent a ceremony of mystical revelation that left a deep and indelible impression on her soul for her entire life:

> In this valley [the region of Katerina's native village, to which she returns at the end of her life] I heard a voice from on high for the first time—actually, it was in the lowest slopes of this valley, where it opens up and flows into a broad plain. I remember the voice with great clarity. I was seven, and suddenly I heard a voice, not my mother's or father's, and the voice said to me, "Don't be afraid, my daughter. You shall find the lost cow." It was an assured voice, and so calm that it instantly removed the fear from my heart. I sat frozen and watched. The darkness grew thicker. There was no sound, and suddenly the cow emerged from the darkness and came up to me. Ever since then, when I hear the word *salvation,* I see the brown cow I had lost and who came back to me. (*Katerina,* p. 6)

Thus Katerina, too, is described from the start as someone in whom contradictory elements are mingled. She is the different daughter, reviled and rejected, and, at the same time, the chosen one. She is beaten and humiliated, but she has the privilege of hearing "a voice from on high." The intermediary situation that characterizes her from her childhood—a gentile girl who, like a Jew, was "afraid of every shadow"—dictates her fate. She leaves home, taking "the back road everyone calls the Jewish road" (p. 17). All her life Katerina will walk on that trail, which symbolically connects the Christian and Jewish domains, and she will try to mix these extremely different existential experiences.

The Liminal Stage (A): The Mundane, Realistic Stage

The pattern of Katerina's liminal stage is similar to that of Tzili's. Both contain two central portions of almost equal length. At the beginning of this stage in both novellas, the heroines wander in an existential limbo. They are characterized as having lost their original attributes and at the same time as combining those attributes in strange mixtures. Toward the conclusion of this stage the heroines are found in decidedly liminal regions, closed and isolated and/or cut off from the social and historical context. In these regions they undergo ritual ceremonies that symbolize their transition to the final stage of their rites of passage. The only conspicuous difference between the two patterns is expressed in the character of the concluding ceremonies of the liminal stage, which expresses the essential difference in the teleology of the two rites of passage. Tzili's concluding ceremony, her ritual seclusion with Mark in the marvelous bunker and her internalization of it, symbolizes the passage from the stage of childhood to that of adulthood, whereas Katerina's concluding ceremony includes two ritual stages separate from each other in time and place. One takes place in the prison where she is sent after killing the man who killed her son, and the second takes places just before her release from that prison. This concluding ceremony is not sexual (the significant sexual event takes place at the end of the first part of this stage) but mystical, and it reflects Katerina's ultimate deliverance from the "human sewer" and her transformation into a mystical personage.

The opening ceremony of Katerina's intermediate stage takes place in the nocturnal world:

I got to Strassov one night, a town consisting of a street and a busy railroad station. Maria had told me a lot about the town, but the sight of it wasn't the way I had imagined it. The people poured out and crowded together near the exit, trains came and went, and tall, hearty men stood on the platforms and loaded sacks of grain.

"Don't let them nuzzle you," Maria had warned me.

Later, the station emptied out, the trains stopped running, the buffet was locked, and beggars and drunks popped out of the dark corners.

"Who are you?" one of the drunks asked me.

I was startled, and my mouth was dumb.

"From what village?" he kept asking.

I told him.

"Come with us; soon we'll make some coffee."

That's how I got to know the night world of the railroad station. I was sixteen years old. They all called me the baby girl. That wasn't an indulgent term there. If a person doesn't give his due, he's thrown out even from that cold, dark corner.

The next day I started washing dishes in the restaurant. Anyone born in a village is used to abuse. My mother beat me and my father didn't spare my body either. The restaurant owner was no better than they. In the evening, before paying me, he would feel my breasts. At night, many hands pawed me. It was cold and dark, and the poor people's clothing gave off a strong smell of damp. The foul smell came to cling to my clothes, too. *The body's not holy, nothing will happen to you,* said one of the drunks, reaching out and feeling my crotch. (*Katerina*, pp. 22–23)

Already on her first night in the new place, Katerina joins a marginal community *par excellence*. In the following nights she undergoes many more experiences connected with sexual humiliation, with violation and pollution of the body, with the loss of equilibrium because of drunkenness. The purpose of these liminal experiences is to bring Katerina to a stage that Avidov Lipsker calls "departure of the ego from its body,"[58] a necessary stage in the apprenticeship of the mystical personage.

Railroad stations and, parallel to them, taverns—places that are, by virtue of their location and purpose, existential intermediary realms—present the dark side of the existential limbo in which Katerina wanders. The bright side is represented by the two Jewish families for whom she works as a servant. The intimate encounter with the members of these families—who neither look nor behave like the gentile antisemitic stereotype—creates a situation of partial conversion in Katerina's soul. On the one hand, she identifies with the fate of the "chosen people" and adopts Jewish ceremonies and customs—sometimes with devotion exceeding that of her employers. But on the other hand, she continues to see the Jews as "those who raised their hand against God and His Messiah" (p. 38).

Katerina's first intimate encounter with the Jewish world takes place in the railroad station. A Jewish woman meets Katerina, who is already sunk up to her neck in human sewage, and offers her a job. Katerina is won over by the strange woman's charm (she seems to Katerina like an "angel of God," and her voice sounds like "a voice from on high" [p. 25]), so she goes home with her. The moment they reach the house, Katerina experiences a reception ceremony similar to the one experienced by Tzili upon entering the home of a different Katerina. The Katerina of this novel relinquishes her old clothes, "which were sodden with the odor of damp, vodka, and tobacco" (p. 25), and bathes for the first time since leaving her home. Then she puts on clothes that Rosa gives her ("cast-off clothes . . . that fit me. They were clean, odorless, for some reason aroused my suspicion that they had belonged to dead Jews," p. 27). Finally she burns her old clothes. The ceremony of changing clothes symbolizes the "strange" state of identity into which Katerina has fallen. The removal of the old clothes, the only item that Katerina has taken from home, and their burning symbolize the severance of ties of affiliation to the old world. By contrast, putting on the "new" clothes (which, "for some reason" make her suspect that they belonged to dead Jews) symbolizes renewed connection with those affiliations, but in a strange, new blend.

Before the ceremonial changing of the clothes, Katerina conceives the world as based on a solid and clear dichotomy. Strong, gentile Christians persecute the "killers of God," on the one hand, and weak Jews, who are unwilling to admit their sin, are persecuted mercilessly, on the other. In the course of that ceremony, during the symbolic bath and the following night, that dichotomy crumbles. In its place is a pattern based on components of the former one, but in a new, threatening mixture. In the new pattern it is not at all clear who are the guilty and who are the accusers, who are the persecutors and who, the persecuted, who are strong, and who, weak. Here the boundaries blur between concrete sights and memories and primordial tribal dreads:

> Now, as I stood naked, fear coursed through my entire body and made me shudder. From every side Jews came up and stood next to me, and they

were all in the same image: a thin man with a drawn sword in his hand. I fell to my knees and crossed myself. My sins had reached the high heavens, and now I was about to pay.

That night I remembered the Jews who used to wander through our village, skipping among the trees and courtyards or standing next to their improvised stands, living ghosts, talking ghosts, and I remembered the peasants who would appear and crack their whips at them. Now, for some reason, it seemed that they were lighter, skipping over trenches and fences; their earthly weight seemed to have been removed. "You can't vanquish them,"—I heard Maria's laugh. "A ghost's body feels no pain." The peasants kept on whipping, and Maria's laughter, her hearty laughter, was swallowed up in the crack of the blows. I awoke. (*Katerina*, pp. 25–26)

Katerina tries to extricate herself from the tangle of identity in which she was caught following her meeting with Rosa, and later also following her meeting with Henni, her second Jewish employer, who also appeared to her in the railroad station as "an angel" (p. 65) in a way that again reflects her strange situation. She makes four efforts to create a new human species, a hybrid that unites what seems to her to be the chosen attributes of both Jews and gentiles. Two of these attempts at creation (or "genetic engineering") are made in the first part of the liminal stage, and the other two in the second part of that stage.

Katerina makes her first attempt at "genetic engineering" with Abraham and Meir, the delicate sons of Rosa and Benjamin, whom she decides to raise by herself after their parents are murdered in a pogrom. She takes the two boys to a rural area (which is similar neither to their native region nor to the village where she herself grew up), and there she educates them in her own pattern and image. On the one hand, she is "careful not to eat nonkosher food, . . . so that not a speck of impurity would cling to them" (pp. 52–53). She speaks to them in Yiddish, "and warn[s] them . . . that they must retain their language" (p. 53). On the other hand, she has them work in the garden, stuffs them with country food, and even shows them a butcher knife and explains to them "that this is our weapon in times of trouble" (pp. 53–54). She does all this to make them sturdy and bold, because "frightened Jews arouse the devils" (p. 54). This effort ends in utter failure. The children's aunt, escorted by two "Ruthenian thugs" (p. 55), discovers the "family's" hiding place and seizes Katerina's wards from her.

Katerina makes her second attempt to create a hybrid, Jewish-gentile creature in a more fundamental manner. This time she does not begin at the stage of education but at creation, the stage of coupling. She becomes pregnant from union with a Jew, Sammy, and she bears a son to him, whom she calls Benjamin. Katerina watches over little Benjamin, the mixed child, as if he were the apple of her eye. Her attention is in total contrast to her relationship to her daughter from union with a gentile, Angela, whom she abandoned immediately after her birth (p. 32).

Katerina's method of educating Benjamin is identical to her previous educational effort. On the one hand, she has him circumcised (despite the reservations of all the Jews she encounters), teaches him Yiddish, and inculcates him in the holidays and customs of the Jews. On the other hand, she drills him: "You must be strong" (p. 130), "You must be a brave boy. . . . You have to make your muscles firm and be a lion cub" (pp. 137–38). For, as she repeatedly explains to him, "without courage, there's no life" (p. 137), and "a weak Jew arouses dark instincts" (p. 130).

However, this effort, too, is nipped in the bud. A gentile from Katerina's village snatches Benjamin from her arms and smashes him against a wall, shattering his skull, "the vessel more precious than all vessels" (p. 140).

The Liminal Stage (B): The Mystical, Visionary Stage

Katerina's first two efforts to create a new "species of man" were made on the earthly and realistic level. She makes the other two efforts, which, together, produce the concluding ceremony of her mystical journey of apprenticeship, on the visionary and mystical level. These efforts, unlike the earlier ones, are crowned with success and fit into three-act ritual patterns. The first two acts reconstruct, in accelerated form, Katerina's biography until her imprisonment, returning her to the earlier stage of separation and to the liminal stage, and conclude with moments of religious self-revelation.

The first part of the concluding ceremony begins with an act indicating Katerina's complete separation from the domain of her prior existence and with a description of her entry into a realm of existence in which her life receives an entirely different character: "That was half my life. From now on the color of my life is red. I too was murdered that evening [when Benjamin was murdered]. What remains of me is a stump" (p. 141). The second act of the ceremony is marked by the return to the liminal stage. It begins, like the parallel act in Katerina's "earlier life," with a scene that takes place in the nocturnal world. This act is a strange amalgam of death and rebirth:

> In the end they brought me back to the cell. I don't know how many days I was kept away from the light of day. The darkness in the cell was great. All that time I felt that I was being swept away in a broad, deep river. Black waves covered me, but I, with a fish's gills, overcame the drowning. When I managed to open my eyes, I saw that it was the Prut River; its flow heavy and red. (*Katerina*, p. 144)

Several of Katerina's expressions point to her return to the liminal condition. Thus, among other things, she reports, from a distance in time, that "my life was narrow, like that of a beast of burden" (p. 146), that "my life was truncated, as though it no longer belonged to me" (p. 147), that "the whole matter of time didn't concern me" (p. 147), that "my thoughts shriveled, and my legs moved along as though by themselves. I was . . . buried in a kind of hard hollowness" (p. 157), and that my "previous life grew ever more distant and vague, as though it wasn't [mine]" (p. 161).

Katerina is removed all at once from the stage of "hard hollowness" (p. 157) by means of a visionary revelation. The focus of that visionary revelation, which is the heart of the third act of the concluding ceremony, is "the great secret" (p. 163) to which Katerina is exposed all at once. This great secret at last permits her to create the desired human species, by means of the incarnation of Jesus the Savior in a new image: "That winter was very long. Occasionally, strong feelings would assail me, acute beliefs that would make my head spin till I felt faint" (p. 158). "But even to myself, I didn't reveal the great secret. My Benjamin had gone up to heaven and he was the true Jesus" (p. 163).

The two acts that open the second part of the concluding ceremony, in which Katerina once again experiences the story of her life until her imprisonment, take place in "the dreadful nineteen forties" (p. 182). That period, from Katerina's point of view, is entirely cut off from her earlier world. It is an existential limbo with new force, more threatening and horrifying: "During the nineteen forties, darkness descended upon me. All my bonds with my dear ones were severed. I knocked on the doors at night in vain. No sign, or any word, came from them, only darkness upon darkness and a great abyss" (p. 182). Her return to the liminal stage is also expressed here on the level of physical characteristics: "At that time a skin disease spread over my body. The disease ravaged my face and made it hideous. 'The monster,' the prisoners used to whisper. My face was covered with red and pink spots, and my hands swelled" (p. 182). To these physical traits, which also typified Tzili in the liminal stage, is attached a sentence that expresses Katerina's nature as a liminal personage in an image that seems inevitable: "I was like an uninhabited cave, with no sights and no thoughts" (p. 182).

Katerina is once again, as in the first part of the concluding ceremony, saved from sinking into "a great abyss" by a visionary revelation or, to be precise, by several visionary revelations. The first one takes place soon after her release from prison, where she had been kept for more than forty years:

> I turned toward the hilltops. . . . No one was within sight, just fields of yellowish stubble with glowing hues like darkened amber. For many years I had not seen a yellow like that. Fear of God fell upon me, and I knelt. . . . Suddenly, I knew that everything I saw was merely a fragment of a vision whose beginning was far from me, whose middle was within me, and what was revealed before me now was merely an illuminated passage leading to a broad tunnel. (*Katerina*, pp. 191–92)

Katerina's renewed perception of the world as a segment of a vision with a beginning, middle, and end symbolizes the conclusion of the process that transforms her from a liminal personage into a mystical personage.[59] Her new condition is announced as she perceives herself, for the first time in her life, as liberated from all the attributes that trammeled her in the past: "I drank from the pond, and for the first time I saw my face: not Katerina of the meadows, nor Katerina of the railroad station, and not Katerina of the Jews" (pp. 196–97). Liberation from social bonds and from an earthly view of the world prepares Katerina for the revelation that reenacts the burning bush:

> While I was standing there, given over to my desire, the heavens opened, and a light from on high covered the blue meadows with a mighty splendor. I covered my face and knelt down.
> "Katerina," I heard a voice.
> "Your servant, my Lord," I answered immediately.
> "Remove your shoes from your feet, because you are standing on a holy place."(*Katerina*, p. 198)

For Katerina this visionary revelation in a "holy place," the ruins of a Jewish home, complements the visionary revelation in the course of which she discovered the "true Jesus." For her the combination of these two revelations is a final confirmation of the renewed covenant between her and her God. Here she sheds the last sign of the liminal stage ("the dreadful rash had left my hands," p. 199), and here, "among those straight-standing remains" (p. 202), she joins "that hidden tribe" (p. 202). Thus she becomes a perfect, and unique, at least as she sees it, representative of the much-desired (primitive) mixture between Judaism and Christianity.

The Stage of Reintegration: Everything Stopped Moving

The reintegration stage in Katerina's rite of passage is very different from the parallel stage in Tzili's rite of passage. Tzili's reintegration stage is composed of a series of events that constitute a reconstruction, devoid of content and sterilized of all the ritual events she had experienced in the liminal stage. At the end of that frustrating series of events, Tzili is represented as having returned to the point of departure where she began her journey of coming of age and self-knowledge, as one of the objects in the yard of her house. Katerina, too, returns to the point of origin from which her journey of apprenticeship began. She returns to her native village and ancestral home, but in *Katerina* that return signals the conclusion of the mental process undergone by the protagonist in the course of her long journey. Katerina, the eighty-year-old woman who tells her story, successfully completed the task assigned to her. The various and opposed sources of her faith, to which she has been exposed in her long and tempestuous life, combine in her soul into a single religious essence, which she represents faithfully as the "guardian of the flame."

Nevertheless one cannot help noticing that the successful conclusion of the mystical initiation ceremony in *Katerina* is illuminated in an acutely ironic light because that success, the mystic-pagan combination of Judaism and Christianity, is based on what seems to the modern reader as gross disregard of the facts.[60] For Katerina creates the longed-for combination in her mind, on the basis of her categorical conclusion that "there are no longer any Jews left in the world" (p. 204). The fact that Katerina concludes her emotional and conscious development by ignoring reality is doubtless the high point in the artistic and conceptual structure of this novella.

The clash created here between Katerina's angle of vision and that of the reader, whose interpretation of the story depends on extraliterary knowledge as well, is important in its immediate context. Beyond that context, the main function of that clash is to provide a visible indication of the conflict of ideas upon which the entire novella is based (as are most of Appelfeld's later works): the clash between a mythic, cyclical world-view and a historical, linear one.

   The mythical worldview is represented here by Katerina in all her actions, both as a character in a fictional world and also as the narrator who organizes and structures that world. Katerina's central actions in the fictional world all derive from the same teleology. They are intended to reconstruct fundamental faith experiences. Only against this background is it possible to understand, for example, the renewed experience of the crucifixion and resurrection of Jesus and of the burning bush. Katerina's mythological worldview is also reflected in her actions as a narrator. For example, Katerina's confessionlike story is based entirely on a pattern of repeated cycles. This pattern is expressed, for example, in the fact that the opening and concluding passages of the novella are almost identical. It is also expressed in the astonishing fact that all the important events of the story take place, as one discovers by carefully noting the narrator's indications of time, at or near the Passover-Easter season.[61] Both of these holidays (which Katerina tries to combine) mark the renewed covenant between the believer and his or her God, and renewed association with the tribe's collective myth. The mythic, cyclical, repetitive worldview is also reflected in the saying with which Katerina chooses to conclude her story, one that concisely expresses the ideological justification of the story of her life: "Now, as the proverb says, the water has flowed back into the river, and I have returned here" (p. 212).

   The second worldview, which is historical and linear, is created as a result of cooperation between the author and the reader. This cooperation is based, in the present context, upon exposure of the narrator's unreliability, as expressed in the representation of the dimension of time in the story. This unreliability, which is repeatedly alluded to throughout the novella, is revealed in full after the end of the war. From Katerina's point of view, that event means that there are no more Jews in the world. That is, history has come to an end, or, in the words of Sigi, Katerina's friend in prison, "Everything has stopped moving" (p. 189). Now comes the turn of the longed-for age, the mythical period above and beyond time.

   In *Katerina* the clash between the mythical and historical worldviews is represented from a position very similar to that from which the parallel conflicts between the naive and modern worldviews are represented in the hasidic stories and in *Tzili*. In several places we find an ambivalent attitude that reflects religious and intellectual distress with no solution. On the one hand, the work shows a deep yearning to sink back into a mythological, tribal continuum. On the other hand, that very yearning is represented as ridiculous, and, at the same time, it arouses dread. Ridicule is appropriate because the character who becomes attached to that mythological, tribal continuum succeeds in doing so only by shutting her eyes to reality. Dread arises because the yearning to sink back into that tribal, mythological continuum contains a dark and murderous aspect, a frightening aspect, that even a "perfectly kosher" gentile woman like Katerina cannot manage to overcome.

We cannot conclude our discussion without trying, with all appropriate caution, to grapple with the question of the status of the Holocaust in the context of Appelfeld's religious attitude. Indeed, the Holocaust is conceived in this context, as in all of Appelfeld's works, from two points of view. From the more understandable perspective, it is described as an experience of enormous loss: the loss of parents, of a home, of childhood; the loss of faith in humanity and human psychology, in ideologies, in culture in general, in literary language in particular, and even in innocent objects. From the other perspective—and this is surprising, at least at first glance—the Holocaust is described as an experience of mighty revelation. Here, in the domain of horror, and only here, occurs the encounter between man and the metaphysical sphere. Here, and only here, is created the deep connection between the individual and the tribe.

Hence it may be said, again with caution, that the Holocaust is grasped in Appelfeld's works as a liminal period, an intermediary time in which there rule, in utter disarray, illness and health, life and death, and also, principally, chaos and sanctity.

The question to be asked here is how Appelfeld sees the status and function of the Holocaust as a liminal period within the overall existence of the Jewish people in the modern age. Do his writings suggest that one can grasp the Holocaust as a private and collective experience, the status and function of which in the overall existence of the Jewish people in the modern age is similar to the status of rites of passage in primitive societies? Is the Holocaust an experience that, by its very existence, as Turner and Eliade repeatedly state with regard to the liminal state in rites of passage, makes possible the continued existence of the intact framework of individual and tribal life? Perhaps one could go even further and state that, like Eliade, Appelfeld believes that the mythical suspension of history is in effect redemption from "the horror of history."[62]

It seems to me that the answer to both aspects of this question emerges clearly from our discussion. The period of the Holocaust does indeed have decidedly liminal characteristics in Appelfeld's works, but it does not fulfill the function that liminal periods fulfill in primitive societies. In primitive societies the liminal period is simultaneously both extraterritorial and also essential to the cultural system of the tribe. By contrast, with Appelfeld the liminal period is extraterritorial and nothing else. The religious experiences undergone by the initiates in primitive rites of passage have meaning because the communities they come from and return to are connected to their tribal, mythological roots. In contrast, the religious experiences of Tzili and Katerina in their rites of passage have no meaning, or at best their meaning is placed in great doubt because the community whose heroine has left it and to which she will return has lost its ties to its mythological roots in *Tzili,* or because "her" community, "the hidden tribe," which she finally dares to seek to join, has "simply" disappeared in *Katerina.* One way or another, Appelfeld's works repeatedly express a historiosophical position to which other great Jewish writers also subscribe:[63] the "entry into history" of the Jewish people in the eighteenth and nineteenth centuries severed it from its roots, thus bringing catastrophes down upon it before the ultimate catastrophe.

Notes

The Hebrew titles of novels and short story collections, as well as of poems, stories, and articles, including those that have been translated, are given in transliteration for those who wish to consult them in the original. Translations are also provided. However, the Hebrew titles of some essays appear in English translation because their meaning is relevant to the content of the notes.

Part 1 (pages 1–28)

1. With regard to the "Lot's Wife's Syndrome," Appelfeld said that he was influenced, among others, by S. Y. Agnon, all of whose stories—even those that take place in Israel—are gripped by the experience of his childhood home. See Schwartz 1991. Thus it is not surprising that the book by Agnon which Appelfeld says influenced him most is *A Guest for the Night* (1968). See also Appelfeld, "Hagarin" (The Kernel), in *Masot Beguf Rishon* (Essays in the First Person, 1979), pp. 101–7. Regarding Appelfeld's narrative art and worldview in his stories in relation to various historical periods, see Barzel 1973 and G. Shaked 1994b.

2. Ezrahi 1984; Ramras-Rauch 1994a, pp. 10, 16.

3. Schneider 1982, pp. 8, 6.

4. See Nevo 1969; Remba 1969; Gutkind 1969; Balaban 1980; Ben-Shaul 1983; Fuchs 1982a; Gingold-Gilboa 1984; Sarna 1989; Adlau 1990–91. On this matter, see also the perceptive remarks of Rochman 1964.

5. Shifra 1975.

6. Sadan 1979 claims that Appelfeld does not possess true powers of memory.

7. Appelfeld has spoken about his years of wandering in Transnistria in many contexts. See, among others, his "Remarks upon Receiving the Ussishkin Prize for 1966" (in Hebrew 1967); and his essays: "Edut" (Testimony) and "Haeima Vehahithayevut" (The Dread and the Obligation) in *Masot Beguf Rishon* (1979); and his lecture before the Board of Trustees of the Hebrew University (1993). See also the following interviews: Halfi 1962; Razili 1963; Schneider 1982; Golan 1971; Roth 1988; Moskona-Lerman 1991; Levit 1991; Schwartz 1991, 1992; Besser 1995; and Pagis 1995, p. 36. Regarding the Holocaust in Transnistria, see, among others, the survey by Ancel 1990 and the article by Ofer 1991. On the fate of Jewish children during the Holocaust in Transnistria, see the comprehensive study by Ben Zion 1989.

8. Appelfeld says in his essay "Hatrada Nimshekhet" (Continued Nuisance, 1993): "True, those were the war years when every moment was stamped in your

flesh, but nevertheless I do not remember even a single village from the dozens of villages that I crossed fearfully over the length of the Ukraine. I was together with hundreds of refugees, and I don't even remember a single name. The war crushed you. Everything became a long, dark convoy on the way to the unknown."

9. Appelfeld confessed: "Everything I knew from home was forgotten. Like a chameleon, I wanted to resemble my surroundings more and more." Schneider 1982, p. 8.

10. See the following stories from *Bekomat Hakarka* (On the Ground Floor, 1968): "Habreiha" (The Escape), "Hahishtanut" (Transmutation), "Rushka," "Haazuva" (Neglect). And see also the following stories from *Adnei Hanahar* (The River Banks, 1968): "Hagilgul" (Metamorphosis), "Hagilui Haaharon" (The Last Revelation). Tzili Kraus undergoes a somewhat different sort of process of memory effacement in *Hakutonet Vehapasim* (The Cloak and the Stripes; trans. 1983 by Dalya Bilu as *Tzili: The Story of a Life*).

11. See the following stories from *Bagai Haporeh* (In the Fertile Valley, 1963): "Kittie" and "Masaotav shel Andriko" (Andriko's Journeys). Also see "Beeven" (In Stone) and "Habehira" (The Choice) in *Kefor al Haaretz* (Frost on the Earth, 1965). Appelfeld talked about his experiences from this period in interviews with Zinger 1971 and Fuchs 1982a. In the interview with Fuchs he said, "The motif of the abandoned child in the monastery symbolizes a dreadful possibility for me—the cutting off of (family and tribal) roots."

12. Gingold-Gilboa 1983, pp. 28–29.

13. Aharon Appelfeld, "Remarks at an Evening in Honor of Gershon Shaked" (in Hebrew, 1993). Appelfeld made similar remarks in his essays: "Hatrada Nimshekhet"; "Heshbon Beinayim" (Subtotal, 1994); "Hamishim Shana Aharei" (Fifty Years after the Great War, 1995). See also the following interviews: Nevo 1969; Allon 1978; Balaban 1980; Leskli 1985; Sarna 1989; and Evron 1994.

A fascinating document that came into the hands of Tzvi Tzameret provides insight into the nature of the encounter between Appelfeld and the pioneering Zionist establishment of the time. It is a composition by Appelfeld submitted as an examination at the end of an accelerated course in the teachers' seminary of the religious workers' movement in Jerusalem on May 30, 1952. The subject of the composition is "The Function of the School in Absorbing Immigration and the Integration of the Exiles," and it includes, among other things, the following sentences: "The Hebrew school today must serve as a melting pot to create a unified generation, unified in its language, in its ideas, and in the goals of its life. . . . The scattered remnants of Zion are infected with mortal illnesses of exile and must find a cure in the homeland. For adults who return to their country it is difficult to free themselves from the shackles of exile . . . but this is not true of our children—the venom of exile has not yet touched their tender hearts, and it is still possible to bend them like a soft branch, to repair and immunize them. . . . The Hebrew school must faithfully serve the purposes of the Hebrew nation: to remove the barriers between the ethnic groups, to implant love of the nations and love of the homeland."

This composition does not contain enough information to determine whether it is the authentic expression of the twenty-year-old Appelfeld, or whether (which

is more likely) it expresses attitudes he assumed he had to present to the two com-
mittees that were to judge whether he was worthy of employment as a Israeli
teacher. One way or another, this document reflects the difficulties he had to confront at that time.

Regarding the relation of Appelfeld's work to Zionism and Zionist indoctrination, see also Ezrahi 1984, 1985–86.

14. See, mainly, "Beein Manos" (With No Escape 1961), "Hirhurei Kayitz
Hatufim" (Passing Summer Thoughts 1961), "Rega" (Moment 1961), and "Diukan" (Portrait 1968).

15. The processes of indoctrination and those opposed to it in *Mikhvat Haor*
(The Scorch of Light, 1983) have been noted in various ways by Moked 1980; G.
Shaked 1980; Shalev 1980; Einat 1980; Schwartz 1981; Ben Barukh 1981; Toker
1982; Dudai 1983; Ratok 1989, pp. 137–49; and Gertz 1994.

16. This is perhaps the place to emphasize that Appelfeld was unable to construct his artistic persona from true family memories. He arrived in mandatory
Palestine in 1946 with no relatives, and he was reunited with his father only
eleven years later. From Appelfeld's remarks in this context (Schwartz 1992), it
appears that the two did not speak at length about the family's past.

At the end of the 1950s Appelfeld received five photographs from distant relatives (see photos following page 102): a portrait of his father, one of his mother,
one of his mother and her two cousins in their youth, a picture of himself at the
age of four or five, and another at about the age of six.

Nor did he possess a mother tongue that could serve as a bridge to the period
of his lost childhood, as with other authors in exile. This happened, as he says,
for several reasons. First, in the course of his wanderings during the Holocaust he
learned to make use of several languages (German, Yiddish, Ruthenian, Rumanian, Russian) that jumbled in his head. Another reason was his ambivalent attitude toward his "Germanized" parents' heritage and because he viewed German
as the language of the murderers. Finally, at a later stage, in his youth in Israel, he
was required to give up the remnants of his "diaspora language." The fact that
Appelfeld abandoned German as a language for literary writing and turned to
Hebrew, which had been completely foreign to him, made him—at least in several
significant respects—a homeless person in terms of language. For more on this
important topic, which demands separate discussion, see Appelfeld's essay, "Al
Hargasha Ahat Manha Venimshekhet" (On One Leading and Prolonged Feeling"
(*Masot Beguf Rishon*, pp. 36–37). Also see Ezrahi 1984, 1985–86; and the fol-
lowing interviews: D.K. 1962; Halfi 1962; Balaban 1980; Gingold-Gilboa 1983;
Shor 1987; Schwartz 1992; and Roth 1988.

17. To the best of my knowledge, Georges Perec is the only author whose narrative art is based on a "process of recollection" similar to that embodied in
Appelfeld's narrative art. The deep similarity between these two writers is apparently connected to the similarity in their biography. Perec lost his parents at a very
early age, and the memories remaining from his early childhood during the Second World War were few. Regarding the affinity among Perec's biography, his
"process of recollection," and his narrative art, see Schnitzer 1991, pp. 167–79;
and Heizner 1994, pp. 92–117).

Another more limited and problematic similarity—though not without interest in several respects—can be found between the "process of recollection" in Appelfeld's fiction and that of German Holocaust fiction (Heinrich Böll, Günter Grass, and others) on the one hand, and that of African American literature (Toni Morrison and others), on the other hand.

18. See, for example, Gorfein 1981; Zahavi 1966; Kremer 1968; Moked 1975; Yudkin 1974; Mazor 1986; and Alter 1985.

19. Schneider 1962, p. 6.

20. I prefer the term "creative tendencies" rather than "creative stages" because the chronological variable in the process discussed here—as well as the chronological variable in other processes that characterize the development of Appelfeld's work—is difficult to specify with the necessary precision. This difficulty derives from the fact that the order in which Appelfeld's stories were published does not exactly reflect the order of their writing. After their completion, certain stories underwent a long "cooling-off period," while others were published closer to the time of their composition. In any event, it may be assumed that the order of publication also represents a process of maturation.

21. The exception who proves the rule is Holtzman 1994.

22. The word "visions" here is a key word in Appelfeld's fiction, as was noted by Barzel 1974, pp. 125–48. The word has two relevant connotations: the aura of taboo that arouses sharp feelings of sanctity and sin, and a sense of *déjà vu,* an image of reality as though remembered, as though it really existed and is, at the same time, fictional.

23. See also the poems "Mah Dinam" (What Is Their Judgment, 1958), "Ad Keev" (Until It Hurts, 1958), "Veshuv" (And Again, 1958), and "Din" (Judgment, 1958), and also, in a less direct and blunt manner, the poems "Lo Eda Khenot Otam Beshem" (I Cannot Tell Them by Name, 1957), and "Lo Esov Leahor" (I Shall Not Turn Back, 1957).

All the personae who serve as intermediaries between the present and the obscure past in Appelfeld's poetry, fiction, and plays are endowed with connotations, on the one hand, of sanctity and might, and, on the other, of sin and great vulnerability. The power of these mediating personae is expressed mainly in their ability to control the fate of other characters. Their vulnerability is expressed, for the most part, in a conspicuous physical handicap and/or in severely restricted mobility. The examples are evident: the girl Bertha in the story named after her in *Ashan,* the handicapped old man in "Bekomat Hakarka" (*Ashan*), the narrator in "Bagova Hakar" (In the Cold Height, *Bagai Haporeh*), the narrator in "Gonev Marot" (The Thief of Visions, *Kefor al Haaretz*), Bettie in *Haor Vehakutonet* (The Skin and the Cloak, 1971), the dwarf in *Mikhvat Haor,* the *yanuka* (youth) and the rabbi in *Badenheim, Ir Nofesh* (Badenheim, Resort Town, 1975; trans. by Dalya Bilu 1980 as *Badenheim 1939*), the rabbi in *1946* (in *Shanim Veshaot* [Years and Hours, 1978], the rabbi in *Beet Uveona Ahat* (At One and the Same Time, 1985, trans. 1990 by Jeffrey M. Green as *The Healer*), the district rabbi in *Al Bariah* (Bolted In, *Sefer Yitzhak Bakun,* 1992), and many others. I shall discuss mediating personae from another point of view in Part 3.

24. Noted by G. Shaked 1971, pp. 153–54.

25. See Schneider 1982, p. 17. See also the essays "Hamoreh" (The Teacher, *Masot Beguf Rishon,* pp. 61–66), and "Hakoreh Vehabayit" (The Beam and the House, 1987), which Appelfeld dedicated to Dov Sadan, and the interview with Roth 1988.

26. G. Shaked 1971, p. 165.

27. Following the terminology of Brinker 1990, pp. 30–31, 46.

28. In the retrospective interview with Roth 1988, p. 64, Appelfeld stated that only when he reached the age of thirty—as he was writing the stories in *Kefor al Haaretz*—did he feel that he was at liberty to struggle as an artist with his early childhood experiences.

29. I refer to the assimilated Jewish families to whom a central place is given in the Austro-Hungarian novellas, first of all, in *Keishon Haayin* (Like the Pupil of the Eye, 1973), *Tor Hapelaot* (The Age of Wonders, 1978, trans. 1981 by Dayla Bilu) and *The Healer,* and also to the assimilated Jewish family to which a more marginal place is given in the novellas that are set in the same time frame, with the same *Zeitgeist*—mainly the Jewish families in *Katerina* (1988, trans. 1992 by Jeffrey M. Green), (*Timyon* [Oblivion], 1993, trans. 1998 by Jeffrey M. Green as *The Conversion*), *To the Land of the Cattails* (trans. 1986 by Jeffrey M. Green, published in Hebrew as "El Eretz Hagomeh," 1990–91, 1992); and *Ad Sheyaaleh Amud Hashahar* (Until the Dawn Rises, 1995).

30. Dov Sadan, who undoubtedly had a decisive influence on Appelfeld's conception of "Jewish geography" (Feldman 1992, p. 232), said of that Jewish community: "It was a large group of Jews who turned to Vienna as a concrete cultural presence before the First World War, and as a cultural fiction after it. Those Jews [meaning the generation of Appelfeld's parents, Y.S.], worshiped a fictional creation" (Sadan 1979).

A similar picture of the community emerges from encyclopedia articles and historical studies. See Ancel and Lavi 1980, pp. 487–511; Yavetz 1994.

31. See Hertz 1972; Sokoloff 1992a; and Schwartz 1986c.

32. In discussing literary autobiography, I use the terminology of Menachem Brinker 1990, pp. 36–37.

33. For example, Elie Wiesel, *Night* (New York: Hill and Wang, 1960); Samuel Pisar, *Of Blood and Hope* (Boston: Little Brown, 1980); Saul Friedlander, *When Memory Comes* (New York: Farrar, Strauss, Giroux, 1979); Shmuel Hacohen, *Kemo Avanim Shotkot* (Like Silent Stones) (Jerusalem: Keter, 1988); Shlomo Breznitz, *Sedot Hazikaron* (The Fields of Memory) (Tel Aviv: Am Oved, Sifriyat Ofakim, 1993). On the works by Wiesel, Pisar, and Friedlander as "artistic autobiographies," see Sungolowsky 1990.

34. Schneider 1982, p. 6.

35. As pointed out by Cohn 1989, p. 13.

36. Schneider 1982, p. 6.

37. Gingold-Gilboa 1983, pp. 28–29.

38. Again I make use of the extensive structure of distinctions offered by Brinker 1990, pp. 29–64.

39. As shown by Miron 1979.

40. Shalom Kremer is, to the best of my knowledge, the only critic whose

views are consistent with the overall approach presented here. He states (1968, pp. 210–12): "The sights that Appelfeld shows us are not true sights. . . . Appelfeld deals with the emotional and essential while sowing external details and spinning out thoughts. . . . These are not realistic stories in the ordinary sense. . . . [Appelfeld's] stories are like a lyric and speculative commentary on chosen sections of reality, upon which Jewish fate is loaded."

41. Moretti 1985, p. 115.

42. Langer 1991, p. xi, argues that all oral testimony about the Holocaust consists, at least on one level, of stories that have broken down. On the portrayal of people after the Holocaust as suffering from a psycho-existential crisis that will not soon be repaired, see Hartman 1994 and Friedländer 1994.

43. Freud [1920], Hebrew ed. 1968, pp. 95–137. On parallel efforts to master traumas that are connected with the Holocaust by means of telling stories, see Rimmon-Kenan 1987 on Günter Grass's novel, *Katz und Maus* (Cat and Mouse, 1967), and Heizner 1994, which refers both to belletristic texts (of Saul Friedländer, Georges Perec, and others) and also to written and oral testimony.

Part 2 (pages 29–94)

1. These are the settings of most of the stories collected in Appelfeld's first book, *Ashan*. The exceptions here prove the rule. They are "Shlosha," "Aviv Kar" (Cold Spring), "Al Yad Hahof" (By the Shore), and, in part, "Pitzuim" (Compensation). The same settings are used in all the stories published in the late 1950s and early 1960s that Appelfeld chose not to include in *Ashan:* "Yom shel Osher" (Day of Happiness, 1959), "Sehor Sehor" (Round and Round, 1959), "Beitzumo shel Hamahzor" (At the Height of the Cycle," a sketch, 1959), "Nisyonot" (Trials, 1959), "Shtei Nefashot" (Two Souls, 1959), "Leyad Hamorad" (Near the Downslope, 1959), "Hagveret Stein Metzapa Lebaala" (Mrs. Stein Expects Her Husband, 1960), "Etzel Harofe" (At the Doctor's, 1960), "Beein Manos" (With No Escape, 1961), "Beyahad" (Together, 1961), "Tapuhim" (Apples, a sketch, 1961), "Ahavato shel Moreh" (A Teacher's Love, 1961), "Yuli" (July, a sketch, 1961), "Hirhurei Kayitz Hatufim" (Passing Summer Thoughts, 1961), "Preda" (Leavetaking, 1961), "Habaita" (Homeward, 1961), and "Rega" (Moment, 1961). One sketch not set against an Israeli background is "Shohet" (Ritual Slaughterer), which was included, with slight changes, in *Bagai Haporeh.*

2. I have included in Appelfeld's fictional realm those regions that receive relatively detailed treatment. This realm is actually far greater, extending throughout most of the Jewish diaspora in the twentieth century, including, among others, the United States, Argentina, Brazil, Australia, and New Zealand.

3. By posing these questions and seeking to answer them systematically, we benefit from the comprehensive work of Davis 1987, pp. 52–101, and Said 1993, pp. 3–61.

4. Gingold-Gilboa 1983. In a later interview (Evron 1994) Appelfeld again referred to himself as an architect, and again in the context of a built-up area containing many units: "I am an architect, but not of a single building, rather of an entire neighborhood. I have a picture of the whole neighborhood in my head. I

know exactly where trees [are missing] and where a house is missing." See also Harel 1995.

5. This is in contrast to lifelike literary realms as defined by G. Shaked 1977, p. 275.

6. I refer, among others, to the essay by Wisse 1983, the critical article by Hagorni 1986, and the scholarly work of Feldman 1992 and of Bernstein 1994. I am grateful to Abraham Holtz for calling my attention to the essay by Ruth Wisse.

7. See Part 1 and Schwartz 1986c.

8. See Tzoran 1982b. Tzoran also made use of the same important and pioneering distinctions in later studies of the same subject: Tzoran 1982a, 1984. His main study (1982b) was preceded by an article that summarizes its principal hypotheses (1981).

9. Here it should be noted that Appelfeld almost never refers to the Germans at all or to the Nazis in particular. This phenomenon can be explained in two ways. First, during the Holocaust Appelfeld was in places where he encountered few Germans. Second, and most significant, Appelfeld focuses on the effort to understand the human condition of the victims and not the relations between them and the executioners. The Ruthenians, too, who play a substantial role in the later works, serve primarily as mirror figures in which various aspects of the Jewish condition are reflected.

10. In an interview with this writer (Schwartz 1992), Appelfeld claimed that "relations between Jews and Arabs are a new topic, at least for me, and therefore they are not yet ripe for artistic-literary representation."

11. Evron 1994.

12. See Part 1 and Schwartz 1986a.

13. The fact that the Institute for Advanced Studies is situated on a high mountain is no coincidence. The setting is meant to indicate the potential importance, even sanctity, of the institution. As Cirlot 1962, pp. 208–11, points out, high places are always associated with cultural connotations of importance and sanctity. Appelfeld makes use of this connotation in many of his stories. Thus, for example, in the early stories "Bagova Hakar" and "Mimrom Hadumiya" (From the Height of Silence, in *Kefor al Haaretz)* and later in *Tzili* and *The Healer* (as noted by Ratok 1989, pp. 125–26), and in *To the Land of the Cattails* and *Ad Sheyaaleh Amud Hashahar.*

14. The contrast between Jewish and gentile life, on a botanical or zoological basis, appears in Appelfeld's stories in dozens of guises. Thus, for example, in "Nisayon Retzini" (A Serious Effort, *Ashan)*, the weak Zimmer, who is compared to a bird (p. 113), is contrasted with Rozina, who is like "a sturdy peasant girl" (p. 109), and she looks at him with "a mad sparkle kindled in her eyes" (p. 113). This scene takes place, it should be added, in Rozina's house, which stands in a courtyard "in fertile and pungent greenery . . . swallowed in an abundance of mighty creepers, and the thick foliage rises above the flat roof" (p. 108). Not surprisingly, Rozina and her house remind Zimmer of "those deep caves that were scattered on the mountainsides around his village, and the village girls who would go down to the well, and the same silence would accompany their heavy steps" (p. 110). "Hamahaseh Haaharon" (The Last Refuge, *Bagai Haporeh)* is

entirely built around the parallel between the gentiles who grow stronger from drinking the potion produced from "the fertile vegetation" (p. 27) that grows in the monastery where the Jewish refugee is hiding, and the refugee, whom the potion ultimately kills.

15. This simile, which appears in various versions in many of Appelfeld's stories, becomes a central motif in the imagery of *Haor Vehakutonet*.

16. Contemplation of the landscape through a glass barrier is a basic experience for all Appelfeld's main characters in the stories of the Land of the Cattails. This, for example, is the activity most characteristic of the father who stays with his family in the Carpathian village in *The Healer,* and also of the boy narrator and his father in *The Age of Wonders.* Similarly, it is the principal activity, almost the only one, of Trude, the landlord's sick wife in *Badenheim.* In this context, perhaps one should note the interesting argument of Robert G. Cohen in his article on Mallarmé's windows (cited in Sebeok and Margolis 1981, p. 4), that the window is a miniature theater, the meeting place of outer life with the innermost life.

17. Shifra 1975. Appelfeld has said similar things in other interviews. See Shor 1987; Levit 1986; and Roth 1988; and see also the comments of Karton-Blum 1986.

18. This phenomenon is especially characteristic of young women in Appelfeld's stories of the Land of the Cattails, as well as in the work of many decadent Austro-Hungarian writers. Notable examples are Paulina in *Keishon Haayin,* Aunt Theresa in *The Age of Wonders,* Isidora in *The Retreat,* Helga in *The Healer,* and Henni in *Katerina.* Some of the women who suffer from this incurable disease are hospitalized in various sanitoriums, often in convents, and some even commit suicide. On this matter, treated from a different point of view, see Pelai 1981.

19. Particularly prominent in this context are the young men in *Keishon Haayin* and *The Age of Wonders.* It appears that no shade of chiaroscuro escapes their inquiring eyes. Bruno in *The Age of Wonders* "would stand next to the window and measure the circles of light crowding against the window screens" (p. 80). Similarly, the young man in *Keishon Haayin,* who has "eyes like an investigating angel" (p. 212), goes back to stand near the window so that he can better "absorb the slow flow" (p. 198).

20. The members of the family in *Keishon Haayin,* for example, are described by the young man who observes them, as though they are swallowing the music "like a drug of pleasure" (p. 205). From their non-Jewish servant, Carola, we learn that "they are devoted to music the way a peasant is to his bottle" (p. 234). A significant number of the characters in the stories of the Land of the Cattails devote most of their time to music. However, not one of them is satisfied with his playing, a phenomenon that is often accompanied by extreme responses: Henni in *Katerina* commits suicide; and Danzig, the violin teacher in *The Age of Wonders,* emigrates to Australia.

Appelfeld made fascinating remarks on this subject in the interview with Anat Levit (1986): "Some of my [Austro-Hungarian] characters are involved in music, and not for nothing. . . . Music became a kind of substitute for religion. Since it is a substitute, it is flawed by nature. The assimilated Jew left the Jewish community and tried to find refuge in literature, music, and theater. For him these took the place of father, mother, faith, roots, homeland, tribe. It couldn't keep going that way. Art can perhaps be a supplement. The assimilated Jew tried to obtain everything he had lost by way of art. That's where the flaw comes from. Art cannot bear all of that on its shoulders, and it collapses."

21. Many characters declare, in various ways, that "the purpose of life" is fulfilled in fine cognac, fresh cheese cake, or even a cigarette (for example, *Ritzpat Esh* [Fiery Ember, 1988], p. 25; *The Healer*, p. 60; *To the Land of the Cattails*, p. 84; and *Mesilat Barzel* [The Iron Tracks, 1991, trans. 1998 by Jeffrey M. Green], p. 6). The culinary festival grows to monstrous proportions in *Badenheim*, a grotesque illustration of the expression, "Eat, drink, and be merry, for tomorrow we die."

22. On this decline, see Bar-Yosef 1994, pp. 14–30. The philosophy of history implied by Appelfeld's Austro-Hungarian novels no doubt derives from the tradition of decadent thought as expressed in the works of many Austrian and German authors, both Jewish and non-Jewish. I refer to such writers as Thomas Mann, Arthur Schnitzler, Stefan Zweig, Jacob Wassermann, and Hugo von Hoffmannsthal, whose names are frequently mentioned in the stories of the Land of the Cattails. For example, Stefan Zweig is mentioned in *Keishon Haayin* (p. 222), in *The Age of Wonders*, p. 45, and in *The Conversion*, p. 46. Jacob Wassermann and Arthur Schnitzler are mentioned in *The Age of Wonders*, p. 151. Franz Werfel is mentioned in *Keishon Haayin* (pp. 198, 236, and elsewhere). And in *The Age of Wonders* there is even a discussion of a group of writers, as a school, explicitly connected with decadence (pp. 107–8). It is likely that Appelfeld was also exposed to "the germs of decadence" (p. 108) in Hebrew writers such as Uri Nissan Gnessin, Dov Kimhi, Aharon Reuveni, and of course David Fogel.

23. See Part 2, note 1, above.

24. The exceptional stories that prove the rule are "Pegisha" (Meeting, *Kefor al Haaretz*) and "Bamekomot Hanemukhim" (In the Low Places, *Kefor al Haaretz*). In these stories Appelfeld developed the patterns that typify the early stories he did not include in his collections of stories.

25. Bachelard 1994, pp. 3–37.

26. Compare the effort of the merchant Schimmer to find a way to the depths of the past by clinging to the memory of Artur Stahl and his daughter Dina, who lived in a cellar crammed with religious books, "a narrow space that was always full of ancient aroma" ("Hakikar" [The Square], *Adnei Hanahar*, p. 177); the actors of the Yiddish theater, some of whom are blind, burrow into a building "that seemed to be an abandoned synagogue that was visited only seldom" ("Halahaka" [The Troupe], *Adnei Hanahar*, p. 19); Bettie, who clings to her memory of the time of her exile in Siberia, especially to May Day celebrations every year; she and her friends "crawled" to the Siberian priest "who had lived underground all those years" in a "dark hut" that had "just one narrow window extended to the light" (*Haor Vehakutonet*, p. 66).

Burrowing into a cellar existence also has similar status—a combination of destructive processes, on the one hand, with preservation of precious scraps of memory, on the other—in some of Appelfeld's stories set in Europe during the

Holocaust or directly afterward. See, for example, the bunker and the dark shed of "The Sorcerer," who serves as a medium for the survivors and raises the dead in "Aviv Kar" (*Ashan*); the cellar of the castle where the major part of the plot takes place in "Keshet Hakimron" (The Arch of the Vault, 1964); the cellars that hide the girl Kittie ("Kittie") and the orphan boy in "Baeven" (*Kefor al Haaretz*); "the synagogue on the cellar floor" belonging to Max in *The Iron Tracks;* and also the pit where Tzili and Mark hide in *Tzili,* and the solitary prison cell of Katerina in *Katerina.*

27. This fetal curling up has, of course, ironic meaning and is one of the major elements in the body language of Appelfeld's protagonists, especially (though not only) the Holocaust survivors who reached Israel. See for example (and dozens of references could be provided), "Bekomat Hakarka," *Ashan,* p. 147; "Ashan," *Ashan,* p. 123; "Bertha," *Ashan,* p. 63; "Bronda," *Adnei Hanahar,* p. 16; *Haor Vehakutonet,* pp. 22, 30, 68, 80, 87, et passim; *Mikhvat Haor,* pp. 25, 33, 35, 94, 108, et passim; and *Bartfuss ben Almavet* (in *Hakutonet Vehapasim;* trans. 1988 by Jeffrey M. Green as *The Immortal Bartfuss*), pp. 8, 22, 74, et passim.

28. See, for example, "Pitzuim," *Ashan,* p. 23; "Ashan," *Ashan,* p. 135. G. Shaked 1971, p. 154, noted the artistic function of this action.

29. Compare "Bronda," *Adnei Hanahar,* p. 13; *Haor Vehakutonet,* p. 77; *Mikhvat Haor,* p. 61; and *The Immortal Bartfuss,* p. 8.

30. See "Rega"; "Leyad Hamorad"; sections from the opening and conclusion of "Nisayon Retzini," *Ashan,* pp. 89, 124; and "Pitzuim," *Ashan,* pp. 19, 21.

31. Also in "Leyad Hamorad": "a very sharp movement, a very sharp movement." The expression appears in slightly different fashion in "Nisayon Retzini," *Ashan,* pp. 110–11 and elsewhere.

32. See especially the opening chapter of *Haor Vehakutonet.*

33. See Part 1, pp. 5–8, above.

34. The three farms where Appelfeld lived are the Mikve Yisrael agricultural school, the agricultural school in Nahalal administered by Hannah Meisel, and the Zionist Youth Village in Jerusalem run by Rachel Yanait Ben-Zvi. The character of the headmistress of the agricultural farm in *Mikhvat Haor,* who is sarcastically called the "Old Maid," is most probably based on Rachel Yanait and Hannah Meisel, and also on Manya Shohat, who frequently visited those institutions. Appelfeld described his stay in these schools in general, and in the Zionist Youth Village in particular (including the antics of Rachel Yanait and her attitude toward him) in the following interviews: Schneider 1982; Moskona-Lerman 1991; and Schwartz 1992.

35. This passage contains many scraps of pictures of hidden childhood typical of the Land of the Cattails in Appelfeld's fiction: typical smells ("the smell of baked cheese"), typical body language (serving coffee without a tray, the way the pipe is smoked), the shape of personal effects (the old man's curved cane), the varieties of German, the linguistic terms that "suit" the objects, the names given to foods (use of the word *omelette* rather than the Hebrew word, *havita*), the color of the light, and the way it is scattered in space, and of course the prolonged and precise examination of these things. Similarly, as Sokoloff 1992a points out, certain expressions ("of the rare kind," which is reminiscent of "old-fashioned," and

"the way we once") imply an invitation to the reader to enter a seemingly private and intimate world that is at the same time familiar and known to everyone.

36. This phenomenon refutes, though this time from another direction, the claims of various scholars regarding Appelfeld's "Zionism" or "anti-diasporism."

37. Zborowski and Herzog 1962.

38. Miron 1979.

39. See Bar-Yosef 1980, p. 14.

40. See G. Shaked 1971, pp. 271–86. I have discussed this topic at length in Schwartz 1993, pp. 15–98.

41. This romantic, Darwinist position is implied in all of Appelfeld's later works. It was apparently consolidated both by the direct influence of German romantic sources and also by the indirect influence of those sources as expressed in a very influential tradition in modern Hebrew culture, which may be termed "the Berdyczewski tradition."

42. The similarity between Appelfeld's "uprooted" characters and those of Hebrew literature in the early part of the twentieth century was pointed out by G. Shaked 1971, p. 150; and Oren 1987, pp. 67–97. See also Schwartz 1986b.

43. The term "Penal Colony" obviously refers to Kafka's story of that name and is used by Appelfeld in his memoir. See "Haeima Vehahithayevut," *Masot Beguf Rishon*, p. 22.

44. "Al Yad Hahof" (*Ashan, Bagai Haporeh*); "Begova Hakar" (*Bagai Haporeh*); "Hashayara" (The Convoy, *Bagai Haporeh*), "Bashemesh Hadromit" (In the Southern Sun, *Bagai Hapore*); "Bemakom Aher" (In Another Place, *Kefor al Haaretz*); "Bahanuka 1946" (Hanukah 1946, *Adnei Hanahar*); and the novella *1946*.

45. See Yaoz 1991.

46. Similar descriptions appear in most of the stories from the Italian region. See "Hashayara," *Bagai Haporeh*, p. 194; "Bemakom Aher," *Kefor al Haaretz*, pp. 140–45; and *1946*, p. 111.

47. See M. Shaked 1967.

48. See "Bashemesh Hadromit," *Bagai Haporeh*, p. 177; "Bemakom Aher," *Kefor al Haaretz*, pp. 140, 142, 143, 144, 147, et passim.

49. "Shlosha" (*Ashan*), "Hamahaseh Haaharon," "Shohet," "Kittie," "Matzod" (Hunt), "Bamidbar" (In the Desert), and "Bagai Haporeh" (In the Fertile Valley), all in *Bagai Haporeh*; "Habriha," "Habegida" (The Betrayal), "Hahishtanut," and "Rushka," all in *Bekomat Hakarka*; "Hamatzod" (The Hunt), "Haofot" (The Fowl), "Hagilgul," "Hagilui Haaharon," all in *Adnei Hanahar*. To these stories may be added, with some reservations, most of the first part of *Tzili*.

50. Appelfeld has spoken about his experiences at that time on many occasions. See pp. 4–5 above for a detailed account, and also Part 1, note 7.

51. In Appelfeld's stories, especially those of the Penal Colony, both horses and birds (not identified by species) are always connected with metaphysical entities. Especially notable in this regard are "Haofot" in *Adnei Hanahar* and, in a different way, the novella, *Keishon Haayin*. See Hupert 1979; Yaoz 1981, pp. 172–75; and Barzel 1981.

52. See also "Habegida" and "Hahishtanut," both in *Bekomat Hakarka*; "Hagilgul," *Adnei Hanahar*; and many passages in the first part of *Tzili*.

53. Langer 1975, pp. 166–204 discusses this at length.

54. See, for example, "Hamatzod," *Adnei Hanahar,* pp. 65, 68, 71; and "Ha-breiha," *Bekomat Hakarka,* pp. 10–12. The "black Jews" also look like insects and birds in stories that do not belong to the Penal Colony region.

55. Even-Zohar 1966, pp. 71–74, views this version of transformation as a spiritual victory of the persecuted over their persecutors.

56. See Bakhtin 1978, pp. 492–528.

57. My distinction between stable and inexorable regions in Appelfeld's fictional realm is consistent with the distinction made by Yaoz 1981, between what she calls historical and transhistorical literature (see especially pp. 105–16).

58. For example, Tomashevsky 1965, pp. 61–95; Bremond 1966, pp. 60–70; Bakhtin 1978; Todorov 1977, pp. 108–10; and Rimmon-Kenan 1984, pp. 15–34.

59. Tzameret 1994 noted the connection between *Layish* and the travel stories of Rabbi Nahman of Bratslav. See also Part 3.

60. Barzel 1994; Gertz 1994; Ezrahi 1994; Katz 1994; Shay 1994; G. Shaked 1994b; and Mazor 1995.

61. The ambiguous reading of the scene that concludes *Ad Sheyaaleh Amud Hashahar* can be supported by two pieces of evidence. Earlier in the novel a local gendarme says to Blanca, "If someone wants to flee . . . in [this] spacious country with the woods and forests, swamps and whatever, . . . the arm of the law won't reach him" (p. 62). He adds emphatically that "we don't even find murderers, unless they give themselves up of their own free will" (ibid.). Second, the scene that concludes this book is significantly different from the manuscript in the penultimate version. In the earlier version, Blanca is caught by the two gendarmes by mistake. In contrast, in the printed version, she virtually seduces the two gendarmes into arresting her. Perhaps she does this because she cannot completely free herself from her desire for the "Corner Coffee House" and the cheesecake served there. In any event, the later version of the ending is consistent with the ambivalent endings of all the novellas set in the Land of the Cattails.

62. I refer to the oxymoronic expression, "darkness glowed in the windows" and to the synesthetic combinations "the space soaked up our voices without returning an echo" (as though sound were a liquid and space were a material that could absorb a liquid), and "everything was silent and empty, so that the hand of the wind alone could have knocked us over" (as though there were a substantive connection between silence and emptiness and weakness or instability). "Haderekh ben Drovna Ledrovitz" [The Road from Drovna to Drovicz], *Kefor al Haaretz,* p. 13.

63. See Lotman 1979, pp. 161–84.

64. The only story by Appelfeld in which the plot deviates from the pattern described here is *Katerina,* which is named after the novel's main character. She seems to find her "lost center point," the parental home that she had left decades earlier. However, Katerina is not Jewish, and she also suffers from a defective image of reality, at least from the point of view of the modern reader.

65. See the extensive treatment in Ratok 1989, pp. 119–36.

66. The tension between voluntary human action and mechanical movement produced by an external force such as a train is undoubtedly a dominant compo-

nent in the composition of these two novels. An example is found in the opening scene of *The Age of Wonders,* which, like many of the opening scenes of Appelfeld's stories, previews the theme and plot of the entire novel. See Moked 1975; Schwartz 1986a, 1986b; Ramras-Rauch 1994a, pp. 45–46; and Treinin 1996. Here the opening scene takes place in a railway carriage, "and on one of its rounded walls was a poster of a girl holding a bunch of cherries in her hand." Right afterward the narrator reports that "the compartment door was open and a girl, very like the one in the poster, stood there with a wooden tray in her hands." He adds, "She stood in the doorway for a long time and then suddenly, as if set in motion by some external command, started walking down the aisle serving coffee" (*The Age of Wonders,* p. 3). See also Nagid 1978; Shenhar 1978; Melamed 1991; and Hazanovitch n.d.

67. See especially *Bagai Haporeh:* "Masa," p. 13; "Matzod," pp. 75–76; "Bamidbar," p. 107; "Masaotav shel Andriko," pp. 171, 173. And see, in *Kefor al Haaretz:* "Haderekh ben Drovna Ledrovitz," p. 8; and "Hagerush" (The Expulsion), p. 57. In *Layish* (1994) the descent of the Jacob's household to Egypt, centered on the sale of Joseph, and the journey of the Israelites to the Land of Israel serve almost as an explicit plot. The novel is studded with dozens of references to these mythic journeys.

68. The reference to Israel's War of Independence is found on page 85 of *Mikhvat Haor,* a novel that has 155 pages. Also, in *Haor Vehakutonet* the date of summer 1964 is mentioned, the date when Betty is released from Siberia (p. 99) and "the immigration from the East" (p. 130). In *The Immortal Bartfuss* the following references occur: the self-hating Jewish remarks of Bartfuss's son-in-law who lives on a moshav (p. 42); a local reference to a former friend of Bartfuss who was once elected to "the neighborhood council" and even was listed as a "party member" (p. 45); and, in the course of a conversation in which Bartfuss happened to take part, a fleeting reference to Israel's dependence on the United States and its connection with the oil reserves of the Arab neighbors (p. 107).

69. Thus, for example, Harry Perlshnik, the protagonist of *Haimut* (The Confrontation, 1975) by K. Tzetnik, is well integrated with what goes on around him. Moreover, all of the climaxes in this novel are based on fateful conjunctions between the life of the individual and that of the nation. One conclusive example is the coincidence of the sexual union of Harry (a Holocaust survivor) with Galila (a Sabra) and the declaration of independence by David Ben-Gurion.

The separation of the arena of action of Appelfeld's Israeli stories from the historical context is more marked when one compares his stories about educational institutions to writing about educational institutions by other Holocaust survivors such as *Shoshan Lavan, Shoshan Adom* (White Rose, Red Rose) and *Yoman Hazahav* (The Golden Diary) by David Schuetz. It is especially marked when one compares Appelfeld's stories to Yoram Kaniuk's novel, *Adam ben Kelev* (Man Son of Dog), which takes place in a distant and isolated insane asylum. Nevertheless, the novel is crammed with various references to contemporary life in Israel and the world.

70. Many scholars have noted this reading process. See Frye 1957, p. 77; Perry 1968; and G. Shaked 1976, pp. 47–64. More indirectly, see also Frank 1948, pp. 379–92; Shklovsky 1965, pp. 3–24; and Hrushovski 1976.

71. For more on this matter, see Schwartz 1981; Parry 1981; Dudai 1983; Barzel 1985; Ratok 1989; and Gertz 1994.

72. See Miron 1979, p. 53.

73. See Schwartz 1992.

74. This has been noted by several scholars and critics. See Hirschfeld 1994; Navot 1985; Josipovici 1985; Laor 1986; and Shaham 1994. Regarding Appelfeld's connections with Austro-Hungarian literature, see also the following interviews: D.K. 1992; Fuchs 1982a; and Roth 1988. I am grateful to Professor Emily Budick for calling my attention to the article by Josipovici.

75. In the novellas *The Age of Wonders, To the Land of the Cattails,* and *Ad Sheyaaleh Amud Hashahar,* and mainly in the novella, *Katerina,* where the central portion takes place in prison.

76. Appelfeld gradually moved away from a lyric-meditative style influenced by Anton Chekhov, Uri Nissan Gnessin, and the Viennese impressionist authors, to a more dramatic style reminiscent of Heinrich von Kleist. It is difficult to point out exactly the stage of transition between the two styles. At the same time, it may be said that the first style reached its high point and full development in *Haor Vehakutonet* (1971), and the second style became more pronounced in *Hakutonet Vehapasim* (1983), the volume that contains *Tzili* and *The Immortal Bartfuss.* Commentary on the changes in Appelfeld's style are included in Miron 1979; Dudai 1983; Marmonchik 1985; G. Shaked 1985; Green 1994; and Fishler 1994.

77. See Dudai 1983.

78. Refraining from describing the faces of characters is a descriptive choice typical of all of Appelfeld's stories. For example, it is possible to count on the fingers of one hand the characters of whose hair and eye color we know. In contrast, all of the characters, especially the awkward Holocaust survivors who arrive in Israel, have very rich body language.

79. Prominent examples include *Mikhvat Haor,* pp. 139–46; *The Healer,* pp. 84–90; *Ritzpat Esh,* p. 69; and *The Conversion,* p. 167.

80. See Zandbank 1975, pp. 31–48, and Holtz 1973.

81. Question marks occur only in Appelfeld's early stories that were not reprinted in collections.

82. Appelfeld spoke in a similar vein in his lecture before the Board of Trustees of the Hebrew University (1993).

Part 3 (pages 95–142)

1. See Golumb 1962; Kremer 1962; Miron 1962; Schweid 1962a, 1962b; David 1962; Schneider 1962; Shabtai 1962; and Zandbank 1963. The central characteristics of the reviews of *Ashan* written soon after its appearance have been discussed at length by Holtzman 1994.

2. Miron 1979, p. 50.

3. G. Shaked 1993, p. 143, has written incisively on this topic: "Appelfeld is the most Jewish author in Israel. . . . More than a decidedly Israeli author, he is

essentially a Jewish author who writes in Hebrew and lives in the Land of Israel."
The identification of Appelfeld as a "Jewish author," an identification that always leans upon the distinction between him and other authors of his generation
who are identified as "Israeli authors" (primarily Amos Oz and A. B. Yehoshua),
serves as a basic assumption, explicit or implicit, in dozens of critical articles, essays, and scholarly studies: Yudkin 1974; Zahavi 1967; Barzilai 1976; Yaoz -Kest
1977; Amir-Coffin 1978; Aderet 1979; Miron 1979; Sadan 1979; Yaoz 1983;
Wisse 1983; Tzameret 1983; Harel-Fisch 1983; Mintz 1984; Barzel 1985; Oren
1987; Lipsker 1992; Ramras-Rauch 1994a; Gouri 1994; Laor 1994; Parush
1994; Ezrahi 1994; Schwartz 1995; and Katz 1996. Appelfeld himself played a
considerable role in creating his image as a "Jewish author," for he has repeatedly
spoken of himself, in many interviews, lectures, and literary symposia, as one
who sees himself, first of all, as a Jewish author. See, for example, D.K. 1962;
Razili 1963; Betzalel 1965; Remba 1969; Nagid 1977; Schwartz 1992; G. Shaked
1994a; and Besser 1995. See also Appelfeld, "What Is Jewish in Jewish Literature?" (1993), and "Heshbon Beinayim."

4. Schweid 1964; G. Shaked 1971.

5. Miron 1979.

6. G. Shaked 1971; Miron 1979; Dudai 1983; Marmonchik 1985; Gold
1994; Green 1994; Fishler 1994; M. Shaked 1994; Treinin 1996.

7. The only critics who have devoted considerable space to this in their works
on Appelfeld are Barzel 1974, 1981, 1985; Oren 1987, 1989; and Schweid 1964,
1992, 1995.

8. The poems that could not be included in these two groups fall into several
smaller categories, such as poems about biblical figures and subjects ("Uriah Hahiti" [Uriah the Hittite, 1953], "Shaul" [Saul, 1953], "Aharei Mot Avshalom"
[After the Death of Absalom, 1953], and "Avraham" [Abraham, 1958]), poems
about nature and the landscape written in a lighter style ("Horef Shav" [Winter
Returns, 1953], and "Stav-Esh" [Autumn-Fire, 1952]), and others.

9. Compare "You are solitude, God, / And I am your desperate talon, / The
scored, cut flesh. . . . I am the emissary of your solitude / In my body of chill / Which
is flesh and blood" ("Shelihut I" [Mission I, 1956]), or "He who rules me / Who
writes me prohibitions and permissions / Who tramples my body to a cord / Who
dwells near me in secret / Who tells me to sit / At his feet today / And to learn the
judgment / In detail" ("Lemargelotav" [At His Feet, 1959]). See also "Bamerhakim
Hatzorvim" (In Searing Distances, 1959), and "Shelihut II" (Mission II, 1957).

10. Compare the second stanza of "Mishirei Iyov" (From the Poems of Job,
1955), "Meamkei Hastav" (From the Depths of Autumn, 1955), and "Kolot Lohashim" (Whispering Voices, 1958).

11. "Yitzhak Katznelson, Poet with a Mission" (in Hebrew, 1956); "The Late
Y. Z. Rimon (Thirty Days since His Death)" (in Hebrew, 1959); "The Special
Character of the Poetry of Aharon Zeitlin" (in Hebrew, 1960).

12. See Halfi 1962; Meizlish 1964; Nevo 1969; Fuchs 1982b; Levit 1991;
and Schwartz 1992. At a symposium with Israeli writers held at Harvard University, "What Is Jewish in Jewish Literature?" in remarks that were later published (1993), Appelfeld said that he feels himself to be very Jewish but that his

connection to Judaism is that of an outsider (pp. 23–24). I am grateful to Professor Emily Budick for bringing this publication to my attention.

13. See, for example, the stories "Pitzuim" (*Ashan*), and "Hayom" (The Day, *Adnei Hanahar*), and the novellas, *Haor Vehakutonet, 1946, Mikhvat Haor,* and *The Immortal Bartfuss.*

14. For example, the interviews with Adlau 1990–91, p. 194, and Levit 1986, 1991. In his conversation with Philip Roth (1988, p. 78), Appelfeld says, in this context, among other things: "Antisemitism directed at oneself was an original Jewish creation. I don't know of any other nation so flooded with self-criticism. Even after the Holocaust, Jews did not seem blameless in their own eyes. On the contrary, harsh comments were made by prominent Jews against the victims. . . . The Jewish ability to internalize any critical and condemnatory remark and castigate themselves is one of the marvels of human nature."

15. See, for example, the descriptions of the "black Jews" through the eyes of the gentile fisherman in "Hamatzod" (*Adnei Hanahar*), or the descriptions of the "black Jews" through the eyes of Katerina in *Katerina,* before she leaves her village.

16. The other protagonists who suffer from "the disease of auto-antisemitism" include Doctor Langman and Professor Fussholt in *Badenheim;* Felix, the father in *The Healer;* the Great Balaban in "Hapsiga" (The Summit, 1982; trans. 1985 by Dalya Bilu as *The Retreat*); Lucy in *Ritzpat Esh;* Sammy in *Katerina;* Hochhut, the industrialist in *The Conversion;* and the father in *Ad Sheyaaleh Amud Hashahar.*

17. See also the rabbi in *1946,* who is carried from place to place on a stretcher until the day of his death. In *Mikhvat Haor,* "The old rabbi does not utter a word. . . . His sister's sons ply him with sardines and cigarettes. People have stopped asking him advice. They ask for confirmation from him, make him sign affidavits and all sorts of documents before he understands the matter properly. . . . Now he no longer insists. He signs whatever document his sisters' sons hand him" (p. 21). The rabbi in *The Conversion* is old and blind, and ruffians live in his courtyard.

18. See Tal 1989, pp. 17–45.

19. Buber 1960, pp. 80–88.

20. See his essays "Hamoreh" (on Dov Sadan) and "Yedid Nefesh" (Soulmate, on Leib Rochman), both in *Masot Beguf Rishon* and "Hakoreh Vehabayit" (also on Dov Sadan). Also see interviews with Schneider 1982, pp. 11–12, and Schwartz 1992.

21. See Ratok 1989, p. 125.

22. See G. Shaked 1994, p. 166.

23. On this subject, see Part 2, and Levit 1986.

24. See also the description of Professor Zauber in *The Conversion,* who calls the Jews of the Carpathians "the true worshipers of God" (p. 24), and Katerina's description (in *Katerina*): "The village Jews were creatures of a special kind. The trees and the silence purified their faith" (p. 125). This idea also is expressed by Rabbi Kurt in the fragment "Hafrada," in whose eyes the regions of Galicia appear as "enchanted provinces of nature and innocence."

25. The centrality of the figure of the holy man in this novella is evidenced in its English title, *The Healer*. Other, shorter descriptions of the village rabbi or judge appear in the story "Haakarot" (The Barren Women, *Bekomat Hakarka*) and in *The Iron Tracks*.

26. Buber 1965, p. 10.

27. See "Bamidbar," "Siber" (Siberia), "Matzod," "Hashayara," "Bashemesh Hadromit," all in *Bagai Haporeh*.

28. Regarding the plot and conceptual structure of the story of Rabbi Nahman of Bratslav's journey to the Land of Israel ("Seder Hanesiya shel Rabi Nahman Mibratslav Leeretz Israel"), I have based my discussion on the concise remarks of Dan 1966, pp. 187–88. The relation in principle between *Layish* and the stories of Rabbi Nahman was pointed out by Tzameret 1994. Regarding the similarity and difference between *Layish* and "In the Heart of the Seas" by S. Y. Agnon, see Barzel 1994. The relation between *Layish* and the tradition of travel stories in general, and "In the Heart of the Seas" and *Ad Mavet* by Amos Oz in particular, was noted by Katz 1994 and G. Shaked 1994b.

29. See Rosenfeld 1990.

30. Appelfeld's complex attitude toward the vision of a return to a kind of Jewish fundamentalism is notable also in the ways that Martin Buber, the "High Priest" of that vision, is presented in his works.

Buber exerted enormous influence upon the assimilated Jewish intelligentsia of Central Europe between the two World Wars (as noted, for example, by Weltsch 1984). In Appelfeld, Buber always appears in two contrasting aspects, respectively positive and negative in connotation. This dual attitude follows two principal patterns. In the first, Buber is portrayed as either a faithful guide to the Jewish myth, or else as a charismatic personality whose doctrine is a mixture of Judaism and Christianity and leads to apostasy. Appelfeld expresses this doubt in principle about Buber's effect, among other things, by placing the words of praise for Buber's effort to return to original faith in the mouths of Christians or converts to Judaism, who are addressing assimilated Jews whose ears are blocked or half-blocked. For example, we have the sermon delivered by Hauptmann, the German convert, to the family of assimilated Jews in *Keishon Haayin* (pp. 254–55) and the short lecture given by Zauber, the Christian geography teacher, to the Jewish apostate, Karl, the protagonist of *The Conversion* (pp. 23–25). Alternatively, the words are addressed by assimilated Jews (who are in the midst of a process of "return") to entirely indifferent gentiles, both rural and urban. For example, Lotte Schloss tries to explain who Buber is and why he is important to the gentile wagon driver, who is taking her to a "spiritual center," and the driver imagines that she is speaking about a "priest or saint" (*The Retreat*, p. 9). Blanca makes an inane effort, already mentioned here, to convince the Austrian gendarmes of the importance and greatness of Jewish holy men, with the assistance of reference to Buber and his "marvelous" book about the faith of the *zaddikim* (*Ad Sheyaaleh Amud Hashahar*, p. 187).

The second way in which Buber is presented is as "a prophet or a professor" (*Badenheim*, p. 62). The doubt about Buber's nature reflects the unsolved problem of Jewish characters who try to return to their origins from another direction. For it is not clear to them (or at least it is clear to us that it is not clear to them) whether Buber and his teaching provide entry to true religious experience or to merely an intellectual peephole, distant and alienated. This doubt is hinted at as early as the short story "Yamim Noraim" (High Holy Days, *Ashan*), and it is dramatized in various ways in two later short stories, "Bamekomot Hanemukhim" and "Mimrom Hadumiya" (*Kefor al Haaretz*) and in the novellas, *The Age of Wonders, Badenheim,* and *The Retreat.* Regarding Appelfeld's attitude to Buber, or at least one aspect of it, see his remarks in an interview with Cohen 1990, p. 132.

I would like to thank Professor Yakov Elboim, who referred me to some of the sources consulted in the course of my work on Appelfeld's relation to hasidic literature.

31. On this matter see Part 1, pp. 4–8.

32. I refer mainly to the paths taken in their wanderings by girls and young women as documented in books such as those that were before Appelfeld, according to his own testimony (Schwartz 1992), as he wrote the novella. See, for example, Yona Melaron, *Od Tetzi Mikan* (You Will Leave Here) (Jerusalem: Yad Vashem, 1981)), Sonia Palti, *El Meever Ladniester: Naara Beeretz Gezera* (Across the Dniester: A Young Woman in Exile) (translated from Rumanian by Yotam Reuveni, Tel Aviv: Moreshet, Beit Edut al shem Mordecai Anielewicz, Sifriyat Poalim, 1983).

33. Leclair 1993; Birmelin 1983; Malin 1983.

34. The motifs characteristic of the coming-of-age stories to which the story of Tzili relates, either as a serious imitation or as a distorted copy, are the young daughter wins (Aarne Thompson, Motif L50); persecution of the young daughter (Aarne Thompson, Motif L52); abandonment in the forest (Aarne Thompson, Motif S143); the king/prince discovers a girl in the forest and marries her (Aarne Thompson, Motif N711.1); lovers are reunited after many adventures (Aarne Thompson, Motif T96). This list was compiled by my student, Ms. Orit Kruglansky.

35. Especially Ludwig Tieck, "Der Blonde Eckbert."

36. Roth 1988, p. 69, emphasis added.

37. Schiller [1795–96]; Hebrew trans. 1985; Kleist 1983.

38. The strong affinity between folk tales and primitive rites of passage from childhood to maturity has been noted by scholars of folklore such as Propp 1968, p. 196; Luthi 1984, p. 160; and Zipes 1983, pp. 26–28. This subject was approached from slightly different angles by Eliade 1975, pp. 126–27; and by the psychologist Bruno Bettelheim (1976).

This is the place to thank Professor Galit Hazan-Rokem and Dr. Dina Stein, who referred me to the studies of folklore I consulted in my work on *Tzili* and *Katerina.*

39. Van Gennep [1909] 1960.

40. Turner 1967, 1969; Eliade 1975.

41. The characteristics of the setting in time and place in *Tzili* are identical to the characteristics of the settings in time and place of those of Appelfeld's stories whose plots are located by the reader during the Holocaust. For an extended discussion of this subject, see Part 2, pp. 63–68.

42. Eliade 1975, p. xiv.

43. Ibid., p.16; Turner 1967, p. 99.

44. Appelfeld often links blindness and/or darkness with sex, on the one hand, and with religion or faith, on the other. In some of his stories he creates a link between blindness and/or darkness and both religion and faith. Conspicuous examples are "Masaotav shel Andriko" and "Kittie" (both in *Bagai Haporeh*), and "Bronda" (*Adnei Hanahar*).

45. Eliade 1975, pp. 41–4.

46. Turner 1967, p. 45; Turner 1969, p. 104.

47. According to the dictionary of symbols, Cirlot 1962, pp. 208–11. Regarding the semantic status of high places in Appelfeld's work, see Part 2.

48. On this matter see the extended discussion in Part 2, pp. 63–68.

49. Halprin 1988; Lipsker 1992.

50. On primitive rites of passage as a common source for folk tales of coming of age and legendary novellas, see Eliade 1975, pp. 118–20; Shoham 1992, p. 30.

51. See Lipsker 1992. See also the sensitive comments of Grossman 1992.

52. Roth 1988, p. 69.

53. On the connection between non-Jewishness and nature in Appelfeld, see Part 2, pp. 43–46.

54. Toren 1989.

55. Neeman 1989; Oren 1989; Hagorni 1989; G. Shaked 1989; Roiphe 1992; Parush 1994.

56. In this regard one may mention Carola, the housekeeper in *Keishon Haayin;* Maria, the housekeeper in *Ritzpat Esh,* and Gloria, the housekeeper and ultimately the wife of Karl, the main protagonist of *The Conversion.*

57. On this matter see the interesting comments of Eliade 1975, pp. 115–21.

58. Lipsker 1992, p. 90.

59. A very similar image of a tunnel, which also symbolizes renewed absorption in the world, though it is only apparent, emerges in Blanca's mind at the end of her journey of return in *Ad Sheyaaleh Amud Hashahar* (p. 182). The use of these two images is in jarring contradiction to the use of the tunnel image in *Tzili,* where it symbolizes Tzili's retreat, as a grown woman, to the status of an object.

60. See Lipsker 1992; and Parush 1994.

61. The mention of return to the ancestral home appears in the opening passage of the first chapter of the novella (p. 3); Katerina's few pleasant hours in her parents' company, the only hours in the year when "a kind of piety that didn't belong to this place" clung to her mother (p. 10); the murder of the Jew Benjamin, in whose house Katerina worked and whom she sees as her only love (pp. 44–45); the murder of her son Benjamin (p. 140); the mention of the return to the ancestral home that appears again in the paragraph beginning the final chapter of the novella.

62. The periodic deferral of historical time by means of myth and ceremony is, as Yerushalmi 1982, p. 107 n. 2, states, a subject that Eliade repeatedly treats. Yerushalmi refers to Eliade's principled stand on this subject and criticizes it.

63. See Mintz 1984; and Roskies 1993.

Bibliography

Aharon Appelfeld: Poetry, Fiction, Essays, and Lectures

I. POEMS

"Stav-Esh" (Autumn-Fire). *Bemaaleh* 22, no. 22 (Heshvan 5713/November 7, 1952): 312.

"Horef Shav" (Winter Returns). *Bemaaleh* 23, nos. 5–6 (Nissan 5713/March 20, 1953): 65.

"Aharei Mot Avshalom" (After the Death of Absalom). *Bemaaleh* 23, no. 10 (1 Sivan 5713/May 15, 1953): 125.

"Shaul" (Saul). *Bemaaleh* 23, nos. 13–14 (20 Tammuz 5713/July 3, 1953): 173.

"Uriah Hahiti" (Uriah the Hittite). *Bemaaleh* 23, nos. 24–25 (19 Teveth 5714/December 25, 1953): 355.

"Nedava" (Charity). *Bemaaleh*, nos. 2–12 (18 Shevat 5714/January 1, 1954): 6.

"Birfot Hayom" (The Waning of the Day). *Bemaaleh* 24, no. 7 (28 Adar B 5714/April 2, 1954): 87.

"Pegisha" (Meeting). *Bemaaleh* 24, no.13 (24 Sivan 5714/June 25, 1954): 172.

"Bikhfari Harahok" (In My Distant Village). *Hapoel Hatzair* 25, no. 48 (4 Av 5714/August 3, 1954): 15.

"Geshem" (Rain). *Niv Hakevutza* 3, no. 4 (Elul 5714/September 1954): 807.

"Mul Pesel Shtikatkha" (Before the Statue of Your Silence). *Niv Hakevutza* 3, no. 4 (Elul 5714/September 1954): 807.

"Shekheni" (My Neighbour). *Bemaaleh* 24, nos. 17–18 (Erev Rosh Hashana 5715/September 27, 1954): 239.

"Veosif Lo Shir" (And I Will Add a Song for Him). *Bemaaleh* 24, no. 20 (9 Heshvan 5715/November 5, 1954): 291.

"Shekiya" (Sunset). *Bemaaleh* 25, nos. 1–2 (29 Shevat 5715/January 23, 1955): 8.

"Tefila" (Prayer). *Niv Hakevutza* 4, no. 2 (Adar 5715/1955): 380.

"Shovakh Hayaldut" (The Dovecote of Childhood). *Niv Hakevutza* 4, no. 2 (Adar 5715/1955): 380.

"Horef" (Winter). *Bemaaleh* 25, no. 6 (24 Adar 5715/March 18, 1955): 69.

"Birekiekha Hagevohim Elohim" (In Your Lofty Heavens, God). *Hapoel Hatzair* 26, no. 26 (28 Adar 5715/March 22, 1955): 17.

"Yomano Hahiver" (His Pale Diary). *Mevoot*, no. 20 (April 1, 1955): 17.

"Headam Eino Ela . . ." (Man Is Nothing But . . .). *Lamerhav*, April 22, 1955.

"Erev" (Evening). *Lamerhav*, April 22, 1955.

"Elohai Haoleh Min Hastav" (My God Who Rises from Autumn). *Hapoel Hatzair* 26, no. 31 (4 Adar 5715/April 26, 1955): 18.

163

"Stav" (Autumn). *Zemanim,* May 13, 1955.

"Yatmut" (Orphanhood). *Bemaaleh* 25, no. 11 (6 Sivan 5715/ May 27, 1955): 147.

"Etzim Bashalekhet" (Trees in Autumn). *Gazit* 14, nos. 5–6 (Av-Elul 5715/ August–September, 1955): 45.

"Meamkei Hastav" (From the Depths of Autumn). *Gazit* 14, nos. 5–6 (Av-Elul 5715/August–September 1955): 45.

"Hatzot" (Midnight). *Niv Hakevutza* 4, no. 4 (Elul 5715/September 1955): 766.

"Mishirei Iyov" (From the Poems of Job). *Bemaaleh* 25, nos. 21–22 (3 Kislev 5716/November 18, 1955): 267.

"Bisearat Haavelut" (In the Tempest of Mourning). *Mevoot* , no. 27 (December 5, 1955): 11.

"Tamtzit" (Essence). *Molad* 14, no. 95 (Tamuz–Av 5716/June–July, 1956): 223.

"Nof" (Landscape). *Molad* 14, no. 95 (Tamuz–Av 5716/June–July, 1956): 223.

"Mishpat" (Trial). *Mevoot,* no. 27 (December 5, 1955): 11.

"Shelihut I" (Mission I). *Molad* 14, no. 95 (Tammuz–Av 5716/ June–July 1956): 223.

"Meara" (Cave). *Molad* 14, nos. 100–2 (Tevet–Adar 5717/December, 1956): 575.

"Ribon Hasaarot" (Lord of the Storms). *Molad* 14, nos. 100–2 (Tevet–Adar 5717/December 1956): 575.

"Akhshav" (Now). *Gazit* 15, nos. 3–10 (171–78) (Shevat–Av 5717/January–August 1957): 30.

"Shelihut II" (Mission II). *Gazit* 15, nos. 3–10 (171–78) (Shevat–Av 5717/January–August 1957): 30.

"Hayom Lo Dibart Imi" (Today You Did Not Speak to Me). *Moznayim* 6, no. 1 (Kislev, 5718/December, 1957): 41.

"Lo Eda Khanot Otam Beshem" (I Cannot Tell Them by Name). *Moznayim* 6, no. 1 (Kislev 5718/December 1957): 41.

"Lo Esov Leahor" (I Shall Not Turn Back). *Moznayim* 6, no. 1 (Kislev 5718/December 1957): 41.

"Hayom Tzamud Imkha Hashir" (Today You Are Armed with A Poem). *Gazit* 16, nos. 11–12 (Tevet–Shvat 5718/January–February 1958): 12.

"Begadim" (Clothes). *Ogdan* 2 (5718): 31.

"Shirim" (Poems). *Ogdan* 2 (5718): 31.

"Beshiva Derakhim" (By Seven Paths). *Deot* 5 (Pesah 5718/1958): 22–23.

"Kol Hahelkot Deshuot" (All the Plots Are Covered with Grass). *Deot* 5 (Pesah 5718): 22–23.

"Mah Dinam" (What Is Their Judgment). *Deot* 5 (Pesah 5718/1958): 22–23.

"Meever Lapargod" (Beyond the Curtain). *Deot* 5 (Pesah 5718/1958): 22–23.

"Merotz" (Race). *Deot* 5 (Pesah 5718): 22–23.

"Yadata" (You Knew). *Deot* 5 (Pesah 5718/1958): 22–23.

"Hine Bati Kimaat" (Here I Have Almost Arrived). *Molad* 16, no. 120 (Av 5718/July 1958): 410.

"Kolot Lohashim" (Whispering Voices). *Molad* 16, no. 120 (Av 5718/July 1958): 410.

"Avraham" (Abraham). *Perakim* 1 (August 1958): 182.

"Baderech Limehozot Aherim" (On the Road to Other Districts). *Haaretz,* August 8, 1958).

"Ad Keev" (Until It Hurts). *Gazit* 17, nos. 7–8 (Heshvan–Kislev 5719/October–November 1958): 17.

"Din" (Judgment). *Gazit* 17, nos. 7–8 (Heshvan–Kislev 5719/October–November 1958): 17.

"Veshuv" (And Again). *Gazit* 17, nos. 7–8 (Heshvan–Kislev 5719/October–November 1958): 17.

"Bamerhakim Hatzorvim" (In Searing Distances). *Gazit* 17, nos. 1–2 (Sivan–Tammuz 5719/June–July 1959): 9.

"Lemargelotav" (At His Feet). *Gazit* 17, nos. 1–2 (Sivan–Tammuz 5719/June–July 1959): 9.

"El Malkhut Hamerumim" (To the Kingdom of the Deceived). In *Et Asher Baharti Beshira,* p. 277. Tel Aviv: Hadar 1959.

II. FICTION

"Sehor Sehor" (Round and Round). *Deot* 9 (1959): 70–72.

"Yom shel Osher" (Day of Happiness). *Gazit* 17, nos. 11–12 (Nissan–Iyar 5719/1959): 14–15.

"Beitzumo shel Hamahzor" (At the Height of the Cycle). *Haaretz,* August 7, 1959.

"Nisyonot" (Trials). *Deot* 10 (1959): 40–46.

"Shtei Nefashot" (Two Souls). *Gazit* 17, nos. 5–6 (1959): 9–12.

"Leyad Hamorad" (Near the Downslope). *Davar,* September 9, 1960.

"Hagveret Stein Metzapa Lebaala" (Mrs. Stein Expects Her Husband). *Yediot Aharonot,* October 21, 1960.

"Etzel Harofeh" (At the Doctor's). *Haaretz,* November 11, 1960.

"Beein Manos" (With No Escape). *Maariv,* April 14, 1961.

"Beyahad" (Together). *Davar,* April 14, 1961.

"Tapuhim" (Apples). *Davar,* June 23, 1961.

"Ahavato shel Moreh" (A Teacher's' Love). *Davar,* June 23, 1961.

"Yuli" (July). *Maariv,* July 7, 1961.

"Hirhurei Kayitz Hatufim" (Passing Summer Thoughts). *Davar,* August 4, 1961.

"Preda" (Leavetaking). *Lamerhav,* September 19, 1961.

"Habaita" (Homeward). *Davar,* October 27, 1961.

"Rega" (Moment). *Maariv,* October 27, 1961.

Ashan (Smoke). Jerusalem: Akhshav, 1962. "Shlosha" (Three); "Pitzuim" (Compensation); "Aviv Kar" (Cold Spring); "Bertha" (Bertha); "Leat" (Slowly); "Nisayon Retzini" (A Serious Effort); "Ashan" (Smoke); "Yamim Noraim" (High Holy Days); "Shutfut" (Partnership); "Al Yad Hahof" (By the Shore); "Sippur Ahava" (Love Story); "Bekomat Hakarka" (On the Ground Floor).

Bagai Haporeh (In the Fertile Valley). Jerusalem: Schocken, 1963. "Masa" (Journey); "Hamahaseh Haaharon" (The Last Refuge); "Shohet" (Ritual

Slaughterer); "Kittie" (Kittie); "Haredifa" (The Pursuit); "Matzod" (Hunt); "Sibir"(Siberia); "Bamidbar" (In the Desert); "Bagai Haporeh" (In the Fertile Valley); "Al Yad Hahof" (By the Shore); "Bagova Hakar" (In the Cold Height); "Hashayara" (The Convoy); "Masaotav shel Andriko" (Andriko's Journeys); "Bashemesh Hadromit" (In the Southern Sun); "Mukar" (Known).

"Keshet Hakimron" (The Arch of the Vault). *Hauma* 2, no. 8 (1964): 581–92.

Kefor al Haaretz (Frost on the Earth). Ramat Gan: Masada, 1965. "Haderekh ben Drovna Ledrovitz" (The Road from Drovna to Drovicz); "Gonev Marot" (The Thief of Visions); "Mota shel Hashtadlanut" (The Death of Intercession); "Tzel Harim" (The Shadow of Mountains); "Misodot Hamishar Hazair" (The Secrets of Petty Commerce); "Hakhanot Lamasa" (Preparations for a Journey); "Batahana" (In the Station); "Hagerush" (The Expulsion); "Bimlo Hastav" (In the Fullness of Autumn); "Baeven" (In Stone); "Habehira" (The Choice); "Kefor al Haaretz" (Frost on the Earth); "Mimrom Hadumiya" (From the Height of Silence); "Habesora" (The Tidings); "Beei Sant George" (In the Isles of St. George; translated by Dalya Bilu, *Jerusalem Quarterly*, no. 28 [Summer 1983]: 48–72; reprinted in *Six Israeli Novellas* [Boston: David Godine, 1999], pp. 304–38); "Pegisha" (Meeting); "Bamekomot Hanemukhim" (In the Low Places); "Bemakom Aher" (In Another Place).

Bekomat Hakarka (On the Ground Floor). Tel Aviv: Daga, 1968. "Habriha" (The Escape); "Habegida" (The Betrayal); "Haakarot" (The Barren Women); "Beyahad" (Together); "Hahishtanut" (Transmutation); "Hashiva" (The Return); "Baderekh" (On the Way); "Rushka" (Rushka); "Haazuva" (Neglect); "Haaliya Lekatzansk" (The Ascent to Katszansk).

Adnei Hanahar (The River Banks). Tel Aviv: Hakibbutz Hameuchad, 1968: "Bronda" (Bronda); "Halahaka" (The Troupe); "Regina" (Regina); "Akhsanya"(Hostel); "Hasoher Bartfuss"(Bartfuss the Merchant); "Hilufei Mishmarot" (Changing of the Guard); "Hamatzod" (The Hunt); "Haofot" (The Fowl); "Hagilgul" (Metamorphosis); "Hagilui Haaharon" (The Last Revelation); "Bahanukah 1946" (Hanukah 1946); "Hayom" (The Day); "Hashod" (The Robbery); "Lahashei Hakor" (Whispers of the Cold); "Ahar Hahupa" (After the Wedding); "Shemesh shel Horef" (Winter Sun); "Lydia" (Lydia); "Hakikar" (The Square); "Orekh Hadin Shelanu" (Our Attorney).

"Diukan" (Portrait). *Hayom*, November 29, 1968.

Haor Vehakutonet (The Skin and the Cloak). Tel Aviv: Am Oved, 1971.

Keishon Haayin (Like the Pupil of the Eye). Tel Aviv: Hakibbutz Hameuchad, 1973.

Badenheim, Ir Nofesh (Badenheim, Resort Town). Tel Aviv: Hakibbutz Hameuchad, 1975. Translated by Dalya Bilu as *Badenheim 1939*. Boston: Godine, 1980.

Kemeah Edim (Like a Hundred Witnesses). Tel Aviv: Hakibbutz Hameuchad, 1975. "Aviv Kar" (Cold Spring); "Bertha" (Bertha); "Ashan" (Smoke); "Al Yad Hahof" (By the Shore); "Kittie"(Kittie); "Bagova Hakar" (In the Cold Height); "Hashayara" (The Convoy); "Bashemesh Hadromit" (In the Southern Sun); "Haderekh ben Drovna Ledrovitz" (The Road from Drovna to Drovicz); "Beei Sant George" (In the Isles of St. George); "Beyahad" (Together);

"Haaliyah Lekatzansk" (The Ascent to Katszansk); "Halahaka" (The Troop); "Hamatzod" (The Hunt); "Haofot" (The Fowl); "Hayom" (Today); "Mitokh 'Haor Vehakutonet'" (from The Skin and the Cloak); "Keishon Haayin" (Like the Pupil of the Eye).

Shanim Veshaot (Years and Hours). Tel Aviv: Hakibbutz Hameuchad, 1978 (contains the novellas *Badenheim, Ir Nofesh* and *1946*). Translated by Dalya Bilu as *Badenheim 1939*. Boston: Godine, 1980.

Tor Hapelaot (The Age of Wonders). Tel Aviv: Hakibbutz Hameuchad, 1978. Translated by Dalya Bilu as *The Age of Wonders*. Boston: Godine, 1981.

"Hapisga" (The Summit). In *Bitzaron* 4, nos. 13–14 (1982), pp. 18–88. Translated by Dalya Bilu as *The Retreat*. London, Melbourne, and New York: Encounters, Quartet Books, 1985.

Mikhvat Haor (The Scorch of Light). Tel Aviv: Hakibbutz Hameuchad, 1983.

Hakutonet Vehapasim (The Cloak and the Stripes). Jerusalem: Hakibbutz Hameuchad, 1983 (contains the novellas *Hakutonet Vehapasim* [translated by Dalya Bilu as *Tzili: The Story of a Life*. New York: E. P. Dutton, 1983] and *Bartfuss ben Almavet* [translated by Jeffrey M. Green as *The Immortal Bartfuss*. New York: Weidenfeld and Nicolson, 1988]).

"Hafrada" (Separation, chapter from a novel in progress). *Iton 77*, no. 68 (1985): 38–39.

"Haminyan Haavud" [The Lost Minyan, chapter from a novel in progress). *Alei Siah* 23 (1985): 129–36.

Beet Uveona Ahat (At One and the Same Time). Jerusalem: Hakibbutz Hameuchad and Keter, 1985. Translated by Jeffrey M. Green as *The Healer*. New York: Grove Weidenfeld, 1990.

"Hatzar Hamatara" (Courtyard of the Gaôl, chapter of a novella). *Iton 77*, nos. 84–85 (1987): 10–11.

"Al Kol Hapeshaim." *Davar,* May 8–29, 1987. Translated by Jeffrey M. Green as *For Every Sin*. New York: Weidenfeld and Nicolson, 1989.

Ritzpat Esh (Fiery Ember). Jerusalem: Hakibbutz Hameuchad and Keter, 1988.

"El Eretz Hagomeh" (To the Land of the Cattails). Chapters 1–3 published in *Bitzaron* 10 (1990–91): 13–63; chapter 4 published in *Bitzaron* 11 (1992): 9–54. Translated by Jeffrey M. Green as *To the Land of the Cattails*. New York: Weidenfeld and Nicolson, 1986.

Mesilat Barzel (The Iron Tracks). Jerusalem: Keter, Tzad Hatefer, 1991. Translated by Jeffrey M. Green as *The Iron Tracks*. New York: Schocken Books, 1998.

Al Bariah (Bolted In). In *Sefer Yitzhak Bakun,* edited by Aaron Komem, pp. 1–32. Beersheva: Ben Gurion University of the Negev, 1992.

Katerina. Jerusalem: Keter, Tzad Hatefer, 1988. Translated as *Katerina,* by Jeffrey M. Green. New York: Random House, 1992.

Timyon (Oblivion). Jerusalem: Keter, Tzad Hatefer, 1993. Translated by Jeffrey M. Green as *The Conversion*. New York: Schocken Books, 1998.

Layish. Jerusalem: Keter, Tzad Hatefer, 1994.

Ad Sheyaaleh Amud Hashahar (Until the Dawn Rises). Jerusalem: Keter, Tzad Hatefer, 1995.

Mikhre Hakerah (The Ice Mine). Jerusalem: Keter, 1997.
Kol Asher Ahavti (All That I Have Loved). Jerusalem: Keter, 1999.
"Shefatim" (Blows).

III. ESSAYS AND LECTURES

"The Function of the School in Absorbing Immigration and the Integration of the Exiles" (in Hebrew). MS. May 30, 1952.
"The Holocaust in Yiddish Literature in the Soviet Union" (in Hebrew). *Yediot Yad Vashem*, no. 14 (1955): 15–16.
"Yitzhak Katznelson, Poet with a Mission" (in Hebrew). *Yediot Yad Vashem*, nos. 8–9 (March 1956): 19.
"The Late Y. Z. Rimon (Thirty Days since His Death)" (in Hebrew). *Moznayim* 8, no. 3 (February 1959): 194–95.
"Empty Well" (play review, in Hebrew). *Bama* 3, no. 56 (November 1959): 43–44.
"The Special Character of the Poetry of Aharon Zeitlin" (in Hebrew). *Gazit* 18, nos. 5–8 (August–November 1960): 97–98.
"The Stories of Yehuda Amihai" (in Hebrew). *Orot* 8, no. 42 (June 1961): 48–49. Reprinted in *Yehuda Amihai: Mivhar Mamarei Bikoret al Yetzirato* (Yehuda Amihai: Selected Critical Essays on His Work), pp. 187–90. Tel Aviv: Hakibbutz Hemeuchad, 1988.
"Remarks upon Receiving the Ussishkin Prize for 1966" (in Hebrew). *Am Veadmato*, January 1967, pp. 21–22.
"Introduction to *Miolamo shel Rabi Nahman Mibratzlav*" (in Hebrew). Jerusalem: Sidrat Yalkut, 1971.
"The Path of Suffering to the Source" (in Hebrew). *Hadoar*, 5 Iyyar 5738/1978, pp. 426–28.
Masot Beguf Rishon (Essays in the First Person). Jerusalem: Hasifriya Hatzionit, 1979. "Edut" (Testimony); "Haeima Vehahithayevut" (The Dread and the Obligation); "Hanesiga" (The Retreat); "Al Hargasha Ahat Manha Venimshekhet" (On One Leading and Prolonged Feeling); "El Meever Latragi" (Beyond the Tragic); "1946"; "Hamoreh" (The Teacher); "Sfat Mahalato Usfat Kisufav" (The Language of His Illness and the Language of His Longing, on Y. H. Brenner); "Yedid Nefesh" (Soulmate, on Leib Rochman); "Hamazor Vehapesher" (The Pain and the Meaning); "Haprudot Hayekarot" (The Precious Seed); "Hagarin" (The Kernel); "I Hashlama" (Disagreement).
"The Harvest of Madness" (in Hebrew). *Davar,* June 13, 1987.
"Hakoreh Vehabayit" (The Beam and the House, on Dov Sadan). *Davar,* June 14, 1987.
"The Final Clarity" (on Dan Pagis, in Hebrew). *Mehkarei Yerushalayim al Sifrut Ivrit* 10 (1987): 11–16.
"What Is Jewish in Jewish Literature?" A Symposium with Israeli Writers, Harvard University Library, The Max and Irene Engel Levy Memorial Lecture, March 31, 1992, Cambridge Mass., 1993.

"Remarks at an Evening in Honor of Gershon Shaked" (in Hebrew). Tel Aviv, June 29, 1993, MS.

Lecture before the Board of Trustees of the Hebrew University in Jerusalem (in Hebrew). MS, 1993.

"Hatrada Nimshekhet" (Continued Nuisance, remarks following the appearance of *Timyon). Yediot Aharonot,* December 10, 1993.

"Heshbon Beinayim" (Subtotal). *Yediot Aharonot,* September 5, 1994.

Beyond Despair: Three Lectures and a Conversation with Philip Roth, translated by Jeffrey M. Green. New York: Fromm International, 1994.

"Hamishim Shana Aharei Hamilhama Hagedola" (Fifty Years after the Great War). *Yediot Aharonot,* April 20, 1995.

"The Writers and Between Them—S. Y. Agnon and David Fogel," lecture series at the Hebrew University in Jerusalem, January–June 1995.

Sippur Hayim (The Story of a Life). Jerusalem: Keter, 1999.

References and Other Sources

Aarne, Antti, and Stith Thompson. 1961. *The Types of the Folktale.* Helsinki: Suomalainen Tiedeakatema.

Aderet, Avraham. 1979. *"The Age of Wonders* and the Crisis of Jewish Identity" (in Hebrew). *Alei Siah* 7–8 (1979): 191–98.

Adlau, Yaakov. 1990. "Aharon Appelfeld, on *Eretz Hagomeh"* (interview with Appelfeld, in Hebrew). *Bitzaron* (Nissan 1990–Nissan 1991): 192–96.

Allon, Dafna. 1978. "We Have a Silence That Is Not Relieved" (interview with Appelfeld, in Hebrew). *Bemahane Gadna,* May 1978.

Alper, Rivka (Litka). 1990. "The Woman Who Plants" (in Hebrew). In *Bnot Benir: Korot Mishkei Hapoalot Vehavot Halimud.* Tel Aviv: Am Oved.

Alter, Robert. 1986. "Mother and Son, Lost in Continent" (on *To the Land of the Cattails). New York Times,* November 2, 1986.

Amir-Coffin, Edna. 1978. *"Badenheim, Ir Nofesh"* (in Hebrew). *Hadoar,* 17 Adar 1, 5738/1978.

Ancel, Jean. 1990. "Transnistria" (in Hebrew). In *Haentziklopedia shel Hashoah,* 3:537–39. Jerusalem: Yad Vashem.

Ancel, Jean, and Theodor Lavi, eds. 1980. "Romania" (in Hebrew). In *Pinkas Hakehilot,* 2:487–511. Jerusalem.

Bachelard, Gaston. 1994. *The Poetics of Space.* Boston: Beacon Press.

Bakhtin, Mikhail. 1978. "The Forms of Time and the Chronotopos in the Novel: From the Greek Novel to Modern Fiction." *PTL* 3 (1978): 493–528.

Balaban, Avraham. 1980. "The Great Difficulty Is How Not To Falsify" (interview with Appelfeld on *Mikhvat Haor,* in Hebrew). *Yediot Aharonot,* June 1980.

Bar-Yosef, Hamutal. 1980. Introduction to *Yalkut Sipurim shel Aharon Reuveni,* pp. 7–26. Tel Aviv: Yahdav.

———. 1994. *Mavo Lesifrut Hadekadens Beeiropa* (Introduction to the Literature of Decadence in Europe). Tel Aviv: Universita Meshuderet.

Barzel, Hillel. 1973. "The Formula of Aharon Appelfeld" (in Hebrew). *Gazit* 29, nos. 9–12 (Kislev–Adar 5733/1973).

———. 1974. "Aharon Appelfeld's World of Mirrors" (in Hebrew). In *Sipporet Ivrit Metarealistit* (Metarealistic Hebrew Fiction), pp.125–48. Ramat Gan: Masada.

———. 1981. "Appelfeld's Affinity with Kafka" (in Hebrew). *Zehut* 1 (1981): 112–20.

———. 1985. "Aharon Appelfeld: Historiosophy and Poetics" (in Hebrew). *Alei Siah* 23 (1985): 139–55.

———. 1994. "Aharon Appelfeld and S. Y. Agnon: The Way to Jerusalem—A Comparative Analysis, *Layish* and *Belevav Hayamim*" (in Hebrew). Lecture at "From Czernowitz to Jerusalem," conference at the Hebrew University, December 20–21, 1994.

Barzilai, Itzhak. 1976. "Jewish Society before the Holocaust according to the Stories of Aharon Appelfeld" (in Hebrew). *Hadoar,* 9 Nissan 5736/1976.

Ben Barukh. Yosi. 1981. "The Long Journey to the Plundered Self; or, The City, the Scorch of Light, and the Cloak That Covers Nothing" (in Hebrew). *Alei Siah* Nissan (5741/1981): 270–72.

———. 1983. "The Black Hole and the White Page: Aharon Appelfeld's Literary Production after 1983" (in Hebrew). *Zehut* 3 (Summer 1983): 116–29.

Ben-Shaul, Moshe. 1983. "Appelfeld: The Bottom of the Well" (on his receiving the Israel Prize 1983, in Hebrew). *Hadoar,* January 21, 1983.

Ben Zion, Shmuel. 1989. *Yeladim Yehudiim Betransnistria Bitekufat Hashoah* (Jewish Children in Transnistria during the Holocaust). Jerusalem: Yad Vashem and Haifa: University of Haifa Press.

Bernstein, Michael. 1994. *Foregone Conclusions, Against Apocalyptic History.* Berkeley, Los Angeles, and London: University of California Press.

Besser, Yaakov. 1995. "Horsethieves and Whores Adopted Me. I Spent the War with Them" (interview with Appelfeld, in Hebrew). *Davar Rishon,* December 29, 1995.

Bettelheim, Bruno. 1976. *The Uses of Enchantment.* New York: Knopf.

Betzalel, Yitzhak. 1965. "In Question Marks" (interview with Appelfeld, in Hebrew). *Lamerhav,* July 9, 1965.

Birmelin, Blair T. 1982. "The Age of Wonders." *San Francisco Review of Books,* January 1982.

———. 1983. "A Folk Tale of the Holocaust" (on *Tzili*). *The Nation,* April 16, 1983.

Blake, Patricia. 1983. "Exact Fit" (on *Tzili*). *Time,* April 11, 1983.

Bremond, Claude. 1966. "Le Logique des Possibles Narratifs." *Communications* 8 (1966): 60–76.

Brinker, Menahem. 1989. *Haim Torat Hasifrut Efsharit?* (Is Literary Theory Possible?). Tel Aviv: Sifriyat Poalim.

———. 1990. *Ad Hasimta Hateveriyanit* (Up to the Alley in Tiberias). Tel Aviv: Am Oved.

Buber, Martin. 1960. *Teuda Veyeud* (Essays on Judaism). Jerusalem: Hasifriya Hatzionit.

———. 1965. *Or Haganuz* (Hasidic Stories). Jerusalem and Tel Aviv: Schocken.

Cirlot, Juan Eduardo. 1962. *A Dictionary of Symbols,* pp. 208–11. New York: Philosophical Library.

Cohen, Joseph. 1990. *Voices of Israel.* Albany: State University of New York Press.

Cohn, Dorit. 1989. "Fictional versus Historical Lives: Border Lines and Borderline Cases." *Journal of Narrative Technique* 19 (Winter 1989): 3–24.

D.K. 1962. "Conversation with Aharon Appelfeld" (interview with Appelfeld on *Ashan,* in Hebrew). *Pi Haaton,* November 21, 1962.

Dan, Yosef, ed. 1966. *Hanovela Hahasidit* (The Hasidic Novel). Jerusalem: Sifriyat Dorot, Bialik Institute.

David, Yonah. 1962. "The Stories of Aharon Appelfeld" (on *Ashan,* in Hebrew). *Hauma* 2 (August 1962): 314–15.

Davis, Lennard J. 1987. *Resisting Novels, Ideology, and Fiction,* pp. 52–101. New York and London: Methuen.

Decker Kennedy, Constance. 1983. "Against Grim Odds, A Will To Live Prevails" (on *Tzili*). *Philadelphia Inquirer,* April 10, 1983.

Dor, Moshe. 1980. "Conversation with Appelfeld on the Publication of *Mikhvat Haor* (in Hebrew). *Maariv,* July 4, 1980.

Dudai, Rina. 1983. "Examination of the Subterfuges of Participation in Creating the Impression of Restraint and Delicacy in a Loaded Narrative Text, According to *Mikhvat Haor* by Aharon Appelfeld" (in Hebrew). Master's thesis, Tel Aviv University.

Einat, Amala. 1980. "Silhouettes in *Mikhvat Haor*" (in Hebrew). *Iton* 77, nos. 22–23 (September–October 1980): 48–49.

Elad-Lender, Pinhas. 1980. "Appelfeld on His Childhood and Youth" (interview with Appelfeld, in Hebrew). *Temurot,* July 1980, pp. 51–52.

Eliade, Mircea. 1975. *Rites and Symbols of Initiation: The Mystery of Birth and Rebirth.* New York: Harper Torch Books.

Even-Zohar, Itamar. 1966. "'Matzod' by Aharon Appelfeld" (in Hebrew). *Iyunim Basifrut.* Jerusalem: Misrad Hahinukh Vehatarbut.

Evron, Edna. 1994. "Aharon Appelfeld, Simply an Author" (conversation on the occasion of the publication of *Layish,* in Hebrew). *Yediot Aharonot,* June 17, 1994.

Ezrahi, Sidra DeKoven. 1980. *By Words Alone: The Holocaust in Literature.* Chicago: University of Chicago Press.

———. 1984. "Aharon Appelfeld: The Search for Language." *Studies in Contemporary Jewry* 1 (1984): 366–80.

———. 1985–86. "Revisioning the Past: The Changing Legacy of the Holocaust in Hebrew Literature." *Salmagundi* (Fall–Winter 1985–86): 245–70.

———. 1994. "*Layish* and the (Anti-)Teleological Pattern in the Voyage to the Land of Israel" (in Hebrew). Lecture at "From Czernowitz to Jerusalem," conference at the Hebrew University, December 20–21, 1994.

———. 1995. "You Ask How I Write" (in Hebrew). *Alpayim* 10 (1995): 94–110.

Feldman, Yael. 1992. "Whose Story Is It, Anyway? Ideology and Psychology in the Representation of the Shoah in Israeli Literature." In *Probing the Limits of*

Representation: Nazism and the Final Solution, edited by Saul Friedlander, pp. 223–45. Cambridge, Mass.: Harvard University Press.

Fishler, Brakha. 1994. "*Haor Vehakutonet* and *Timyon:* Two Language Choices" (in Hebrew). Lecture at "From Czernowitz to Jerusalem" conference at the Hebrew University, December 20–21, 1994.

Frank, Josef. 1948. "Spatial Form in Modern Literature." *Criticism* 10 (1948): 379–92.

Freud, Sigmund. [1920]. *Beyond the Pleasure Principle.* Cited in Hebrew translation, *Kitvei Sigmund Freud,* trans. Hayim Isak (Tel Aviv: Dvir, 1968), pp. 95–137.

Friedlander, Saul. 1994. "Trauma, Memory and Transference." In *Holocaust Remembrance: The Shapes of Memory,* edited by Geoffrey H. Hartman, 252–63. Cambridge, Mass.: Blackwell.

Friedland, Yehuda. 1971. "An Intermediary Stage on the Way to the Novel *Haor Vehakutonet* by Aharon Appelfeld" (in Hebrew). *Davar,* October 1, 1971.

Frye, Northorp. 1957. *Anatomy of Criticism.* Princeton, N.J.: Princeton University Press.

Fuchs, Esther. 1982a. "Interview with Aharon Appelfeld." In *Encounters with Israeli Authors,* pp. 52–63. Marblehead, Mass.: Micah.

——. 1982b. "Thematic Distraction: Structural Underpinnings in the Writing of Aharon Appelfeld." *Hebrew Studies* 23 (1982): 223–27.

Gertz, Nurit. 1994. "'From Darkness to a Great Light': The Zionist Story in *Mikhvat Haor*" (in Hebrew). Lecture at "From Czernowitz to Jerusalem" conference at the Hebrew University, December 20–21, 1994.

Gingold-Gilboa, Shulamit. 1983. "Between Trauma and Awareness" (conversation with Aharon Appelfeld upon his receiving the Israel Prize 1983, in Hebrew). *Iton 77,* no. 46 (1984): 28–29.

——. 1984. "Aharon Appelfeld: All the Contradictions Are Visible" (interview with Appelfeld, in Hebrew). *Yediot Aharonot,* January 13, 1984.

Golan, Yaron. 1971. "Interview with Appelfeld on the Publication of His Book, *Adnei Hanahar*" (in Hebrew). *Pi Haaton,* May 5, 1971.

Gold, Nili. 1994. "*Haor Vehakutonet:* Literary Language and the Riddle of the Artist" (in Hebrew). Lecture at "From Czernowitz to Jerusalem," conference at the Hebrew University, December 20–21, 1994.

Golumb, Dikla. 1962. "Novellas of Aharon Appelfeld" (in Hebrew). *Davar Literary Supplement,* May 4, 1962.

Gorfein, Rivka. 1981. *Leever Hof Alum* (Toward a Hidden Shore). Tel Aviv: Hakibbutz Hemeuchad.

Gouri, Haim. 1994. "A Jewish Author in a Hebrew State" (in Hebrew). Lecture at "From Czernowitz to Jerusalem" conference at the Hebrew University, December 20–21, 1994.

Green, Jeffrey. 1994. "The Art of Aharon Appelfeld from the Translator's Point of View" (in Hebrew). Lecture at "From Czernowitz to Jerusalem" conference at the Hebrew University, December 20–21, 1994.

Grossman, Judith. 1992. "The Only Redemption Was in the Heart" (on *Katerina*). *New York Times,* September 2, 1992.

Gutkind, Naomi. 1969. "Appelfeld: Portrait of an Artist and a Witness to the Holocaust" (interview with Appelfeld, in Hebrew). *Hatzofeh,* March 25, 1969.

Guvrin, Nurit. 1986. "Paradox and the Effort to Escape It" (in Hebrew). *Alei Siah* 23 (1986): 157–65.

Hagorni, Avraham. 1986. "The Magic Mountain and the Dissolution of the Palmach" (in Hebrew). *Davar,* May 16, 1986.

———. 1989. "The Uprooted Woman" (on *Katerina,* in Hebrew). *Davar,* October 6, 1989.

Hakak, Herzl, and Balfour Hakak. 1983. "Looking toward the Past: A Conversation with the Author Aharon Appelfeld" (in Hebrew). *Maalot* 15, no. 1 (1983): 31–36.

———. 1987. "My Childhood Was Passed in the Holocaust" (interview with Appelfeld, in Hebrew). *Hauma* 86 (1987): 441–49.

Halfi, Rahel. 1962. "*Ashan:* Gloomy and Tragic" (interview with Appelfeld, in Hebrew). *Maariv,* November 23, 1962.

Halprin, Sara. 1986. "Innocence and Resilience in *Hakutonet Vehapasim* by Aharon Appelfeld" (in Hebrew). *Hadoar,* December 27, 1986.

———. 1988. "Katerina's Journey of Awakening" (in Hebrew). *Moznayim* 65, nos. 1–2 (Fall 1988): 50–53.

Harel, Orit. 1995. "The Architect of Memories" (interview with Appelfeld, in Hebrew). *Maariv,* December 20, 1995.

Harel-Fisch, A. 1981. "Time To Be Silent and Time To Speak" (on *Tor Hapelaot,* in Hebrew). *Zehut* 1 (1981): 150–54.

———. 1983. "Aharon Appelfeld and Jewish Fiction after the Holocaust" (in Hebrew). In *Tarbut Yehudit Beyamenu: Mashber o Hithadshut* (Contemporary Jewish Culture: Crisis or Renewal), pp. 125–31. Ramat Gan: Bar-Ilan University.

Hartman, Geoffrey, ed. 1994. "Darkness Visible." Introduction to *Holocaust Remembrance,* pp. 1–22. Cambridge, Mass.: Blackwell.

Hazanovitch, Naomi. N.d. "The Theme of the Locomotive in *Tor Hapelaot* by Aharon Appelfeld" (in Hebrew). MS.

Heizner, Zmira. 1994. "The Rhetoric of Trauma" (in Hebrew). Ph.D. diss., Hebrew University.

Hertz, Dalya. 1972. "*Keishon Haayin:* Literature at Its Best" (in Hebrew). *Davar,* December 29, 1972.

Hirschfeld, Ariel. 1994. "The Comb of the Lorelei: Aharon Appelfeld and German Romanticism" (in Hebrew). Lecture at "From Czernowitz to Jerusalem," conference at the Hebrew University, December 20–21, 1994.

Holtz, Avraham. 1973. "The Open Parable as the Key to *Sefer Hamaasim* by S. Y. Agnon" (in Hebrew). *Hasifrut* 4, no. 2 (April 1973).

Holtzman, Avner. 1994. "The Appearance of Aharon Appelfeld against the Background of the Literature of the New Wave" (in Hebrew). Lecture at "From Czernowitz to Jerusalem," conference at the Hebrew University, December 20–21, 1994.

Howe, Irving. 1980. "Novels of Other Times and Places" (on *Badenheim 1939*). *New York Times,* November 23, 1980.

Hrushovski, Benjamin. 1976. "Segmentation and Motivation in the Text Continuum of Literary Prose: The First Episode of War and Peace." In *Papers of Poetics and Semiotics,* edited by Benjamin Hrushovski and Itamar Even-Zohar. Tel Aviv: Israeli Institute for Poetics and Semiotics, Tel Aviv University.

Hupert, Shmuel. 1979. "What Did Aunt Amalia See?" (on *Tor Hapelaot,* in Hebrew). *Haaretz,* May 11, 1979.

James, William. 1949. *The Varieties of Religious Experience* (consulted in Hebrew trans.) Jerusalem: Mosad Bialik.

Josipovici, Gabriel. 1985. Introduction to Aharon Appelfeld's *The Retreat,* pp. 5–13. London, Melbourne, and New York: Encounter Quartet Books.

———. 1987. "Time of the Palms of Their Hand" (on *To the Land of the Cattails*). *Times Literary Supplement,* February 27, 1987.

Karton-Blum, Ruth. 1986. "The Jewish Secret" (on *Beet Uveona Ahat,* in Hebrew). *Hadoar,* May 23, 1986, pp. 16–17.

Katz, Avi. 1994. "Everything Is Dirty except Jerusalem" (on *Layish,* in Hebrew). *Haaretz,* July 22, 1994.

———. 1996. "Muteness Is What Strangles Us" (in Hebrew). *Haaretz,* May 3, 1996.

Kermode, Frank. 1968. *The Sense of an Ending: Studies in the Theory of Fiction.* New York: University Press.

Kleist, Heinrich von. 1983. *Über das Marionettentheater.* Cited in Hebrew translation, *Al Teatron Hamarionetot,* trans. Nili Mirsky. (Tel Aviv: Sifriyat Hapoalim, 1983).

Komem, Aharon. 1983. "The What and the Whatness" (in Hebrew). *Moznayim* 4, no. 57 (1983): 41–43.

Kremer, Shalom. 1962. "A Young Modern Writer Whose Tone Is Subtle and Reliable" (on *Ashan,* in Hebrew). *Yediot Aharonot,* May 18, 1962.

———. 1968. "Aharon Appelfeld: Reality and Legend in His Stories." In *Realizm Ushevirato* (Realism and Its Destruction), pp. 203–13. Ramat Gan: Masada and Agudat Hasofrim.

Kurtzweill, Baruch. 1964. "Comments on the State of Our Literature at This Hour" (in Hebrew). *Haaretz Literary Supplement,* September 6, 1964, p. 20.

———. 1966. "Cultural Landscapes and Landscapes of Consciousness in Israeli Fiction." In *Bein Hahazon Levein Haabsurdi* (Between Vision and the Absurd), pp. 340–62. Jerusalem: Schocken.

Langer, Lawrence L. 1975. *The Holocaust and the Literary Imagination.* New Haven and London: Yale University Press.

———. 1990. "Fictional Facts and Factual Fictions: History in Holocaust Literature." In *Reflections of the Holocaust in Art and Literature,* edited by Randolph L. Braham, pp. 117–29. New York: Columbia University Press.

———. 1991. *Holocaust Testimonies: The Ruins of Memory.* New Haven and London: Yale University Press.

Laor, Dan. 1986. "Aharon Appelfeld's 'Magic Mountain'" (on *Beet Uveona Ahat,* in Hebrew). *Haaretz,* January 3, 1986.

———. 1994. "S. Y. Agnon, Aharon Appelfeld, and 'The Jewish Myth'" (in Hebrew). Lecture at "From Czernowitz to Jerusalem" conference at the Hebrew University, December 20–21, 1994.

Leclair, Thomas. 1993. "Passage through the Inferno" (on *Hakutonet Vehapasim*). *Washington Post*, April 3, 1993.

Lejeune, Philippe. 1975. *Le Pacte Autobiographique*. Paris: Le Soil.

Leskli, Hezi. 1985. "Local Geography Lesson" (interview with Aharon Appelfeld, in Hebrew). *Hair*, June 14, 1985.

Levit, Anat. 1986. "With Constant Eagerness To Discover the World" (conversation with Appelfeld, in Hebrew). *Davar*, January 10, 1986.

———. 1991. "Journey To Gather Remains of the Soul" (interview with Appelfeld on the publication of *Mesilat Barzel*, in Hebrew). *Davar*, September 22, 1991.

Linde, Charlotte. 1993. *Life Stories*. New York: Oxford University Press.

Lipsker, Avidov. 1986. "From *Tor Hapelaot* to *Eretz Hagomeh*: Autobiographical Testimony and Its Historiosophical Lesson in Appelfeld's Book, *El Eretz Hagomeh*" (in Hebrew). *Alei Siah* 23 (1986): 167–73.

———. 1992. "Mystical and Ecstatic Education of the 'Saint' against the Legendary Background of the Novella *Katerina* by Aharon Appelfeld" (in Hebrew). *Efes Shtayim* 1 (Spring 1992): 87–98.

Lotman, Jury M. 1979. "The Origins of Plot in the Light of Typology." *Poetics Today* 1, nos. 1–2 (1979): 161–84.

Luthi, Max. 1984. *The Fairytale as Art Form and Portrait of Man*. Bloomington: Indiana University Press.

Malin, Irving. 1983. "Holocaust Fairy Tale" (on *Hakutonet Vehapasim*). *Newsday*, April 24, 1983.

Marmonchik, Penina. 1985. "Halashon Hafigurativit shel Aharon Appelfeld Kemafteah Lehavanat Yetzirotav" (Aharon Appelfeld's Figurative Language as Key to Understanding His Work). Ph.D. diss., Bar Ilan University.

Mazor, Yair. 1986. "The Song of the Author, or, The Correct Story of Emotion" (on the conscious orchestration of language in Aharon Appelfeld's work, in Hebrew). *Alei Siah* 23 (1986): 183–91.

———. 1995. "You Will Not See Her Before You, You Will Not Get To Her" (on *Layish*, in Hebrew). *Hadoar*, February 17, 1995, pp. 18–20.

Meizel (Shohat), Hannah. 1967. *Letoldot Hinukh Habat Lehityashvut: Pirkei Kineret Venahalal* (Toward a History of Educating Girls for Settlement: The Stories of Kineret and Nahalal). Tel Aviv: Hotzaat Tarbut Vehinukh.

Meizlish, Penina. 1964. "An Hour with Aharon Appelfeld" (interview, in Hebrew). *Haboker*, July 10, 1964.

Melamed, Ariana. 1991. "Late Revenge" (in Hebrew). *Hadashot*, September 6, 1991.

Mintz, Alan. 1984. *Hurban: Responses to Catastrophe in Hebrew Literature*, pp. 203–39. New York: Columbia University Press.

Miron, Dan. 1962. "The Stories of Aharon Appelfeld" (in Hebrew). *Haaretz*, May 25, 1962.

———. 1976. "Reflections on the Classical Image of the Shtetl" (in Hebrew). *Yediot Aharonot*, September 24, 1976.

———. 1979. *Pinkas Patuah* (Open Notebook), pp. 49–59. Tel Aviv: Sifriyat Poalim.

Mitgang, Herbert. 1986. "An Interview with Aharon Appelfeld." *New York Times Book Review,* November 15, 1986.

Moked, Gabriel. 1975. "An Artist of Lyrical Prose" (upon Appelfeld's receiving the Brenner Prize, in Hebrew). *Yediot Aharonot,* February 14, 1975.

———. 1980. "On *Mikhvat Haor"* (in Hebrew). *Al Hamishmar,* October 1, 1980.

———. 1994. "The Status of Experiences in the Plot in the Story Collection, *Ashan"* (in Hebrew). Lecture at "From Czernowitz to Jerusalem" conference at the Hebrew University, December 20–21, 1994.

Mondi, Yosef. 1988. "I Am Not a Human Being, I Am Just an Author" (conversation with Appelfeld, in Hebrew). *Maariv,* March 11, 1988.

Moretti, Franco. 1985. "The Comfort of Civilization." *Representations* 12 (Fall 1985): 115–39.

Moskona-Lerman, Bili. 1991. "The Boy from the Cornfield" (interview with Appelfeld, in Hebrew). *Maariv, Sofshavua,* September 6, 1991.

Nabantian, Susanne. 1983. *Seeds of Decadence in the Late Nineteenth-Century Novel: A Crisis in Values.* London and Basingstoke: Macmillan Press.

Nagid, Haim. 1977. "Jewish Literature or Israeli Literature" (symposium with Appelfeld, Haim Gouri, A. B. Yehoshua, and Yehuda Amichai, in Hebrew). *Maariv,* September 30, 1977.

———. 1978."The Age of Horror" (on *Tor Hapelaot,* in Hebrew). *Yediot Aharonot,* March 31, 1978.

Navot, Amnon. 1985. "Smoke and Ashes" (in Hebrew). *Moznayim* 58, nos. 5–6 (1985): 72–73.

Neeman, Mikhal. 1989. "The Last Jews" (on *Katerina,* in Hebrew). *Yediot Aharonot,* July 14, 1989.

Nevo, Yifat. 1969. "Normal Life, Normal Stories" (conversation with Appelfeld, upon his receiving the Prime Minister's Prize, in Hebrew). *Davar,* July 11, 1969.

Oates, Joyce Carol. 1983. "A Fable of Innocence and Survival" (on *Tzili*). *New York Times Book Review,* February 27, 1983.

Ofer, Dalia. 1991. "The Holocaust in Transnistria: A Special Case of Genocide" (in Hebrew). MS, Institute of Contemporary Jewry, Hebrew University, Jerusalem.

Oren, Yosef. 1987. "The Reflection of Jewish Fate in the Stories of Aharon Appelfeld" (in Hebrew). In *Hasippur Hayisraeli Hakatzar* (The Israeli Short Story), pp. 67–97. Tel Aviv: Yahad.

———. 1989. "Katerina, You Are Our Sister!" (in Hebrew). *Maariv,* June 23, 1989.

Pagis, Ada. 1995. *Lev Pitomi* (Sudden Heart). Tel Aviv: Am Oved.

Parry, Idris. 1981. "The Voices of the Sickness." *Times Literary Supplement,* November 20, 1981.

Parush, Iris. 1994. *"Katerina,* Other Chosen Women" (in Hebrew). Lecture at "From Czernowitz to Jerusalem" conference at the Hebrew University, December 20–21, 1994.

Pelai, Moshe. 1981. "Ruin and Illusion before the Holocaust" (on *Badenheim, Ir Nofesh,* in Hebrew). *Hadoar* 20 (February 1981).

Perry, Menahem. 1968. "Analogy and Its Place in the Structure of the Novel of Mendele Mokher Seforim: Studies in the Poetics of Prose" (in Hebrew). *Hasifrut* 1 (1968): 65–100.

Propp, Vladimir. 1968. *Morphology of the Folktale.* Austin: University of Texas Press.

Ramras-Rauch, Gila. 1994a. *Aharon Appelfeld: The Holocaust and Beyond.* Bloomington and Indianapolis: Indiana University Press.

———. 1994b. "The Hidden I: I Write and Erase" (in Hebrew). Lecture at "From Czernowitz to Jerusalem" conference at the Hebrew University, December 20–21, 1994.

Ratok, Lily. 1989. *Bayit al Blima* (House on the Edge of the Abyss). Tel Aviv: Heker.

Razili, Haya. 1963. "They Tell about Themselves" (interview including Appelfeld, in Hebrew). *Davar,* April 8, 1963.

Remba, Isaac. 1969. "Aharon Appelfeld: Shikun Geulim, Block 7, Entrance 2" (interview with Appelfeld, in Hebrew). *Maariv,* March 28, 1969.

Rimmon-Kenan, Shlomit. 1984. *Hapoetika shel Hasiporet Beyameinu* (The Poetics of Fiction in Our Day). Tel Aviv: Sifriyat Poalim.

———. 1987. "A Narration as Repetition: The Case of Gunter Grass's *Cat and Mouse.*" In *Discourse in Psychoanalysis and Literature,* pp. 176–87. London and New York.

Rochman, Leib. 1964. "Aharon Appelfeld: Nayer Shtern in Hebreisher Literatur" (in Yiddish). *Forverts,* January 12, 1964.

Roiphe, Anne. 1992. "A Story To Break Your Heart." *Los Angeles Times,* September 27, 1992.

Rosenfeld, Alvin H. 1990. "Intimacy and Alienation." *Jerusalem Report,* October 1990, pp. 59–60.

Roskies, David. 1993. *Against the Apocalypse.* Cambridge, Mass.: Harvard University Press.

Roth, Philip. 1988. "Walking the Way of the Survivor: A Talk with Aharon Appelfeld." *New York Times,* February 28, 1988. Reprinted in Aharon Appelfeld. *Beyond Despair: Three Lectures and a Conversation with Philip Roth,* trans. Jeffrey M. Green, pp. 59–80. New York: Fromm International, 1994.

Rubin, David, ed. 1986. *Autobiographical Memory.* Cambridge: Cambridge University Press.

Sadan, Dov. 1979. "Narrator and His Purpose" (in Hebrew). *Davar,* May 4, 1979.

Said, Eduard. 1993. *Culture and Imperialism.* New York: Vintage Press.

Sarid, Menachem. 1982. "The Covenant and the Mercy: An Examination of 'Hanukah 1946' by Aharon Appelfeld" (in Hebrew). *Bitzaron* 4, nos.13–14 (1982): 90–93.

Sarna, Yigal. 1989. "Aharon Appelfeld's Bunker" (interview with Appelfeld, in Hebrew). *Yediot Aharonot Musaf 7 Yamim,* May 12, 1989.

Schafer, Roy. 1992. *Retelling a Life: Narration and Dialogue in Psychoanalysis.* New York: Basic Books.

Schiller, Friedrich von. [1795–96]. *Über naive und sentimentalische Dichtung.*

Cited in Hebrew translation *Shira Naivit Vesentamentalit,* trans. David Oren (Tel Aviv: Sifriyat Poalim, Hakibbutz Hameuchad, 1985).

Schneider, Shmuel. 1962. "*Ashan:* Small Accounts Combine into a Great Accounting" (in Hebrew). *Pi Haaton,* June 24, 1962.

———. 1982. "Aharon Appelfeld: On His Life and Work" (interview with Appelfeld, in Hebrew). *Bitzaron* 4, nos. 13–14 (1982): 5–17.

Schnitzer, Dafna. 1991. "*W,* or the Memory of Loss" (afterword to the Hebrew translation of *W,* by Georges Perec, in Hebrew). Tel Aviv: Hakibbutz Hameuchad, Siman Kria.

Schwartz, Yigal. 1979. "The Poetics of Dread" (on *Masot Beguf Rishon,* in Hebrew). *Davar, Masa,* December 28, 1979.

———. 1981. "The Model of the Closed Camp: The Way Out?" (in Hebrew). *Siman Kria* 12/13 (1981): 357–60.

———. 1982. "Without Drums and Bugles!!!" (in Hebrew). *Yediot Aharonot,* December 31, 1982.

———. 1983a. "Aharon Appelfeld" (in Hebrew). In *Haentsiklopedia Haivrit,* suppl. 2 (1983): 170–71.

———. 1983b. "As Though Condemned to Constant Motion: The Basic Plot Pattern and Its Transformations in the Prose of Aharon Appelfeld" (in Hebrew). *Yediot Aharonot,* March 15, 1983.

———. 1986a. "The Carpathian Time: Speech, Consciousness, and Muteness in the Fiction of Aharon Appelfeld" (in Hebrew). *Moznayim* 9, no. 59 (Nisan, 1986): 10–12.

———. 1986b. "The Theme in the Fiction of Aharon Appelfeld" (in Hebrew). *Mehkarei Yerushalayim Besifrut Ivrit* 9 (1986): 201–14.

———. 1986c. "'When No One Is Looking, the Transformations Will Come': The Story 'Bimlo Hastav,' as an Early Version of *Keishon Haayin* and of *Tor Hapelaot.* Remarks on the Structure of the Inner Development of Aharon Appelfeld's Fiction" (in Hebrew). *Alei Siah* 23 (1986): 175–81.

———. 1991. "Neither Apollo Nor Alik" (interview with Appelfeld and introductory essay, in Hebrew). *Kol Hair, Tarbut Uvidur,* September 6, 1991.

———. 1992. "Interview with Aharon Appelfeld" (in Hebrew). *Milim Udemuyot: Proyekt Hasifrut shel Yerushalayim* (Filmed In-depth Interviews with the Major Jewish Authors and Thinkers of Our Day).

———. 1993. *Lihiyot Kedei Lihiyot* (To Live So as To Live). Jerusalem: Magnes Press, Yad Yitzhak Ben Zvi.

———. 1995. "Hebrew Fiction: The Period After" (in Hebrew). *Efes Shtayim* 3 (1995): 7–15.

Schweid, Eliezer. 1962a. "*Ashan* by Aharon Appelfeld" (in Hebrew). *Lamerhav,* June 7, 1962.

———. 1962b. "Three Works and Their Moral" (on *Ashan,* in Hebrew). *Lamerhav,* September 28, 1962.

———. 1964. "From Tragic Catharsis to the Path of Equilibrium" (in Hebrew). *Min Hayesod,* April 9, 1964.

———. 1992. "Revenge on the Path to Homelessness" (on *Mesilat Barzel,* in Hebrew). *Dimui* 4 (Spring 5752/1992): 55–60.

———. 1995. "Religious Morality in the Stories of Aharon Appelfeld" (in Hebrew). *Moznayim* 69, no. 5 (5745/1995): 3–6.

Sebeok, Thomas, and Harriet Margolis. 1981. "Captain Nemo's Porthole and Sherlock Holmes' Windows" (in Hebrew). *Hasifrut* 30–31 (April 1981): 1–19.

Shabtai, Aharon. 1962. "Stories against the Background of the Holocaust" (in Hebrew). *Al Hamishmar,* June 7, 1962.

Shaham, Haya. 1992. "The Double Speech: The Problem of Language in *Badenheim, Ir Nofesh* by Aharon Appelfeld" (in Hebrew). *Bikoret Ufarshanut* 28 (Winter 1992): 71–81.

———. 1994. "The Resort Novel: *Badenheim, Ir Nofesh* by Aharon Appelfeld and *Death in Venice* by Thomas Mann: A Comparative Study of Generic and Thematic Aspects" (in Hebrew). Lecture at "From Czernowitz to Jerusalem" conference at the Hebrew University, December 20–21, 1994.

Shaked, Gershon. 1971. "We Are Only Tired" (in Hebrew). In *Gal Hadash Basipporet Haivrit* (The New Wave in Hebrew Fiction), pp. 149–67. Merhavia: Sifriyat Poalim.

———. 1976. *Omanut Hasipur shel Agnon* (Agnon's Narrative Art). Tel Aviv: Sifriyat Poalim.

———. 1977. *Hasipporet Haivrit, 1880–1970,* vol. 1, *Bagola* (Hebrew Fiction from 1880 to 1970, vol. 1, In the Diaspora). Jerusalem and Tel Aviv: Keter and Hakibbutz Hameuchad.

———. 1980. "The Transport to Palestine" (on *Mikhvat Haor,* in Hebrew). *Haaretz,* July 12, 1980.

———. 1985. *Gal Ahar Gal Basifrut Haivrit* (Wave after Wave in Hebrew Literature), pp. 27–37. Jerusalem: Keter.

———. 1989. "Now There Are No More Victims in the World, Only Victors" (on *Katerina,* in Hebrew). *Haaretz,* June 8, 1989. Reprinted in Gershon Shaked, *Sifrut Az, Kan Veakhshav* (Literature Then, Here and Now), pp. 143–51. Tel Aviv: Zemora-Bitan, 1993.

———. 1993. *Sifrut Az, Kan Veakhshav* (Literature Then, Here and Now). Tel Aviv: Zemora-Bitan.

———. 1994a. "Aharon Appelfeld: Between Him and His Times" (in Hebrew). Lecture at "From Czernowitz to Jerusalem" conference at the Hebrew University, December 20–21, 1994.

———. 1994b. "In Every Generation a Person Must See Himself" (on *Layish,* in Hebrew). *Haaretz,* July 27, 1994.

———. 1994c. "A Thirst for Sources" (interview with Appelfeld). *Modern Hebrew Literature* 12 (1994): 7–9.

Shaked, Malka. 1967. "On 'Beei Sant George' by Aharon Appelfeld" (in Hebrew). In *Madrikh Leleket Sipurim* (Teachers' Handbook). Tel Aviv: Tarbut Vehinukh.

———. 1994. "Style as Content: Some Comments on *Tor Hapelaot*" (in Hebrew). Lecture at "From Czernowitz to Jerusalem" conference at the Hebrew University, December 20–21, 1994.

Shalev, Moti. 1980. "The Nausea of Rebirth" (on *Mikhvat Haor,* in Hebrew). *Davar,* August 8, 1980.

Shay, Eli. 1994. "A Wandering Jewish Circus" (on *Layish,* in Hebrew). *Maariv,* April 5, 1994.

Shenhar, Aliza. 1978. "The Bitter Taste of the Approaching Summer" (in Hebrew). *Al Hamishmar,* June 16, 1978.

Shifra, S. 1975. "The Ability to Live—The Ability to Forget" (interview with Appelfeld, in Hebrew). *Davar, Masa,* October 24, 1975.

Shklovsky, Victor. 1965. "Art as Technique." In *Russian Formalist Criticism,* edited by Lee T. Lemon and Marion J. Reis, pp. 3–24. Lincoln and London: University of Nebraska Press.

Shoham, Giora S. 1992. *Antishemiut: Valhalla, Golgotha Veauschwitz* (Antisemitism: Valhalla, Golgotha and Auschwitz). Tel Aviv: Gome Sifrei Mada Umehkar.

Shor, Arieh. 1987. "There Are So Many Things That Seem Important" (on *Ritzpat Esh,* in Hebrew). *Davar,* September 29, 1987.

Smitten, Jeffrey R., and Ann Daghistany, eds. 1980. *Spatial Form in Narrative.* Ithaca, N.Y., and London: Cornell University Press.

Sokoloff, Naomi B. 1992a. *Imagining the Child in Modern Jewish Fiction,* pp. 129–52. Baltimore: Johns Hopkins University Press.

———. 1992b. *"Tzili,* Female Adolescence: The Holocaust in the Fiction of Aharon Appelfeld." In *Gender and the Text in Modern Hebrew and Yiddish Literature,* edited by Naomi B. Sokoloff, Anne Lapidus Lerner, and Anita Norich, pp. 171–94. New York and Jerusalem: Jewish Theological Seminary of America.

Sungolowsky, Joseph. 1990. "Holocaust and Autobiography: Wiesel, Friedlander, Pisar." In *Reflections of the Holocaust in Art and Literature,* edited by Randolph L. Braham, pp. 131–46. New York: Columbia University Press.

Tal, Uriel. 1989. *Theologia Politit Vehareich Hashlishi* (Political Theology and the Third Reich). Tel Aviv: Sifriyat Poalim and Tel Aviv University.

Todorov, Tzvetan. 1977. *The Poetics of Prose,* pp. 218–33. Ithaca, N.Y.: Cornell University Press.

Toker, Naftali. 1982. "On the Seer of Light and the Fear of Shadows" (in Hebrew). *Moznayim,* March 1982, pp. 292–97.

Tomashevsky, Boris.1965. "Thematics." In *Russian Formalist Criticism: Four Essays,* edited by Lee T. Lemon and Marion J. Reis, pp. 61–95. Omaha: University of Nebraska Press.

Toren, Orli. 1989. "In the Great Lap of Katerina" (interview with Appelfeld, in Hebrew). *Yerushalayim,* May 5, 1989.

Treinin, Avner. 1996. "Lecture on the Publication of *Ad Sheyaaleh Amud Hashahar"* (in Hebrew). Beit Hasofer, Jerusalem, February 13, 1996.

Turner, Victor. 1967. *The Forest of Symbols,* pp. 93–111. Ithaca, N.Y.: Cornell University Press.

———. 1969. *The Ritual Process: Structure and Anti-Structure.* Chicago: Aldine.

Tzameret, Tzvi. 1983. "From the Book of the Volcanic Change" (on Appelfeld's receiving the Israel Prize 1983, in Hebrew). *Davar,* April 17, 1983.

———. 1994. "In Memory Is the Secret of Redemption" (on *Layish,* in Hebrew). *Amudim,* Elul 5754/1994, pp. 346–47.

Tzemah-Verta, Ada. 1962. "A Lot and a Little with Restraint" (on *Ashan*, in Hebrew). *Molad* 20, nos.169–70 (1962): 424–27.

Tzoran, Gabriel. 1981. "Toward a Theory of Space in the Story" (in Hebrew). *Hasifrut* 30–31 (1981): 20–34.

———. 1982a. "The Field of Vision and the World: The Organization of Space in the Fable of Kafka and in the Fable of Aesop" (in Hebrew). In *Sifrut Germanit Lifnei Veaharei* (German Literature Before and After), edited by Gideon Toury, pp. 48–75. Tel Aviv: Sifriyat Poalim.

———. 1982b. "Itzuvo Umivnehu shel Hamerhav Bayetzira Hasifrutit" (The Representation and Structure of Space in the Literary Work). Ph.D. diss., Tel Aviv University.

———. 1984. "Space and Meaning in 'The Pit and the Pendulum' by Edgar Allen Poe" (in Hebrew). *Dapim Lesifrut* 1 (1984): 259–74.

Van Gennep, Arnold. [1909]. *The Rites of Passage*. Reprint, London: Routledge and Kegan Paul, 1960.

Weltsch, Robert. 1984. "Destiny and Purpose" (in Hebrew). Introduction to Martin Buber, *Teuda Veyeud* (Destiny and Purpose). Jerusalem.

Wisse, Ruth. 1983. "Aharon Appelfeld, Survivor." *Commentary* 76 (August 1983): 73–76.

Yanait-Ben-Zvi, Rahel. 1975. *Im Hayeled Bahazit: Havat Hayeladim Biyrushalayim* (With the Child at the Front: The Children's Farm in Jerusalem). Ramat-Gan: Masada.

Yaoz, Hannah. 1981. *Sifrut Hashoah Beivrit, Kesiporet Historit Vetrans-Historit* (Holocaust Literature in Hebrew as Historical and Trans-Historical Literature). Tel Aviv: Eked.

———. 1983. "Existential Jewish Literature" (on the occasion of Appelfeld's receiving the Israel Prize 1983, in Hebrew). *Iton* 77, no. 38 (1983): 22–33.

———. 1991. "How Strange They Are, Everything Around Is Moist: The Jew and the Landscape in Aharon Appelfeld's Fiction" (in Hebrew). *Dimui*, Summer 1991, pp. 62–65.

Yaoz-Kest, Itamar. 1977. "What Is the Generation of the State in Our Literature?" (in Hebrew). *Yediot Aharonot*, October 7, 1977.

Yavetz, Zvi. 1994. "One Year in Czernowitz between the Two World Wars" (in Hebrew). Lecture at "From Czernowitz to Jerusalem" conference at the Hebrew University, December 20–21, 1994.

Yerushalmi, Yosef Haim. 1982. *Zakhor: Jewish History and Jewish Memory*. Seattle: University of Washington Press.

Yudkin, Leon I. 1974. "Appelfeld's Vision of the Past." In *Escape into Siege: A Survey of Israeli Literature Today*, pp. 116–23. London and Boston: Routledge and Kegan Paul.

Zahavi, Alex. 1966. "*Kefor al Haaretz*" (in Hebrew). *Keshet* 30 (1966): 176–77.

———. 1967. "Jews and Judaism in Modern Israeli Literature" (on *Kefor al Haaretz*, in Hebrew). *Hauma* 5 (1967): 571–79.

Zandbank, Shimon. 1963. "The Unfelt Growth" (in Hebrew). *Amot* 1, no. 2 (1963): 100–2.

———. 1975. *Derekh Hahisus: Al I-Havadaut Vegiluyeiha Beyetzirot Kafka* (The

Way of Hesitation: On Uncertainty and Its Manifestations in the Works of
Kafka). Tel Aviv: Hakibbutz Hameuchad.

Zborowski, Mark, and Elizabeth Herzog. 1962. *Life Is with People: The Culture
of the Shtetl.* New York: Schocken.

Zinger, Moshe. 1971. "Writing from Within" (interview with Appelfeld, in Hebrew). *Hadoar* 12 (February 1971): 251.

Zipes, Jack. 1983. *Fairytales and the Art of Subversion: The Classical Genre for
Children and the Process of Civilization.* London: Heinemann.

Zweig, Stefan. 1982. *Haolam shel Etmol: Zikhronot shel Ben Eiropa* (The World
of Yesterday: Memoirs of a European).Tel Aviv: Zmora Bitan.

Zwick, Yehudit. 1971. "The Present That Cannot Be Exhausted in Words" (on
Adnei Hanahar, in Hebrew). *Lamerhav, Masa,* May 28, 1971.

Index

"Abraham" ("Avraham"), 157n.8

Adnei Hanahar ("The Riverbanks"): "Ahar Hahupa" ("After the Wedding"), 107; "Akhsanya" ("Hostel"), 50, 52; "Bronda," 50, 77, 161n.44; characters with blocked consciousness in, 49; erasure of memory in, 5, 144n.10; "Hagilgul" ("Metamorphosis"), 67, 153n.49; "Hagilui Haaharon" ("The Last Revelation"), 64, 65, 153n.49; "Hakikar" ("The Square"), 51, 151n.26; "Halahaka" ("The Troupe"), 52, 151n.26; "Hamatzod" ("The Hunt"), 65, 67, 153n.49, 154n.54; "Haofot" ("The Fowl"), 153nn. 49, 51; "Hasoher Bartfuss" ("Bartfuss the Merchant"), 50; "Hayom" ("The Day"), 6, 103; "Orekh Hadin Shelanu" ("Our Attorney"), 52; Penal Colony depicted in, 64; "Regina," 50

Ad Sheyaaleh Amud Hashahar ("Until the Dawn Rises"): assimilated Jewish family in, 147n.29; auto-antisemitism in, 158n.16; Buber in, 159n.30; Carpathian Hasidism in, 108, 111–12; constant motion in, 70–71, 154n.61; enclosed space in, 156n.75; Jews' and gentiles' relation to surrounding space in, 44; Jews having diminished will to live in, 46; life as not autonomous in, 57; spatial-thematic structure of, 43; tunnel image in, 108, 161n.59

"After the Death of Absalom" ("Aharei Mot Avshalom"), 157n.8

"After the Wedding" ("Ahar Hahupa"), 107

Age of Wonders, The (Tor Hapelaot),
20–28; assimilated Jewish family in, 147n.29; auto-antisemitism in, 103; in *Bildungsroman* tradition, 14; Buber in, 159n.30; contemplation of nature through a glass in, 150.16; decadence in, 151n.22; enclosed area of, 76, 77, 156n.75; first part of, 20; as imaginary autobiography, 22–23, 24–25, 27; Jewish women having diminished will to live in, 150n.18; life as not autonomous in, 57; as mistaken for autobiography, 20–22; obscure origins as subject in, 27; presence of absence in, 25–28; protagonist's birthplace as alien, 72–73; radical transformation of protagonist of, 26–27; reconstruction of memory in, xvii, 21, 23–24, 26; second part of, 20; sensitivity to sensory stimuli in, 150n.19; spatial-thematic structure of, 40; swallowing scene in, 74; tension between memory and forgetfulness in, 23–25; tension between voluntary and mechanical movement in, 154n.66; two parts of, 20; white page in, 20, 25–26, 27; youth of thirteen as protagonist of, 25

Agnon, Shmuel Yosef: and Appelfeld on modern science and literature, xxi; in Appelfeld's "Nisayon Retzini," 102; Appelfeld's view of Jewish world compared with, 3; deracinated characters of, 58; on immigration to Israel, 55; and "Lot's Wife's Syndrome," 143n.1; and process of remembrance in Appelfeld, 7; romantic ethos in work of, 109; *Sefer Hamaasim,* 91

"Aharei Mot Avshalom" ("After the Death of Absalom"), 157n.8

"Ahar Hahupa" ("After the Wedding"), 107

Aharon Appelfeld: The Holocaust and Beyond (Ramras-Rauch), xvii

"Ahavato shel Moreh" ("A Teacher's Love"), 148n.1

"Akhsanya" ("Hostel"), 50, 52

"Akhshav" ("Now"), 99

Al Bariah ("Bolted In"), 76, 103

"Al Hargasha Ahat Manha Venimshekhet" ("On One Leading and Prolonged Feeling"), 6, 26, 49

"Al Kol Hapeshaim" (*For Every Sin*), 70, 71

Almog, Ruth, 88

Alternberg, Peter, 81

"Al Yad Hahof" ("By the Shore"), 13, 61, 148n.1

Amichai, Yehuda, xi

"Andriko's Journeys" ("Masaotav shel Andriko"), 15–16, 161n.44

Animals, 46, 67, 89

Antisemitism, 103, 158n.14

Appelfeld, Aharon Erwin

FICTIONAL REALM OF, xxii–xxiii, 35–94; in Appelfeld's master plan, 32; chronotopic dimension of, 68–82; Closed Camp model in, 75–79; closed space as laboratory for, 79–82; diachronic and synchronic relations in, 69; dual-focus perspective in, 93; extent of, 148n.2; Italian region in, 59–63; Land of Searing Light (Israel) in, 35, 47–59, 70, 87–88; Land of the Cattails in, 35, 37–46, 56–59, 70; Penal Colony in, 59, 63–68, 82, 93; regions of, 35–68; textual dimension of, 82–93

LIFE OF: agricultural schools attended by, 12, 152n.34; army service of, xiv; birth of, xvii; childhood of, xiii; deportation to Transnistria, xiii, xvii, 5; at Dr. Ginigor's orphanage in Czernowitz, 5, 22; as having no memories of his family, 145n.16; Hebrew learned by, xiv, 145n.16; at Hebrew University, xv, 12; Holocaust as crucial and formative for, xiii; Holocaust leaving

"black hole" in biography of, 27; in Italy 1945–46, xiv, 5; Jewishness of, xv, 157n.12; in Palestine, xiv, xvii, 6; pedagogical training of, 12; protest against his Jewishness, 5–6; reunited with his father, 145n.16; separated from his father, xiii, xvii, 5; with Soviet Army, 5; trauma of the war years, xiii–xiv; wanderings in 1944, xiv; wanderings in the Ukraine, xiii, xvii, 4, 64, 113, 143nn.7, 8

RELIGION IN WORK OF: fundamentalism, xxii, 104–42; Hasidism, 105, 106–12; Jewish characters in, xxi; pagan-Christian Judaism, 105–6, 112–42; poems about relation of poet to God, 98–101; science and modern ideologies, xxi–xxii, 101; traditional Judaism, xv, 101–5

WORKS OF: absence of memory in, 4–8; Appelfeld as "architect" of, 32, 148n.4; Appelfeld as Jewish author, 97–98, 156n.3; autobiographical mode in, 14–19; autonomy granted to parts of whole in, 91; Berdyczewski tradition influencing, 153n.41; big subjects in, 81–82; cellars and ground floors in Israeli stories, 49–51; and classical and postclassical Hebrew and Yiddish writers, 56–57; constant motion in, 69–74; decadence in Austro-Hungarian stories, 151n.22; distancing of testimony in, 10–12; equilibrium between formative experience and later knowledge in, 7; expanding the scope of, 31; faces not described in, 156n.78; as fitting together like links in a chain, 3; four main creative tendencies in, 8–19; Germans as almost never referred to in, 149n.9; and Holocaust fiction, xi, xvi, 97; Holocaust in, xviii, xxii, 141–42; and Israeli-regional segment of Hebrew literature, 59; Israel not represented in, xv, xxi; and Jewish-historical segment of Hebrew literature, 58–59; journey stories, 70–74; languages used in, 145n.16; "Lot's

Wife Syndrome" in, 3, 143n.1; as
lyrical-contemplative, 8, 33, 156n.76;
marginal existential regions in, 58;
master plan for, 31–33; mediating
personae in, 146n.23; monastery stories, 5, 75; music and Austro-
Hungarian characters in, 150n.20;
mythical and historical worldviews
clashing in, 140; nature and Jews
contrasted in, 45; as not ideological,
32; "Orphic plunge" of, xviii–xix;
personal confession in, 8–10; poetry
falling into two groups, 98; precategorical experience represented by,
xxii, 82; process of remembrance in,
7–8; reconstruction of his childhood
in, xviii, xxi, 4, 9–10; resort novellas, 40–41, 80, 81; sex linked with
blindness in, 161n.44; shortcomings
turned to advantages in, 8; socio-
cultural range extended, 12–14;
streets and squares in Israeli stories,
51–52; stylistic change in, 156n.76
Appelfeld, Boniah Sternberg (mother),
xiii, xvii, 5
Appelfeld, Michael (father), xiii, xvii, 5
"Apples" ("Tapuhim"), 148n.1
"Arch of the Vault, The" ("Keshet Hakimron"), 76, 151n.26
Arieli-Orlov, L. A., 55
"Ascent to Katszansk, The" ("Haaliya
Lekatzansk"), 72, 107
Ashan ("Smoke") (collection): as
Appelfeld's first published collection,
xi, xvii; and Appelfeld's master plan,
32; "Aviv Kar" ("Cold Spring"), 13,
71, 151n.26; "Bertha," 13, 49–50,
51–52, 54; characters with blocked
consciousness in, 49; critical reception of, 97; distancing of testimony
in, 11–12; as milestone in Appelfeld's
life, xv; "Nisayon Retzini" ("A Serious Effort"), 13, 101–2, 149n.14;
Penal Colony depicted in, 64; "Pitzuim" ("Compensation"), 13,
148n.1; reaction to Zionism in, 6;
settings of, 148n.1; single person or
small group in foreground in, 12–13;

"Yamim Noraim" ("High Holy
Days"), 160n.30. See also "Shlosha"
("Three")
"Ashan" ("Smoke") (story), 13
Assimilation, 18–19, 39, 56, 147n.29
"At His Feet" ("Lemargelotav"), 157n.9
"At One and the Same Time." See
Healer, The
"At the Doctor's" ("Etzel Harofeh"), 51
"At the Height of the Cycle" ("Beitzumo
shel Hamahzor"), 148n.1
Auslander, Rosa, xiii
"Autumn-Fire" ("Stav-Esh"), 157n.8
"Aviv Kar" ("Cold Spring"), 13, 71,
151n.26
Avot Yeshurun, 3
"Avraham" ("Abraham"), 157n.8

Badenheim 1939 (Badenheim, Ir
Nofesh): absence of horror of the
camps in, xii; and Appelfeld's recognition outside Hebrew reading community, xi; arena of action as narrowing
in, 80; auto-antisemitism in, 158n.16;
autonomy given to part of, 91; Buber
in, 159n.30; Carpathian Hasidism in,
108–9; characters identified with
beautiful forms of life in, 46; contemplation of nature through a glass in,
150n.16; enclosed area of, 76; established religion characterized by helplessness in, 104; Jews having diminished will to live in, 45–46; life as not
autonomous in, 57; spatial-thematic
structure of, 40–41, 42, 59; swallowing scene in, 74
"Baderekh" ("On the Way"), 70
"Baeven" ("In Stone"), 16–17, 22, 75,
151n.26
Bagai Haporeh ("In the Fertile Valley")
(collection): abandoned child in monastery in, 144n.11; "Al Yad Hahof"
("By the Shore"), 13, 61, 148n.1; and
Appelfeld's master plan, 32; "Bagova
Hakar" ("In the Cold Height"), 10,
62, 76, 149n.13; "Bamidbar" ("In
the Desert"), 64, 66, 153n.49;
coming-of-age stories in, 15–16;

Bagai Haporeh (continued)
"Hamahaseh Haaharon" ("The Last Refuge"), 65, 75, 149n.14, 153n.49; "Haredifa" ("The Pursuit"), 70; "Hashayara" ("The Convoy"), 61, 70; on Jewish life before the Holocaust, 97; Jewish tribe at center stage in, 13; "Kittie," 15, 65, 67, 75, 151n.26, 153n.49, 161n.44; "Masa" ("Journey"), 15–16, 68; "Masaotav shel Andriko" ("Andriko's Journeys"), 15–16, 161n.44; "Matzod" ("Hunt"), 67, 153n.49; "Mukar" ("Known"), 76; obscure origins as subject in, 15; Penal Colony depicted in, 64; pilgrim stories in, 108; reaction to Zionism in, 6; "Shohet" ("Ritual Slaughterer"), 65, 148n.1, 153n.49; "Sibir" ("Siberia"), 14, 70; tension between memory and forgetfulness in, 24

"Bagai Haporeh" ("In the Fertile Valley") (story), 153n.49

"Bagova Hakar" ("In the Cold Height"), 10, 62, 76, 149n.13

"Bamekomot Hanemukhim" ("In the Low Places"), 37, 47, 76, 151n.24, 160n.30

"Bamidbar" ("In the Desert"), 64, 66, 153n.49

Barash, Asher, 4

"Barren Women, The" ("Haakarot"), 159n.25

Bartfuss ben Almavet. See Immortal Bartfuss, The

"Bartfuss the Merchant" ("Hasoher Bartfuss"), 50

Barzel, Hillel, 146n.22

"Batahana" ("In the Station"), 13, 70

Bayit al Blima (Ratok), xvii

"Beein Manos" ("With No Escape"), 148n.1

"Beei Sant George" ("In the Isles of St. George"), 61, 63, 76

Beersheba, 36

Beet Uveona Ahat. See Healer, The

"Beitzumo shel Hamahzor" ("At the Height of the Cycle"), 148n.1

Bekomat Hakarka ("On the Ground Floor"): "Baderekh" ("On the Way"), 70; "Beyahad" ("Together"), 64–65, 148n.1; cellar figures in, 50, 52; erasure of memory in, 5, 144n.10; "Haakarot" ("The Barren Women"), 159n.25; "Haaliya Lekatzansk" ("The Ascent to Katszansk"), 72, 107; "Habegida" ("The Betrayal"), 153n.49; "Habriha" ("The Escape"), 65, 67, 153n.49; "Hahishtanut" ("Transmutation"), 65, 153n.49; "Hashiva" ("The Return"), 72, 107; material benefit preferred over obligation in, 13; Penal Colony depicted in, 64; reaction to Zionism in, 6; "Rushka," 65, 153n.49

"Bemakom Aher" ("In Another Place"), 59, 76

Ben-Ner, Yitzhak, 88

Berdyczewski, M. Y., 58, 153n.41

Bergman, S. H., xv

Berkowitz, Y. D., 57, 58

"Bertha," 13, 49–50, 51–52, 54

"Beshiva Derakhim" ("By Seven Paths"), 100

"Betrayal, The" ("Habegida"), 153n.49

"Beyahad" ("Together"), 64–65, 148n.1

"Beyond the Curtain" ("Meever Lapargod"), 100

"Beyond the Tragic" ("El Meever Latragi"), 78, 94

Bialik, H. N., 57, 58, 102

"Bimlo Hastav" ("In the Fullness of Autumn"): artificial species of plants in, 67; assimilated Central European Jewry in, 19, 23; on "a colorful bubble," 19, 25; enclosed area of, 76; Jewish archetype in, 13; Jews' and gentiles' relation to surrounding space in, 44; Jews having diminished will to live in, 45–46; life as not autonomous in, 57; real family portrayed in, 17–19; spatial-thematic structure of, 38–40

Blonde Eckbert, Der (Tieck), 104–5

"Blows" ("Shefatim"), 103

"Bolted In" *(Al Bariah)*, 76, 103
Brenner, Yosef Hayim, xxi, 55, 58, 59, 97, 98
Broch, Hermann, xxi
"Bronda," 50, 77, 161n.44
Buber, Martin, xv, 21, 105, 108, 111, 159n.30
Budapest, 36, 58
Bukovina, 3, 36, 56, 69
"By Seven Paths" ("Beshiva Derakhim"), 100
"By the Shore" ("Al Yad Hahof"), 13, 61, 148n.1

Carpathians, 36, 56, 69, 106–12
Castle (Kafka), 70
Celan, Paul, xiii
"Choice, The" ("Habehira"), 75–76
Cirlot, Juan Eduardo, 149n.13
"Cloak and the Stripes, The" (collection). See *Hakutonet Vehapasim*
"Cloak and the Stripes, The" (novella). See *Tzili: The Story of a Life*
Closed Camp model, 75–79
"Cold Spring" ("Aviv Kar"), 13, 71, 151n.26
Coming-of-age literature, 15–16, 81, 114, 125, 129, 160n.34
"Compensation" ("Pitzuim"), 13, 148n.1
"Continued Nuisance" ("Hatrada Nimshekhet"), 143n.8
Conversion, The (Timyon): assimilated Jewish family in, 147n.29; auto-antisemitism in, 158n.16; Buber in, 159n.30; Carpathian Hasidism in, 158n.24; decadence in, 151n.22; enclosed area of, 76; established religion characterized by helplessness in, 158n.17; Jews' and gentiles' relation to surrounding space in, 44; Jews having diminished will to live in, 45–46; life as not autonomous in, 57; spatial-thematic structure of, 42–43
"Convoy, The" ("Hashayara"), 61, 70
"Courtyard of the Gaôl" ("Hatzar Hamatara"), 103
Czernowitz, xiii

"Day, The" ("Hayom"), 6, 103
"Day of Happiness" ("Yom shel Osher"), 148n.1
"Death of Intercession, The" ("Mota shel Hashtadlanut"), 13, 103
Defoe, Daniel, 80
"Dovecote of Childhood, The" ("Shovakh Hayaldut"), 9
Dvir, Ami, 81

"Edut" ("Testimony"), 18, 27, 28, 63
"El Eretz Hagomeh." See *To the Land of the Cattails*
Eliade, Mircea, 115, 141, 142, 161n.62
Eliot, T. S., 79
"El Malkhut Hamerumim" ("To the Kingdom of the Deceived"), 100
"El Meever Latragi" ("Beyond the Tragic"), 78, 94
"Escape, The" ("Habriha"), 65, 67, 153n.49
"Essays in the First Person." See *Masot Beguf Rishon*
"Etzel Harofeh" ("At the Doctor's"), 51
Evron, Edna, 38
"Expulsion, The" ("Hagerush"), 13–14, 70, 103

Feierberg, M. Z., 58
"Fiery Ember." See *Ritzpat Esh*
Fink, Ida, 82
Fogel, David, 81
For Every Sin ("Al Kol Hapeshaim"), 70, 71
"Fowl, The" ("Haofot"), 153nn. 49, 51
Freud, Sigmund, 27
"From the Height of Silence" ("Mimrom Hadumiya"), 76, 149n.13, 160n.30
"Frost on the Earth" (collection). See *Kefor al Haaretz*
"Frost on the Earth" ("Kefor al Haaretz") (story), 72
"Function of the School in Absorbing Immigration and the Integration of Exiles, The," 144n.13

"Gaash" ("Volcano"), 99
Galicia, 36

German folk tales, 113
Gestalt psychology, 90
Gingold-Gilboa, Shulamit, 32
Ginigor, Dr., 5, 22
Gnessin, Uri Nissan, xxi, 58, 59, 156n.76
Golding, William, 80
"Gonev Marot" ("The Thief of Visions"), 13, 31, 76
Grimm brothers, 113
Grossman, David, 81

"Haakarot" ("The Barren Women"), 159n.25
"Haaliya Lekatzansk" ("The Ascent to Katszansk"), 72, 107
"Habaita" ("Homeward"), 148n.1
"Habegida" ("The Betrayal"), 153n.49
"Habehira" ("The Choice"), 75–76
"Habesora" ("The Tidings"), 70
"Habriha" ("The Escape"), 65, 67, 153n.49
"Haderekh ben Drovna Ledrovitz" ("The Road from Drovna to Drovicz"), 13–14, 72, 106–7, 109–10, 154n.62
"Hafrada" ("Separation"), 103, 158n.24
"Hagarin" ("The Kernel)", 143n.1
"Hagerush" ("The Expulsion"), 13–14, 70, 103
"Hagilgul" ("Metamorphosis"), 67, 153n.49
"Hagilui Haaharon" ("The Last Revelation"), 64, 65, 153n.49
"Hagveret Stein Metzapa Lebaala" ("Mrs. Stein Expects Her Husband"), 148n.1
"Hahishtanut" ("Transmutation"), 65, 153n.49
Haimut (K. Tzetnik), 155n.69
"Hakhanot Lamasa" ("Preparations for a Journey"), 13–14
"Hakikar" ("The Square"), 51, 151n.26
Hakutonet Vehapasim ("The Cloak and the Stripes"): Appelfeld's second style in, 156n.76. See also Immortal Bartfuss, The (Bartfuss ben Almavet);

Tzili: The Story of a Life ("The Cloak and the Stripes")
"Halahaka" ("The Troupe"), 52, 151n.26
Halkin, Shimon, 12
Halprin, Sara, 128
"Hamahaseh Haaharon" ("The Last Refuge"), 65, 75, 149n.14, 153n.49
"Hamatzod" ("The Hunt"), 65, 67, 153n.49, 154n.54
"Haminyan Haavud" ("The Lost Minyan"), 103
"Haofot" ("The Fowl"), 153nn. 49, 51
Haor Vehakutonet ("The Skin and the Cloak"): blind forces in, 92; geographical contrast in, 35; Holocaust survivor burrowing in, 151n.26; indistinguishability in, 86, 88–90; isolated scraps of information in, 77, 155n.68; Jews and nature in, 150n.15; linguistic portrayal of space in, 83–92; lyric-meditative style of, 156n.76; nonspecificity in, 86, 87–88; plot fabric of, 90; reaction to Zionism in, 6–7; semantic and syntactic patterns in, 91–92; social and ideological context ignored in, 52; unconnectedness in, 86, 90–91
"Hapisga." See Retreat, The
"Haredifa" ("The Pursuit"), 70
"Hashayara" ("The Convoy"), 61, 70
"Hashiva" ("The Return"), 72, 107
Hasidism, 105, 106–12
"Hasoher Bartfuss" ("Bartfuss the Merchant"), 50
"Hatrada Nimshekhet" ("Continued Nuisance"), 143n.8
"Hatzar Hamatara" ("Courtyard of the Gaôl"), 103
"Hayom" ("The Day"), 6, 103
Hazaz, Haim, 3, 55
Healer, The (Beet Uveona Ahat; "At One and the Same Time"): assimilated Jewish family in, 147n.29; autoantisemitism in, 158n.16; Carpathian Hasidism in, 107, 110–11, 159n.25; contemplation of nature through a glass in, 150n.16; enclosed area of, 76; Jewish women having diminished

will to live in, 150n.18; spatial-
thematic structure of, 42–43; tastes
in, 151n.21
"Here I Have Almost Arrived" ("Hine
Bati Kimaat"), 100
Herzog, Elizabeth, 56
"High Holy Days" ("Yamim Noraim"),
160n.30
"Hine Bati Kimaat" ("Here I Have Almost Arrived"), 100
"Hirhurei Kayitz Hatufim" ("Passing
Summer Thoughts"), 48–49, 148n.1
Holocaust: Appelfeld on artistic response to, 93–94; in Appelfeld's writings, xviii, xxii, 141–42; as crucial
and formative for Appelfeld, xiii; as
leaving "black hole" in Appelfeld's
biography, 27; as liminal period,
141–42; as loss, 141; as revelation,
141. See also Holocaust literature;
Holocaust survivors
Holocaust literature: Appelfeld and, xi,
xvi, 97; enclosed spaces in, 80–81;
people depicted as animals in, 67; resort stories in, 81
Holocaust survivors: burrowing into
depths of the unconscious, 50; constant motion for, 70; passing through
Italy, 61, 62–63; reeducation for, 79;
the street and square as threatening
to, 51; and traditional Jewish way of
life, 101–3
"Homeward" ("Habaita"), 148n.1
"Horef Shav" ("Winter Returns"),
157n.8
"Hostel" ("Akhsanya"), 50, 52
"Hunt" ("Matzod"), 67, 153n.49
"Hunt, The" ("Hamatzod"), 65, 67,
153n.49, 154n.54

Immortal Bartfuss, The (Bartfuss ben Almavet): ethnic contrast in, 36; isolated
scraps of information in, 77, 155n.68;
and the Italian region, 61; life as not
autonomous in, 57–58; social and
ideological context ignored in, 52
"In Another Place" ("Bemakom Aher"),
59, 76

Indistinguishability, 86, 88–90
"In Stone" ("Baeven"), 16–17, 22, 75,
151n.26
"In the Cold Height" ("Bagova Hakar"),
10, 62, 76, 149n.13
"In the Desert" ("Bamidbar"), 64, 66,
153n.49
"In the Fertile Valley" (collection). See
Bagai Haporeh
"In the Fertile Valley" ("Bagai Hapo-
reh") (story), 153n.49
"In the Fullness of Autumn." See "Bimlo
Hastav"
"In the Isles of St. George" ("Beei Sant
George"), 61, 63, 76
"In the Low Places" ("Bamekomot Ha-
nemukhim"), 37, 47, 76, 151n.24,
160n.30
"In the Station" ("Batahana"), 13, 70
Iron Tracks, The (Mesilat Barzel): burrowing into cellar existence in,
151n.26; enclosed area of, 75; forti-
fied basement in, 71; and the Italian
region, 61; swallowing scene in, 74;
tastes in, 151n.21; village rabbi in,
159n.25

Jaffa, 36
Jerusalem, 36, 61, 69
Jews: antisemitism, 103, 158n.14;
Appelfeld's Jewish characters, xxi;
assimilation, 18–19, 39, 56,
147n.29; Hasidism, 105, 106–12; as
having diminished will to live, 45–
46, 150n.18; and nature contrasted,
45; in shtetl, 56–57; traditional Judaism in Appelfeld's work, xv, 101–
5; Zionism, 6, 53, 54, 56. See also
Holocaust; and Appelfeld works by
name
"Journey" ("Masa"), 15–16, 68
Joyce, James, 4
"July" ("Yuli"), 35, 148n.1

Kabbalah, 105
Kafka, Franz, xxi, 27, 70, 91
Kahanah-Carmon, Amalia, xi
Kaniuk, Yoram, 81, 155n.69

Katerina, 128–41; assimilated Jewish family in, 147n.29; auto-antisemitism in, 158n.16; burrowing into cellar existence in, 151n.26; Carpathian Hasidism in, 158n.24; as deviating from cyclic plot pattern, 154n.64; enclosed area of, 76, 156n.75; encounter with Jewish world in, 134–35; experience of covenant between man and God in, 130; as generic hybrid, 128–29; important events occurring at Passover-Easter, 140, 161n.61; Jewish women having diminished will to live in, 150n.18; Jews' and gentiles' relation to surrounding space in, 44; Katerina as guardian of flame of Judaism in, 130, 139; liminal stage in, 132–36; and medieval exemplary tradition, 128; and mimetic tradition, 128; mundane, realistic stage in, 132–33; mystical revelation in, 131, 137, 138–39; mystical, visionary stage of, 136–39; mythical and historical worldviews clashing in, 139–41; naive and modern clashing in, 112–13; the naive in, 129; pagan-Christian Judaism in, 112, 139; reintegration stage in, 139–41; rite of passage as plot topos of, 129, 141; separation stage in, 131–32; tunnel image in, 138

Kaufmann, Yehezkel, 12

Kefor al Haaretz ("Frost on the Earth") (collection): abandoned child in monastery in, 144n.11; and Appelfeld's master plan, 32; assimilated Jewish family in, 147n.29; "Batahana" ("In the Station"), 13, 70; "Beei Sant George" ("In the Isles of St. George"), 61, 63, 76; "Baeven" ("In Stone"), 16–17, 22, 75, 151n.26; "Bemakom Aher" ("In Another Place"), 59, 76; "Bamekomot Hanemukhim" ("In the Low Places"), 37, 47, 76, 151n.24, 160n.30; bifurcated point of view in, 19; in *Bildungsroman* tradition, 14; "Gonev Marot" ("The Thief of Visions"), 13, 31, 76;

"Habehira" ("The Choice"), 75–76; "Habesora" ("The Tidings"), 70; "Haderekh ben Drovna Ledrovitz" ("The Road from Drovna to Drovicz"), 13–14, 72, 106–7, 109–10, 154n.62; "Hagerush" ("The Expulsion"), 13–14, 70, 103; "Hakhanot Lamasa" ("Preparations for a Journey"), 13–14; on Jewish life before the Holocaust, 97; Jewish tribe at center stage in, 13; journeys in stories in, 13–14; "Kefor al Haaretz" ("Frost on the Earth"), 72; "Mimrom Hadumiya" ("From the Height of Silence"), 76, 149n.13, 160n.30; "Mota shel Hashtadlanut" ("The Death of Intercession"), 13, 103; obscure origins as subject of, 15, 16; "Pegisha" ("Meeting"), 151n.24; reaction to Zionism in, 6; tension between memory and forgetfulness in, 24; "Tzel Harim" ("The Shadow of Mountains"), 13, 103. *See also* "Bimlo Hastav" ("In the Fullness of Autumn")

"Kefor al Haaretz" ("Frost on the Earth") (story), 72

Keishon Haayin ("Like the Pupil of the Eye"): artificial species of plants in, 67; auto-antisemitism in, 103; in *Bildungsroman* tradition, 14; Buber in, 159n.30; characters identified with beautiful forms of life, 46; decadence in, 151n.22; enclosed area of, 76; Jewish women having diminished will to live in, 150n.18; Jews' and gentiles' relation to surrounding space in, 44–45; Jews having diminished will to live in, 45–46; life as not autonomous in, 57; music in, 150n.20; sensitivity to sensory stimuli in, 150n.19; spatial-thematic structure of, 39–40; swallowing scene in, 74

Kenaz, Yehoshua, xi, 88

"Kernel, The" ("Hagarin"), 143n.1

Kertesz, Imre, 81, 82

"Keshet Hakimron" ("The Arch of the Vault"), 76, 151n.26

"Kittie," 15, 65, 67, 75, 151n.26, 153n.49, 161n.44

Kleist, Heinrich von, xxi, 114, 129, 156n.76

"Known" ("Mukar"), 76

"Kolot Lohashim" ("Whispering Voices"), 100

Kremer, Shalom, 147n.40

Land of Searing Light (Israel), 35, 47–59, 70, 87–88

Land of the Cattails, 35, 37–46, 56–59, 70

Langer, Lawrence L., 148n.42

"Language of His Illness and the Language of His Longing, The" ("Sfat Mahalato Usfat Kisufav: Mashehu al Yosef Hayim Brenner"), 98, 105, 106, 109, 112

"Last Refuge, The" ("Hamahaseh Haaharon"), 65, 75, 149n.14, 153n.49

"Last Revelation, The" ("Hagilui Haaharon"), 64, 65, 153n.49

Layish, 70, 71, 107–8, 159n.28

"Leavetaking" ("Preda"), 148n.1

"Lemargelotav" ("At His Feet"), 157n.9

Levi, Primo, 81, 82

Levit, Anat, 150n.20

"Leyad Hamorad" ("Near the Downslope"), 51, 148n.1

"Like the Pupil of the Eye." See Keishon Haayin

Lipsker, Avidov, 128, 133

"Lord of the Storms" ("Ribon Hasaarot"), 99–100

"Lost Minyan, The" ("Haminyan Haavud"), 103

"Lot's Wife Syndrome," 3, 143n.1

"Love Story" ("Sippur Ahava"), 13

Mann, Thomas, 81

"Masa" ("Journey"), 15–16, 68

"Masaotav shel Andriko" ("Andriko's Journeys"), 15–16, 161n.44

Masot Beguf Rishon ("Essays in the First Person"): "Al Hargasha Ahat Manha Venimshekhet" ("On One Leading and Prolonged Feeling"), 6, 26, 49;

on Appelfeld's wanderings in Transnistria, 143n.7; in Bildungsroman tradition, 14; "Edut" ("Testimony"), 18, 27, 28, 63; "El Meever Latragi" ("Beyond the Tragic"), 78, 94; "Hagarin" ("The Kernel)", 143n.1; "Sfat Mahalato Usfat Kisufav" ("The Language of His Illness and the Language of His Longing"), 98, 105, 106, 109, 112

"Matzod" ("Hunt"), 67, 153n.49

"Meeting" ("Pegisha"), 151n.24

"Meever Lapargod" ("Beyond the Curtain"), 100

Meisel, Hannah, 152n.34

Melaron, Yona, 160n.32

Memory: Appelfeld having no memories of his family, 145n.16; erasure of, 4–8, 144n.10; process of remembrance, 7–8; reconstruction of, xvii, 21, 23–24, 26; tension between forgetfulness and, 24, 26

Mendele Mokher Sefarim (Shalom Yaakov Abramovitch), 56–57

Mesilat Barzel. See Iron Tracks, The

"Metamorphosis" ("Hagilgul"), 67, 153n.49

Mikhvat Haor ("The Scorch of Light"): in Bildungsroman tradition, 14; central setting of, 53; and Closed Camp model, 75; constant motion in, 70; enclosed area of, 76; established religion characterized by helplessness in, 158n.17; ethnic contrast in, 36; external ties between chapters of, 78; headmistress of the agricultural school in, 152n.34; images of Appelfeld's childhood in, 55, 152n.35; isolated scraps of information in, 77, 155n.68; and the Italian region, 61; nonspecificity in, 88; reaction to Zionism in, 6, 53, 54, 56, 145n.15; reeducation for Holocaust survivors in, 79, 91; social and ideological context in, 53–56; spatial pattern of, 53, 55–56; swallowing scene in, 74

"Mimrom Hadumiya" ("From the Height of Silence"), 76, 149n.13, 160n.30

Miron, Dan, 57, 97, 98
"Mishpat" ("Trial"), 10
"Moment" ("Rega"), 48, 51, 148n.1
Morante, Elsa, 82
Moretti, Franco, 26
"Mota shel Hashtadlanut" ("The Death of Intercession"), 13, 103
"Mrs. Stein Expects Her Husband" ("Hagveret Stein Metzapa Lebaala"), 148n.1
"Mukar" ("Known"), 76
Musil, Robert, xxi, 81

Nahman of Bratslav, 70, 108, 159n.28
Naples, 60, 61
"Near the Downslope" ("Leyad Hamorad"), 51, 148n.1
Netanyah, 36
1946, 59–60, 79
"Nisayon Retzini" ("A Serious Effort"), 13, 101–2, 149n.14
"Nisyonot" ("Trials"), 148n.1
Nonspecificity, 86, 87–88
"Now" ("Akhshav"), 99

"On One Leading and Prolonged Feeling" ("Al Hargasha Ahat Manha Venimshekhet"), 6, 26, 49
"On the Ground Floor" (collection). See Bekomat Hakarka
"On the Way" ("Baderekh"), 70
"Orekh Hadin Shelanu" ("Our Attorney"), 51
Orlev, Uri, 81
"Orphanhood" ("Yatmut"), 9, 17
"Our Attorney" ("Orekh Hadin Shelanu"), 52
Oz, Amos, xi, 156n.3, 159n.28

Pagis, Dan, xiii
Palti, Sonia, 160n.32
"Partnership" ("Shutfut"), 13
Passage rites, 114–15, 129, 141
"Passing Summer Thoughts" ("Hirhurei Kayitz Hatufim"), 48–49, 148n.1
"Pegisha" ("Meeting"), 151n.24
Penal Colony, 59, 63–68, 82, 93
Perec, Georges, 80, 145n.17

"Pitzuim" ("Compensation"), 13, 148n.1
Plants, 44, 46, 67
"Poems" ("Shirim"), 10
Prague, 36, 58
"Preda" ("Leavetaking"), 148n.1
"Preparations for a Journey" ("Hakhanot Lamasa"), 13–14
Proust, Marcel, 4, 7
"Pursuit, The" ("Haredifa"), 70

Ramras-Rauch, Gila, xvii
Ratok, Lily, xvii
Reeducation, 79, 91
"Rega" ("Moment"), 48, 51, 148n.1
"Regina," 50
Resort stories, 40–41, 80, 81
Retreat, The ("Hapisga"; "The Summit"): auto-antisemitism in, 158n.16; Buber in, 159n.30; constant motion in, 71; enclosed area of, 76; Jewish women having diminished will to live in, 150n.18; Jews having diminished will to live in, 45–46; life as not autonomous in, 57; spatial-thematic structure of, 40–42, 149n.13
"Return, The" ("Hashiva"), 72, 107
"Ribon Hasaarot" ("Lord of the Storms"), 99–100
Rites of passage, 114–15, 129, 141
"Ritual Slaughterer" ("Shohet"), 65, 148n.1, 153n.49
Ritzpat Esh ("Fiery Ember"): auto-antisemitism in, 158n.16; constant motion in, 70; enclosed area of, 76; Jews having diminished will to live in, 45–46; life as not autonomous in, 57; spatial-thematic structure of, 40–41, 42; tastes in, 151n.21
"Riverbanks, The." See Adnei Hanahar
"Road from Drovna to Drovicz, The" ("Haderekh ben Drovna Ledrovitz"), 13–14, 72, 106–7, 109–10, 154n.62
Rochman, Leib, 106
Roth, Joseph, 81
Roth, Philip, 113–14, 129, 158n.14
"Round and Round" ("Sehor Sehor"), 148n.1

"Rushka," 65, 153n.49
Ruthenia, 58

Sadan, Dov, xv, 12, 25, 106, 143n.6,
   147n.30
"Saul" ("Shaul"), 157n.8
Schiller, Friedrich, 114, 129
Schneider, Shmuel, 4, 21
Schnitzler, Arthur, 81
Scholem, Gershom, xv, 12
Schuetz, David, 55, 81, 155n.69
Schweid, Eliezer, 97
"Scorch of Light, The." See *Mikhvat
   Haor*
"Sehor Sehor" ("Round and Round"),
   148n.1
Sened, Alexander, 4
Sened, Yonat, 4
"Separation" ("Hafrada"), 103,
   158n.24
"Serious Effort, A" ("Nisayon Retzini"),
   13, 101-2, 149n.14
"Sfat Mahalato Usfat Kisufav: Mashehu
   al Yosef Hayim Brenner" ("The Lan-
   guage of His Illness and the Language
   of His Longing"), 98, 105, 106, 109,
   112
Shabtai, Yaakov, 4, 7
"Shadow of Mountains, The" ("Tzel
   Harim"), 13, 103
Shahar, David, 4
Shaked, Gershon, xi, 13, 97, 156n.3
Shalom Aleichem (Shalom Rabinovitz),
   56-57
Shamir, Moshe, 87
Shanim Veshaot ("Year and Hours"):
   1946, 59-60, 79; pure white page in,
   20. See also *Badenheim 1939 (Baden-
   heim, Ir Nofesh)*
"Shaul" ("Saul"), 157n.8
"Shefatim" ("Blows"), 103
Shenhar, Yitzhak, 55
Shifra, S., 45
"Shirim" ("Poems"), 10
"Shlosha" ("Three"), 11-12; as link to
   Appelfeld's poems, 11; overcoming
   obstacles in, 13; as Penal Colony
   story, 65, 153n.49; setting of, 148n.1;

tension between memory and forget-
   fulness in, 24, 26
Shofman, Gershon, 58
Shohat, Manya, 152n.34
"Shohet" ("Ritual Slaughterer"), 65,
   148n.1, 153n.49
"Shovakh Hayaldut" ("The Dovecote of
   Childhood"), 9
Shtetl, Eastern European, 56-57
"Shutfut" ("Partnership"), 13
"Sibir" ("Siberia"), 14, 70
"Sippur Ahava" ("Love Story"), 13
Sippur Hayim ("The Story of a Life"),
   xii
"Skin and the Cloak, The." See *Haor Ve-
   hakutonet*
"Smoke" (collection). See *Ashan*
"Smoke" ("Ashan") (story), 13
Sokoloff, Naomi B., 152n.35
"Square, The" ("Hakikar"), 51,
   151n.26
"Stav-Esh" ("Autumn-Fire"), 157n.8
"Story of a Life, The" *(Sippur Hayim)*,
   xii
"Summit, The." See *Retreat, The*

Tammuz, Benyamin, 87
"Tapuhim" ("Apples"), 148n.1
"Teacher's Love, A" ("Ahavato shel
   Moreh"), 148n.1
Tel Aviv, 36, 58
Telushim, 58, 59
"Testimony" ("Edut"), 18, 27, 28, 63
"Thief of Visions, The" ("Gonev
   Marot"), 13, 31, 76
"Three." *See* "Shlosha"
"Tidings, The" ("Habesora"), 70
Tieck, Ludwig, 104-5
Timyon. See *Conversion, The*
"Together" ("Beyahad"), 64-65,
   148n.1
Toren, Orli, 129
Tor Hapelaot. See *Age of Wonders, The*
"To the Kingdom of the Deceived" ("El
   Malkhut Hamerumim"), 100
To the Land of the Cattails ("El Eretz
   Hagomeh"): assimilated Jewish fam-
   ily in, 147n.29; connotation of height

To the Land of the Cattails (continued)
in, 149n.13; constant motion in, 72;
enclosed space in, 156n.75; isolated
scraps of information in, 76, 77;
Jews' and gentiles' relation to surrounding space in, 44; Jews having
diminished will to live in, 45–46;
spatial-thematic structure of, 43;
swallowing scene in, 74; tastes in,
151n.21
"Transmutation" ("Hahishtanut"), 65,
153n.49
"Trial" ("Mishpat"), 10
"Trials" ("Nisyonot"), 148n.1
"Troupe, The" ("Halahaka"), 52,
151n.26
Turner, Victor, 115, 141
Tzameret, Tzvi, 144n.13
"Tzel Harim" ("The Shadow of Mountains"), 13, 103
Tzetnik, K., 81, 155n.69
Tzili: The Story of a Life ("The Cloak
and the Stripes"), 113–28; as biographical and historical, 113; connotation of height in, 122, 149n.13;
constant motion in, 70; erasure of
memory in, 144n.10; hybrid character of, 128; and the Italian region, 61;
Katerina compared with, 129, 131,
133, 139; life as not autonomous in,
57–58; liminal stage in, 118–25,
132; naive and modern clashing in,
112–13, 127–28, 141; and naive literature, 113–14; pagan-Christian Judaism in, 112; the pit in, 71, 123–24,
132, 151n.26; pure white page in, 20;
reintegration stage in, 125–28, 139;
rite of passage as plot topos of, 114–
15, 129, 141; ritual scenes in, 118,
122, 125; separation stage in, 116–
18; setting of, 116, 160n.41; three

parts of, 115; tunnel image in, 126,
161n.59
Tzoran, Gabriel, 33, 149n.8

Unconnectedness, 86, 90–91
"Until the Dawn Rises." See *Ad Sheyaaleh Amud Hashahar*
"Uriah Hahiti" ("Uriah the Hittite"),
157n.8

Van Gennep, Arnold, 114–15
Vienna, 36, 38, 58, 61
"Volcano" ("Gaash"), 99

"Whispering Voices" ("Kolot Lohashim"), 100
"Winter Returns" ("Horef Shav"),
157n.8
"With No Escape" ("Beein Manos"),
148n.1
Wolfe, Thomas, 4

"Yadata" ("You Knew"), 101
"Yamim Noraim" ("High Holy Days"),
160n.30
Yanait, Rachel, 152n.34
"Yatmut" ("Orphanhood"), 9, 17
"Year and Hours." See *Shanim Veshaot*
Yehoshua, A. B., xi, 156n.3
Yerushalmi, Yosef Haim, 161n.62
Yiddishkait, 57
Yizhar, S., 88
"Yom shel Osher" ("Day of Happi-
ness"), 148n.1
"You Knew" ("Yadata"), 101
"Yuli" ("July"), 35, 148n.1

Zborowski, Mark, 56
Zionism, 6, 53, 54, 56
Zweig, Stefan, 81